IN THE PAST NIGHT

Selected *Works** of Dmitry Stonov

Novels

Driver Tuzov (1926)
Polyanske Days (1927)
The Family of Raskins (1929)
Novels about Altay (1931)
Esterka (1938)
Tekla and Her Friends (1959)
In the City of Our Fathers (1964)

Collections of Short Stories and Novellas

Fever (1925)
By His Own Hand (1925)
People and Things (1928)
Two, Traveling along Karachay (1930)
The North Changes Its Face (1931)
The Blue Bone (1932)
Out of the Circle (1936)
Early Morning (1947)
Stories (1957)
In the Past Night: The Siberian Collection (1995)

*With the exception of *In the Past Night,* none of these are currently available in translation.

Dmitry
Stonov

IN THE PAST NIGHT

The Siberian Stories

Translated
by
Natasha
Stonov
and
Kathryn
Darrell

Texas Tech University Press

This book was set in Garamond and Joanna and printed on acid-free paper that meets the Guidelines for permanence and durability of the Committee on Production Guidelines for Book Longevity of the Council on Library Resources. ♾

Printed in the United States of America

Design by Ted Genoways
Illustrations by Kerri Carter

Library of Congress Cataloging-in-Publication Data

Stonov, Dmitrii, 1892-1962.
[Short stories. English. Selections]
In the past night : the Siberian collection / Dmitry Stonov ; [translated by Kathryn Darrell and Natasha S. Stonov].
p. cm.
ISBN 0-89672-358-5 (cloth : alk. paper)
1. Siberia (Russia)—Exiles—Fiction. 2. Political prisoners—Russia (Federation)—Siberia—Fiction. 3. Stonov, Dmitrii, II. Darrell, Kathryn. III. Title.
PG3476.S786A27 1995
891.73'44—dc20 95-30998
CIP

95 96 97 98 99 00 01 02 03 04 / 9 8 7 6 5 4 3 2 1

Texas Tech University Press
P. O. Box 41037
Lubbock, Texas 79409-1037 USA
1-800-832-4042

Acknowledgments

The Stonov family would like to express its deepest appreciation to the people named below. They are only a few, however, of the many to whom we owe untold thanks—whose help and unflagging support did, in reality, save our lives.

To Margaret, the Lady Thatcher who, as prime minister of Britain, met with us both in Moscow and London. Her example of strength and courage gave us continued hope.

To President Ronald Reagan, whose method of dealing with the Soviet Union may have received criticism at home but lifted the heart of every Russian dissident.

To President George Bush, who had merely to mention the Stonov name in the Oval Office and our eleven years of refusal came to an end within ten days.

To Pamela Cohen, president of the Union of Councils for Soviet Jews, to Micah Naftalin, its national director, and to all its affiliates; to Marillyn Tallman, chair of the Chicago Action for Soviet Jewry (CASJ), and to the staff of each. Their enormous efforts in our behalf not only introduced us to America, but made it a welcoming home. (Surely, without them, our transition from the Land of Lenin to the Land of Lincoln would never have gone so smoothly.)

Finally, we would like to thank the Chicago Transit Authority, because it was on a CTA "el" platform that Natasha Stonov asked Kathryn Darrell for directions and she came into our lives. Her luminous work as co-translator was only the beginning. Without her energy and dedication, these stories might never have flowered under the light of freedom.

Anna Idlin Stonov
Leonid and Natasha Stonov

Foreword

"DO YOU HAVE a suit at home? It is impossible to release you in such rags, especially to the House of Writers. By morning the whole building would be talking."

So went part of the conversation that took place on the evening of 20 August 1954 at headquarters in Lubyanka. Disguised as an office in a former hotel, Lubyanka was the infamous KGB interrogation prison housed in the heart of Moscow.

"I have not been home for over five years, as you know," said the newly released prisoner, "and my family has been living in poverty."

"We'd better call and find out," said the KGB officer. Thus it was that the telephone rang in the apartment on Lavrushinsky Street, and his family heard for the first time that Dmitry Stonov had been released.

Almost all the events of Russian history in the twentieth century touched the fate of Dmitry Mironovich Stonov—the radical changes, the search for truth, the tragedies, and the inhuman ordeals. He was not only to witness these dramatic events but also to participate actively in them.

Born on 8 January 1898 in the village of Bezdezh (near Kobryn) in the densely populated southwestern part of Byelorussia, Dmitry Stonov (née Vlodavsky) was the sixth child and the youngest son of a successful merchant. As a boy, the first years of the impending thunderstorm of revolution were printed indelibly in his mind "as blazing fires, the hushed and alarming conversations between my parents, the unwarranted arrests of the lowly *muzhiks*, and the wildly shouting police officers with their splendid mustaches." Later, in his autobiography, he would write, "The year 1905 was one that flashed by in a scarlet flame."

That year of excitement was followed by many of boredom and loneliness as Dmitry attended a commercial college in Brest-Litovsk—far away from home. Two years prior to World War I, the future writer moved to Lodz. There he studied the weaving business in a factory, where he worked for one year on the loom. Later he would write: "What a terrible time I had then. I decided to poison myself. Somebody or something stopped me."

With the advent of the war, Stonov's years of wandering began. The October Revolution of 1917 caught up with him at a railway depot 250 miles northwest of Moscow, where he became a Bolshevik. During the Civil War Stonov fought on two different fronts, became a correspondent for two newspapers, and ended up in the Ukraine, in Poltava, where he founded the magazine *Raduga* (*Rainbow*).

Stonov was now twenty-two. He had become a Bolshevik when Lenin fulfilled the promise of the Revolution by granting peasants their own land. Later, these same peasants were labeled "landowners," and their land was declared forfeit. Traveling all over the country, Stonov saw them daily, packed into boxcars and shipped to Siberia as "criminals of the state." But even in Poltava he knew that many people—owners of mills and big farms—were shot without even an investigation or a trial because they did not want their grain to be confiscated by the state.

In spite of himself doubts were growing.

It was in Poltava that Stonov befriended Vladimir Galaktionovich Korolenko. Korolenko, who never recognized Soviet authority, was a Russian author revered next only to Tolstoy. Because of this, the Communists never dared to arrest him. He was well known not only as a brilliant writer but also as a man of character and unwavering morality. His character was revealed in 1913 in his response to the famous Beilis case—a case that divided Russian society in much the same way as the Dreyfus affair had affected France at the end of the last century.

M. Beilis was a Jew falsely accused of the ritual murder of a young Russian boy. Korolenko was not Jewish, but he recognized the case for the rampant anti-Semitism it was. Practically alone among the gentile intelligentsia, he publicly sprang to Beilis's defense.

When Stonov heard that the Korolenko family was near starvation, he tried to help them by getting food from the Communist Party Fund. His efforts came to naught. Korolenko wrote the young man that he refused to receive anything from the bloody hands of the Communist Committee.

Whatever doubts Stonov had, he had suppressed them. His exposure to Korolenko—the friendship that ensued, and the philosophical discussions that stimulated them both—was to have a profound effect on Stonov for the rest of his life. Later he would remark that the character of great Vladimir Korolenko helped him both to endure and to overcome his burdens. In 1921 he threw away his party membership card, changed his name, and left Poltava for Moscow, where nobody knew him.

In Moscow Dmitry Stonov thrived. He became a correspondent for many important newspapers such as *Izvestia.* He was also a primary contributor to Maxim Gorky's magazine *Nashi Dostizhenia* (*Our Achievements*). By 1925 Stonov's first book was published, a collection of short stories called *The Fever. By His Own Hand* followed the same year. His reputation began to build as many more books followed: *Hundreds of Thousands* (1927); *People and Things* (1928); *The Raskin Family* (1929); *Stories about Altay* (1930); *The Blue Bone* (1932); *Out of the Circle* (1936); *Esterka* (1938); *Early Morning* (1947); and others.

To those who met him, Dmitry Stonov was unforgettable. A founding member of the Union of Writers, he formed deep friendships with most of Russia's other promising young authors. Vital, witty and brilliant, his qualities as a leader were apparent from the first meeting. In his autobiography Mikhail Bulgakov would write, "Today I fell in love. With Dmitry Stonov!" Stonov's family life, too, was outstandingly happy. His wife Anna, his son Leonid, and his daughter Yelena were his closest friends, who understood and valued his creativity. They were a small island in the sea of hypocrisy and lies that permeated Soviet society.

The year 1942 found Stonov drafted into the Soviet Army, in which he fought not only in the defense of Stalingrad but also on the fourth Ukrainian front. In 1944, after a serious injury, he was demobilized and worked in the Soviet Informburo and on the Radio Committee. He also returned to teaching at the Literature Institute.

Shortly before midnight on 13 March 1949, Dmitry Stonov's life was to change forever. He was arrested and taken to Lubyanka.

It was during the height of Stalin's campaign against outstanding members of the Jewish intelligentsia. Massive arrests were carried out to further Stalin's plan of resolving the Jewish question. Stonov was a natural target. It was also at this time that many members of the Jewish Antifascist Committee were arrested and, on 12 August 1952, most were shot.

In June 1993 Leonid Stonov (Dmitry's son) accomplished a previously impossible feat. Presenting himself at the offices of the KGB, he was able to gain access to the sealed file of his father's ordeal. The denunciations he found in it shocked him because many were signed by people the family considered their closest associates.

In the arrest decree signed by the terrifying Minister of State Security Abakumov various informers testified as follows:

> D. Stonov showed a hostile attitude to the Soviet system and systematically conducted anti-Soviet propaganda among his writer friends. This propaganda led to the discrediting of the Communist party and Soviet government. He also praised British-American democracy.
>
> Stonov is quoted as saying literary creation was absolutely impossible. Writers are obliged to write according to party request. Their tendency is to rewrite editorial articles from central newspapers in their own words.
>
> D. Stonov said that it was impossible to write what he wanted and that it was impossible to write positively about the Soviet reality when one saw nothing positive in it.

Known only as KGB Major Kosyakov, Stonov's investigator subjected him to months of grueling, intensive questioning and, for several weeks, nonstop sessions of torture and interrogation—demanding admissions of anti-Soviet activity and denunciations against his friends in the Union of Writers. To punish Stonov for his lack of cooperation, he sentenced the writer to a week in the "cabinet," a damp stone isolation closet where it was difficult to sit and impossible to lie down.

For Stonov to break under torture and accuse others was inevitable. If he had not, he would have been shot. It is the nature of the confessions, however, that reveal the man. Stonov named only those writer-comrades he knew were no longer alive. When he ran out of these, he used his extensive knowledge of literature, charging obscure eighteenth- and nineteenth-century poets and novelists. To Stonov's credit, none of his friends who were free at the time ever suffered because of his testimony.

But even under intense questioning at Lubyanka, Stonov kept his head. Profiting from a blunder on the part of a junior interrogator, he discovered that Antonina Shapovalova, a colleague, was an KGB spy. Later, on the only occasion his wife Anna was allowed to see him, he kept telling her, "Don't borrow money from Antonina!"—to whom, of course, they owed nothing. Fortunately, Anna understood him, was able to warn their friends, and Shapovalova's usefulness to the KGB came to an end at the Union of Writers.

Six months later, in September 1949, Stonov was tried in absentia before three civilians and sentenced to ten years in a Siberian prison camp.

Victor Kagan, a physicist and Stonov's fellow inmate in Krasnoyarsky Kray—with whom he remained friends for life—remembers conditions in camp. Life was brutish, prisoners were deliberately starved and required to carry all their water on their backs in huge wooden barrels.

But now, finally recognizing and accepting himself as an enemy of the regime, Stonov felt strangely free. Many years later he would write to Kagan, "I remember the days and years of our communication in prison. We lived so high and in such purity."

Incredibly, had it not been for the massive incompetence of the Communist bureaucracy, Stonov's *In the Past Night* might never have been written. By mistake, he had been sent to a camp exclusively for engineers and scientists. Rather than run the risk of alienating superiors, the camp hierarchy said nothing and Stonov remained there for the first year of his imprisonment. To provide him with work, prison officials volunteered his services "in the freedom," outside of camp, where he worked by day at a library.

For Stonov the real hardship was his inability to pursue his literary career. Writing materials were denied all prisoners. The library was a God-given opportunity, and his solution, as always, was a creative one.

At night he would develop and memorize his stories. During the day, at the library, he would remove the tobacco from his cigarettes and, using a tightly-packed minuscule script, write his manuscripts on the cigarette paper. All throughout his imprisonment at the camp, it was another almost insurmountable task to find a way to smuggle the manuscripts to his family. This he could do only on rare occasions by arranging with prisoners, released "in the freedom," to mail them to relatives—who eventually got them to Anna and his family. Astonishingly, only the middle portion of one story was lost.

Terrified that discovery of the anti-regime stories would add even more years to Stonov's sentence, his wife and son hid the papers in a glass jar and buried them, hoping for his return.

As the problems of getting "safe" people to send his stories became overwhelming, Dmitry decided to sketch only details on the rest of his cigarette paper, send the notes, and hope to complete them if he survived. Immediately after his release he embarked on this task. It was not an easy one. Indeed, it was not until the collection's title came to him that he saw clearly the theme that made his vision so compelling. Stonov realized that from 1917 when the Communists assumed power, until Khrushchev repudiated Stalin in 1956, darkness had covered the land. Each hopeless year had been the same as the last, with no difference at all between them, with no difference between those within the camps and those without; that each month had melded seamlessly into the next until all time had stopped; that all those many days had become just a single night—a long, interminable one.

The title of the book became "In the Past Night," words that described not only the past nights in which the stories had been created, but also the politics of the past that had created the darkness. When completed, the manuscript was returned to the glass jar.

The Stonov family remains ever grateful to Mrs. Deborah Shulman—currently living in Israel—who took the jar with no thought to her own safety and buried it in the soil under her dacha, near Moscow, where the stories were concealed for another twenty-five years.

It was a practice of the Communists to move prisoners from one camp to another as frequently as possible. This served two purposes. It kept the prisoners in a constant state of uncertainty, and it also prevented them from developing friendships with other prisoners or with anyone in authority. To Stonov's dismay, privy as he was to information in his job in the freedom, word came that a huge transfer of prisoners was being planned. It was a devastating blow to his writing opportunities—at least on paper. It also meant the end of any chance to smuggle the stories to Anna.

Transported to a labor camp outside the city of Krasnoyarsk, Stonov was the first writer ever to be sent there. While he was being registered, the commandant asked "Who are you?" to which Stonov answered, "A writer." "What writer!" was the response. "So what on earth have you done if even Zoshchenko and Akhmatova have not been brought to us but you've been taken!" (Mikhail Zoshchenko and Anna Akhmatova were two of twentieth-century Russia's most accomplished writers whose work had been banned.)

From the moment he arrived at the new camp in Krasnoyarsky Krai, until the time off his release, Stonov composed the stories in his mind and recited them over and over every day until they were irrevocably committed to memory.

Victor Kagan, now in Israel, remembers vividly the character and the convictions of the man with whom he carried on philosophical discussions every day they were together, as they braved the snow and subzero weather outside the barracks. His admiration continued to grow with each year of their lifetime correspondence. "Dmitry was not very optimistic about the future of the country. He used to say, 'The fact that people are sitting in prison for no reason is, of course, terrible. But there is something even more terrible—if today all of them were released, absolutely nothing would change.' He went even further. 'If today the authorities were to issue a regulation that people should be fed shit, tomorrow there would be a host of scientists who would prove that shit contains an enormous amount of nutrition.'" But it was Stonov's almost prescient perception of the character of others that impressed Kagan most:

> Dmitry believed that it was possible to judge without mistake a person, based on what he wrote. Once, by listening to the verses of an old friend of mine, he said, "This is a person who keeps everything inside and one can expect anything from him—either good or bad." Later, I learned that my friend was an informer. Another time he told me, "I have just read Howard Fast, his [The Passion of] Sacco and Vanzetti. I think he is a deeply decent person. You will see what kind of scandal will explode when he learns more about the Communists." Of course, he was right. The scandal exploded later, and Fast wrote The Naked God. Of himself, Dmitry would say only, "I have been stopped from saying what I want, but no one can make me say what I don't want."
>
> And always, in his own way, he was a fighter. He fought in his youth during the short time he was a member of the Communist party. After returning from camp, he began to fight again—in the way that was most natural for him. Thus, the Siberian collection of short stories, saved by his family for over a quarter of a century. With his sure instinct for the future, it is not unlikely that Stonov always believed they would someday come to light.

After Stalin's death in March 1953, a group of influential writers worked actively to get Stonov's case reconsidered and, on 20 August 1954, he was released.

In an attempt to forget his ordeal, Stonov threw himself into his work, returning to the places of his youth—Byelorussia, Lithuania, and the western Ukraine—where he gathered material for three more novels: Teklya and Her Friends (1959); In the City of our Fathers; and Short Stories (both published posthumously).

Respected Soviet critic Fyodor Levin wrote about Stonov that "He immersed himself not only in the way his characters lived but in their inner lives as well. Not only did the types of people of whom he wrote cover a wide spectrum but also their geographic background reflected the broad world with which the writer had familiarized himself. Devoted to the tradition of Korolenko, Chekhov, and Bunin, he wrote in a classic yet realistic style that was fascinating not only for its unhurried development, its expressiveness and precise economy of words, but also for the kindness and cordiality with which he related to his characters."

Well-known Russian writer Yury Nagibin remembered, however, that when Dmitry Stonov returned to Moscow—to his family and to literature—although outwardly he remained the same calmly confident and fascinating person, something in him had broken.

Stonov wrote to Kagan seven years after his release, "I cannot write common letters and use common gray words and standard small ideas—I don't know how. That is why I am silent and I torture myself for this silence, for the silent are dead, and we are supposed to be alive."

On 29 December 1962, at age sixty-four, Dmitry Stonov died of a heart attack, eight years after his return from Siberia. About Russia and communism he would quote: "Woe to those who call evil good and good evil, who pretend that the darkness is light and the light is darkness" (Isa. 5:20).

Leonid Stonov

Contents

I

After the Death

1

THE SMALL BUILDING, hollowed out under the earth, is almost obliterated by a three-foot cover of snow. From the chimney a column of smoke curls lazily into the blue, predawn sky. Yanis died, so in the morgue the Tatar orderly is heating the stove. Later this morning, as are the rules, the body will be dissected, so it cannot be allowed to grow stiff.

Yanis is sixty-five years old. Was. From now on, I must speak of him in the past tense. I liked his self-control, the measured calm of his movements, the quiet smile of his gray eyes, his steadiness, his natural talent for industry. And, in listening to him, I could forget I was in camp.

2

Here Yanis sits—broad, stocky, with a long beard and a fox hat. It's clear he received a letter today. Smiling good-naturedly, spreading the bristles on his splendid mustache, he shares the news from home. From the way Yanis speaks, it's as if he had visited there himself—visited his own farm, visited his own neighbors, traveled to the closest city where he could buy supplies and sell his produce—potatoes, grain, and piglets. Imagine! It is only January and already the cow—the only one left for his wife—already the cow has calved. The heifer, of course, must be given to the *kolkhoz,* the collective farm. Other news? Nothing special. Slowly, silently, people live and work. Those who remain are almost never bothered by the authorities. (That means the arrests are slowing down.) His old woman has been accepted into the worker's union; she is now a full member of the *kolkhoz.* It is difficult for her—a woman of sixty—but, like all Letts, she is hardworking and manages to do her share. For instance, she delivered her full quota of milk to the *kolkhoz* even before the deadline. The surplus she drove to the dairy and converted into Holland cheese and butter. She says (Yanis means "she writes") that she has sent him the globe of cheese and a good kilogram of butter because she has enough food. Of course, it would be a good idea to check, since it's possible she left herself with only a very small part or nothing at all. But how can he find out? And there is another mystery—from month to month his woman keeps sending him lard, saying it's from an old boar they killed a Christmas ago. Yanis grins. What strange boars they have in Latvia these days—they keep giving fat a year after they die.

Does Yanis yearn for home? Outwardly, one cannot tell. It so happened that he was arrested. About that nothing can be done—he must be satisfied only with letters. He continues to share the local news. His daughter Marta, who lives a hundred kilometers from where she was born, delivered a boy—her third one. From his sons he has many grandchildren as well, he can recall each of them by name. Of his seven children, five still live and prosper—and that is the immediate clan. But if one takes brothers and sisters, then adds to them uncles and aunts—plus brothers, sisters, uncles, and aunts from an earlier time who live in America, Canada, and Australia—well, there are a lot of them. Of course, some landed in Siberia, as did Yanis, but about that nothing can be done.

Finished with family matters, he moves on to his next favorite subject—physicians. To the physicians working in camp—convict or free—he relates with warm respect. "They are good people and, if allowed, they are always ready to help."

That is not how it was in '44—when the long trains filled with convicts stretched to Siberia from Estonia, Latvia, and Lithuania. "To tell the truth, on these trains there were no physicians at all—just one nurse for everyone, so what could she do? The convoy guards were in complete control; she was powerless." Remembering the deportation, Yanis shakes his head woefully, as if even now, as if looking within himself, he can still see the whole disaster. "Summer. In each car no less than seventy people. They are fed thin soup and drink unpurified water. The dysentery begins. There is no medicine except aspirin or castor oil, no food even for the sick, and the nurse can do nothing. The train crawls slowly—for one week, two weeks, three weeks. Several times it is stalled on the track for several days to give the right-of-way to troops traveling to the front. Finally, all the guards turn into animals, but even our own are worse than wolves. In the night one can hear the muffled sound of struggle and a thin voice crying 'Save me,' then the rattle just before death. A man is sick and weak. Others surround him, suffocate him, remove his clothes, then take his belongings. In the night he simply disappears. And for what? The clothes and belongings they will give to a guard, who will sell them and keep most of the profit himself. With what's left, he may buy them a half loaf of bread or a handful of millet. To make sure others won't take the food, the thieves cram it down their throats instantly, into empty stomachs—and immediately vomiting and diarrhea begin. Later that night, when they too are sick and weak, stronger ones will prey on them in turn. And you must just look and be silent or otherwise even you, the healthy one, will be killed. Yes, it happened. It happened. It is painful to remember."

Sadly, he brings his story to a halt. Then Yanis returns to a subject he likes better—camp physicians. Again his eyes radiate good will. The doctors examined him and—he assures us with artless innocence that it was only because of their special fondness for him—they stated, "You, Yanis, don't have to work—in fact, shouldn't be working at all. Just sit in the invalid barrack and rest." They even furnished him with a certificate warning that any kind of job for Yanis was forbidden.

But can a sound person sit and do nothing? Of course not. So Yanis began to carve things from wood.

I see him working even now. From a small piece of iron he manufactured saws and knives. With these primitive tools he produced his wares—frames, lacquered boxes with secret drawers, spoons, combs. Cross-legged, he sits and works, constantly looking to see if he is watched. The commandant could come in unexpectedly and it's good-bye to all tools, all raw materials, and all finished objects! Even worse, Yanis could be threatened with isolation. He is cautious. In all his time in prison, he has been caught red-handed only twice.

As a rule, Yanis never gave his work away. You want it? You buy it! It seemed he couldn't even imagine giving something away on which he had worked for several days. He would bargain, but only because it was expected of him—and, in the end, he always took what he'd been offered. After all, the money came in handy. Sometimes there was sugar to buy in the commissary, or perhaps paper, envelopes, and stamps—and Yanis couldn't ask anything from either his daughter or his sons; they had problems of their own. Every so often he would make an exception, but only for the physicians. One he might present with a cigarette box, another with a small frame. What else could he do? How else could he repay their kindness—for giving him, an obviously healthy man, a release from physical labor. So? For a favor, one must pay.

Did Yanis ever think about dying? I don't think so. We spoke often and he never mentioned it. "I'm a healthy man. My father lived until ninety, less one year. Besides, they lengthened my life," he said, referring with irony to his twenty-five year sentence. "So I, like my father, will have to live on and on." Did he really take serving his term seriously? About that he also avoided speaking.

3

It took Yanis one hour to die. After the lights-out signal, he suddenly felt sick. Shaking with weakness and dizzy, he threw up several times before they took him to the hospital. At five in the morning, invalid Belyaev, returning from the place where he worked as a substitute, noticed smoke coming from the morgue chimney. "I wonder," he thought. "Who is being heated?" he wondered. It proved to be Yanis.

Belyaev quickened his steps. Was it possible the other invalids had already gotten wind of the Latvian's death? It could not be. Still, he was nervous. In spite of being lame, he limped faster and faster. He would have run had he not feared notice by the guard in the tower. Catching his breath, he entered the barrack. The oil lamp was smoking and the rest of the invalids were either deep in sleep or snoring. Sitting by a table, an orderly dozed. One invalid got up, slipped into his work coat, put his feet into his felt boots and, still stumbling because he wasn't fully awake, left to satisfy his needs. Concealing himself, Belyaev waited.

Sleep is soundest in the hours just before dawn. Removing his shoes, Belyaev crept to the bunk on which Yanis had lain. His neighbors, both above and below, continued to snore. Stretched out, he waited several minutes, listening to their sounds. He even breathed heavily, as if he himself were asleep. Anxiously, he wondered if the mirror Yanis had made was still inside his table. Thick glass—from where it came no one knew—set into a finely crafted frame. Clearly, when a person does something for himself, he doesn't begrudge the time or labor. There was no doubt—nobody in the barrack yet knew of Yanis's death. The sheet, the blanket, the pillow and case—everything was still in place. Carefully, he turned, opened the drawer of the table and, groping inside, sighed with relief. The mirror was in place as well. With the celerity with which people steal, he slipped the mirror into the side pocket of his coat.

It was now possible to return to his own place but—almost sensing through his skin the profit they would bring—the pillowcase, sheet, and towel gave him no peace. He was unable to leave. The sound of his feet impatiently thumping on the bunk brought him back to his senses. "Devil take me," he cursed, afraid of his own noise. Sooner or later, Yanis's bedlinen would be stolen anyway! There was only one problem—the black ink stamps identifying them as camp property were impossible to remove. Should he cut them out, as other prisoners did? And, were he to decide on cutting—which was essential to start immediately—what would he say if someone should wake? He realized it was fear that immobilized him. "You're a fool," he reproached himself savagely. Without waiting another moment, he began to pull off the pillowcase, roll up the sheet, and take the towel from its nail.

Wake-up found Belyaev back in his bunk. Instantly, with a bulging bundle under his arm, he left for the locker room next to the barrack. The locker-room warden took his time in responding, then stamped angrily to the door in his bare feet. An old man from the forest of Altay—short, stocky, with a broken nose—he looked like a wizard, so covered with grey hair that even his bare chest curled like smoke. A small copper cross, buried deep, was barely visible. To the other convicts he related with suspicion—especially the thieves—and made it known that, to all intents and purposes, he was a prisoner purely for religious reasons. "Devil curse you, at such an early hour," he said irritably, crossing himself and staring at Belyaev and his bundle. "What do you want?"

Just a moment before the question, Belyaev hadn't known what he was going to tell the old man. Irresistibly, something had drawn him to the locker room and here he had come. Now, more awake, he scanned the shelves—especially the shelf containing boxes of food. Sent to the inmates from home, the food was kept in this room as well. Quickly he said, "Yanis the Latvian died. Did you hear?" Shifting from one foot to the other, the warden scratched his chest. Still sleepy, he was slow to understand.

"What has that to do with me?" he asked angrily. "He died? So he died! His end came, and he will be buried."

"That's not what I mean. Last week he received a parcel."

"So?" asked the warden.

"So it should be almost full."

Finally, Belyaev's words penetrated into the warden's brain. He became even angrier. His short neck flushed and, in a strange way, the blood rushed to his face from his beard up. "And you? Why do you put your nose into it? It's the commanders' business. Let them say what is to be done with it."

"I'm not interfering—I only wanted to let you know. Will you let me have access to my trunk?"

The old man looked at Belyaev's bundle with sudden understanding—and from then on every moment was precious. But it was necessary to get rid of Belyaev as quickly as possible, without being too obvious.

"What if they search the boxes?" he asked. "Will I be responsible?"

"They'll never search all the boxes," said Belyaev. "The last time they did was for the October Revolution celebration. They won't do it again until May Day or after."

"All right," agreed the warden grudgingly, "just remember—I know nothing, I saw nothing."

4

The warden pulled on his pants and his felt shoes even before the door slammed. He was lazy, and just the idea that he had to hurry oppressed him, but there was no time to think. First, he bolted the door. Of course, he could not contemplate taking Yanis's things. It was impossible for a locker-room warden to steal even a scrap. He was trusted and he had to value that trust. Ah, but food. Yanis's parcel was almost full! From camp practice, he knew that the most reliable storage place was the stomach. What one ate, no one else could take. So, quickly crossing himself and putting the Latvian's box on his knees, he began to work speedily with his self-made knife. To cut and swallow wonderful Latvian lard had always enraptured him—with its thickness, softness, whiteness, and pleasant flavor. With a peasant's eye, he cut the lard into small equal cubes. After gulping each of them down, he followed up with Holland cheese and a thick layer of butter. His eyes bulged. His short neck was strained. One could see the lumps of food pushing each other down through his gullet. Finally, he tired. Sweating profusely, choked with food, he kept swallowing as if he were forced. There was still so much lard left, it didn't even look touched. Frustrated, the warden shook his head. What should he do now? Put another piece inside someone else's box, to eat another day? It might be discovered. Then it came to him. In addition to his trunk, Belyaev had a bag. That would be the best hiding place! He gave the plan about three-minutes' thought. If he were to take more lard, how much? In the invalid barrack, everyone knew that Yanis had recently received a parcel. But the convicts were not important—they would complain and then be quiet. Much worse was Kazashvili, their capo. Cunning, fast, and connected to the guards, he could do whatever he wanted. Although he was still worried, the warden put a brick of lard into Belyaev's bag. To the butter and cheese he was indifferent.

5

About Yanis's death, capo Kazashvili found out just before eight.

"Died? My, my, my." He liked to think aloud. Now he walked back and forth in his small room, moving his hands and muttering. The convicts outside, who didn't yet know of Yanis's death, heard his voice and wondered what had happened. Kazashvili was not clever, but he was uncommonly treacherous. His job was to serve as go-between for both guards and convicts, but he betrayed each of them alike. As the convicts saw it, Kazashvili was dangerous, so it was safer to get along with him—the more so because he was so cheap to buy. He had been imprisoned for smuggling, but he hinted that smuggling was simply a cover. In his time, he hinted, he had been tightly connected with the Georgian counterrevolutionaries on one side and, on the other, had studied brother-to-brother with Lavrenty—in this way, he called Beria by his first name. "If I were to write Lavrenty that someone dared to put Kazashvili in prison . . . " But he would not write and even in that there was implied meaning.

"Such a good man, Yanis—my, my, my." These exclamations didn't prevent him from thinking, "Who is on duty today in the guard's room? Corporal Yevseev. A bad man! If it were Fedyukov, one could present him with Yanis's *moskvichka*. The shabby work jacket would have been enough, and the form The Prisoner Had No Possessions would already be prepared. Yevseev will demand an inventory; he will examine the trunk and the bag and then take the best of everything for himself. That meant it was possible to get only the food. And what kind of person was the locker-room warden?" At this moment, Kazashvili believed that particular warden to be the worst person in the world.

Upset and insulted by fate, he entered the locker room. In a cold sweat, the warden was on his bed under a blanket. He was sick. Breathing heavily, he was gasping for air. Kazashvili asked, "What happened?" The answer was, "God only knows." The warden's body ached and he was nauseated. Obviously it was malaria. What else could it be?

Leaning into the miserable man's face, Kazashvili began to talk in a loud whisper about the scum and the camp ruffians. Some son of a bitch keeps writing the commander, writing and writing that he would like to take the place of the locker-room warden in the invalid barrack. He is arranging this secretly with the overseers, with each one separately. He bribes them. The day before yesterday he, Kazashvili, was called and actually interrogated—and yesterday the commander of the guard had talked to him. He wanted to know, was it true about the warden?—that he rummaged through the trunks and the bags belonging to the convicts, and that they were able to keep vodka in there?

At that point Kazashvili stopped whispering and said aloud, "Can you believe that? Can you believe such people?" Through hooded eyes, he watched the warden. The warden didn't believe a word and knew it was all lies made up on the spot. And even doubled in half with the pain in his stomach, he nevertheless began to swear and justify himself.

"Vodka? Please! Let them search!" He kept a complete record of everything given to him, and he took full responsibility for it. Let them search! He was innocent!

The warden thrashed about in anger, though every move was plagued by pain. His stomach ached and he was nauseated, but it was necessary to keep down all that he had eaten. "Let them check, let them," he croaked.

But Kazashvili had accomplished what he wanted, so he was in no hurry. "Calm down," he said finally, "let me do the job I'm supposed to do." Of course, it was necessary to placate the commander—but that business was now his, Kazashvili's.

In such a way did he talk for a long time, and only then did he bring up the subject of Yanis's parcel. Of course! That was the way to shut them all up—with butter and lard. With butter and lard!

Now it was the warden's turn to whisper. The mere mention of lard made him sicker than ever, but still he struggled with himself. He had to think about tomorrow. It wasn't every day that someone died, and his stomach wouldn't ache forever. "Yes, the world is full of enemies and the envious, and neither lives by the rule of God. They like to take things that don't belong to them and profit from other people's misfortune." He finished by begging Kazashvili not to forget him. He, the warden, received no help from anyone. In Altay, his own relatives were able to live only by begging. He could visualize their pitiful plight, though he had just invented them a moment ago. With that, plus the stabs of pain in his stomach, he was even able to shed a few tears. Too weak to rise, he could barely point to Yanis's parcel with his finger.

"I don't ask for much, only a trifle."

His sorrowful voice was so sincere that Kazashvili, who didn't believe him for a moment, was moved to pity. What a man he was, their capo! And, to allow the warden enough time to appreciate that fact, Kazashvili generously cut a small piece of lard for him.

Mentally adding the brick of lard he had already hidden to the piece just handed to him by the capo, the warden calculated, "It will be near two kilograms." After remembering that, he crossed himself once more and moaned piteously about the sins of man.

6

Death in camp surfaces only at night. Afraid of day, it prefers the secrecy of darkness, although the secret is known to every convict there. At ten in the morning on a glittering, frosty day, a prisoner-physician is directed to the morgue. In his hand he carries a small satchel containing all the instruments necessary for a postmortem examination, plus an ink pot and paper. But ask him where he is going and why, and he will tell you the first thing that pops into his head—though he winks at the same time, as if to say, "Why do you ask? You know I'm not allowed to say. If they discover I did, I'll lose my place on the medical staff."

Meanwhile, in the small half-dark shed adjacent to the morgue, a convict-carpenter is building the coffin. For whom, you ask? "That is not my business" will be the answer. "If you want to know, ask the commander." But, as with most seasoned carpenters who have to spend their lives working in silence, he would like to speak, to share his thoughts. "A man lived and breathed—not of our faith, perhaps—but without a word he disappears. Does he have any countrymen here? No? Then," he says, storing his hammer below and pointing his finger toward heaven as he finishes his usual speech, "then all of us will meet up there."

Once done with the coffin, the carpenter—who is a general handyman as well—takes a rectangular piece of tin and paints it white. The marker is affixed to a tall, thin iron bar. When the paint dries, the carpenter carefully inscribes a number—1192— which is the death number assigned to the deceased Yanis.

After the doctor departs, the Tatar must sew Yanis back up. For this, the medical unit grants him a fee, one hundred grams of alcohol. The Tatar is skillful. To date, no superior has ever seen him drunk, and no convict has ever heard about his payment. As a final duty, he dresses the corpse in underclothes.

There is no longer any need to heat the morgue so, until the middle of night, Yanis will be alone. It is now about forty-two degrees below zero. Slowly, he will begin to stiffen, then ice will silver his eyelids and noticeably whiten his beard. Even his nostrils will be rimmed with a fine border of rime.

Two hours after lights-out, an oxcart will come to the camp gate. Named by the convicts for the sound of the animal drawing it, it is known as "Moo One." The coffin is open, the cover is near. Two guards are on duty in the sentry box. One checks the number on the metal tag, the other checks the wire label affixed to one of Yanis's toes. They tally.

Creaking down the road, the cart is accompanied by two prisoners and a guard, who drag along beside it. At the camp cemetery, cleared in a forest glade, the grave is already dug. Long rows of little hills stretch in every direction, blue in the dim light. Some have already sunk back into the earth and can hardly be seen in the gathering dark. Using a heavy stone, the convicts can now nail down the lid. Then, as they groan under the heavy load—it's difficult for only two men—Yanis is lowered into his grave. The men then fill it with frosty earth and snow. Finally, taking the bar with the number 1192 on it, they pound it into the new little hill, at the head.

Here the coded marker will stay for a year, or perhaps a year and a half. Then it will bend and fall down and, if it hasn't completely rusted, will be repainted and renumbered for the next deceased.

7

In about two weeks, a letter for Yanis will come from the remote farm in remote Latvia. The letter will be returned with the notation, "Addressee Unknown." In a month or so, a parcel will arrive. It, too, will be returned with the same notation. Alerting the family to the death of a convict is not allowed—and, since Yanis had no countrymen in camp, there is no one to smuggle out the news as a hint in a letter home.

That Yanis no longer lives his wife and children will surmise in six months or so, after all the letters and all the parcels have been returned. Nevertheless, to seek solace, they will write the commander and ask. For over a half year they may wait in anguish, but the answer will never arrive.

In Stalin's camp, the commander cannot reply to requests from the family. It is forbidden.

The Jewish Melody

1

OUR CAMP PHYSICIAN, David Israilevich Rivkin, was typical of a particular kind of Jew—shy, nearsighted, always smiling a sad smile and always humming an almost inaudible tune. Bald, bent over, and freckled, he hummed as he examined patients and thumped them percussively on the back; he hummed when he played chess—with the same absentminded indifference whether he was winning or losing—and, in the office of the interrogator, I am sure he hummed the same tune there. Behind his thick glasses, his eyes were so magnified they looked uncommonly large and their color seemed intensified. When he removed his glasses, the eyes he revealed were tired and, like most myopic eyes, a bit crossed—eyes that looked on God's world as if it were not quite clear. He was quiet and withdrawn to such an extent that, even after a five-month-long acquaintance and many meetings, I knew no more about him now than I had known the first month—and what I knew was only general.

In 1931, when Dr. Rivkin was thirty-three, he returned to a Russia he had left when he was only seven. For nine years he lived in the Soviet Union, "as a free cossack," he used to say, and practiced as a pediatrician in a children's hospital in Smolensk. In 1940 he was arrested and sent to a labor camp—the first time for ten years then, later, for ten more. When we met, he was already in his twelfth year of confinement.

Our camp was one of the most strict. Of three thousand prisoners, only a mere twenty were allowed to move about freely without a guard. I was one of them because they needed a highly trained engineer like me to supervise production. In our prison canteen they carried only toothbrushes and plastic cups so, sometimes, when I returned from the city to which I often had to go, I would bring David Israilevich two pounds of margarine or a dozen eggs or a small box of cookies. He would often reproach me, saying "Why? Why do you take such a chance? It is not permitted to bring so much through the checkpoint." Immediately, he would take money and pay me, then shyly remove his glasses and clean them. He was scrupulous about not bothering people or asking for special privileges.

He was right, Rivkin—it was indeed forbidden for unescorted prisoners to bring back extra food from the freedom. But the seasoned prisoner is cunning and sly, and I already knew how to get along with the overseers so they looked at me with hooded eyes or searched me without interest. Such carelessness—which, by the way, I paid for—gave me frequent opportunities to smuggle special treats into camp. On one occasion I was able to get past the checkpoint with two small bottles of pure alcohol hidden inside my high felt boots—alcohol that could be converted to a good liter of vodka. It goes without saying what great luck that was. Thank God my cell mate, a forwarding agent, had to spend the night away. I scrounged up some good appetizers and invited the doctor to a banquet in my tiny room.

A banquet in camp. A banquet behind the locked door of a place of confinement, with nonstop peeking over one's shoulder as a precaution, with the bottle hidden under the table and carefully concealed. But despite the precautions, despite all of the fear of being caught and all the looking behind one's back, there is something exhilarating about an affair like that. Putting the scraps on the table with two cups of tasteless camp tea, constantly checking to see we weren't watched, winking at each other, we drank with pleasure from the bottle. Toasting, David would say, "This is the last time we will endanger ourselves!" And I would toast with an opposite sentiment,

"Let's, God willing, do the same thing tomorrow." In such a manner, we savored the full bottle. After which, hiding it, we began our "tea ceremony" without apprehension.

As with all people who drink rarely and get drunk quickly, the face of my friend became wet and flushed and his eyes became slightly wild. From humming, he moved to singing in full voice. Gesturing like a conductor, he sang a famous folk song about a coachman. Finally drunk, he sang some Jewish songs and even American songs—and then fell into melancholy. Sighing deeply, he said, "Oh, my. Oh, my, maybe you'll tell me a story." I guessed that the doctor wanted to tell a story himself. My guess was correct. Soon, not looking at me and sitting in the corner as if to conceal himself, he began reluctantly. Then more and more rapidly and with some excitement, David Israilevich began to speak . . .

2

"No, my friend, memories are like a river . . . like water that overflows the shore after the floodgate has been opened," he said. It was clear that mentally he had begun this conversation with me earlier but only now began to say the words aloud. "I do not believe people who say they've forgotten their childhood, forgotten the country in which they were born, that they push those memories from their hearts and then live forever without them, without any pangs of homesickness. I will never believe such people. What nonsense! Somewhere I read, I don't remember where, that love for the Motherland is atavistic. Well, let it be atavistic. Calling it that does not make the feeling any less compelling or powerful. From the time I was seven I lived in America. English became my native language, and even now I still think in English. I studied in American schools, went to an American university. The people, the landscape—everything was American and belonged to me. But there were moments when reality would suddenly drop away and, as if from another world, darkly different landscapes and people would appear. I would hear strange voices and their sounds were different. I tell you human beings are bound by their traditions, and whatever is said about the century of atomic energy, we will forever remain like our ancestors—and the places where our ancestors lived and where we ourselves were born and first saw the world will pull us. Oh, but I know—all this is nonsense to you, and you are bored."

His face was as flushed as before and his eyes glittered wildly. As if he wanted to block out their brilliance, he put his glasses back on. I knew after he said "You are bored" that I was supposed to say, "No, no! Please continue, it's interesting," but I didn't say anything. I had the impression he was telling his story not so much for me as for himself.

"You are a Jew," he began again. "You have heard, of course, about the terrible pogroms of 1905. One of those pogroms was in Elisavetgrad. We—that is, my father's family—lived in a small village three miles from there. The rioters came so unexpectedly, we couldn't defend or hide ourselves; there was no warning. Of my entire family—and of brothers alone I had five—only I survived. I was lucky in other respects as well, I never saw how my family was killed. Terrified by the loud cries and the crash of broken glass, I jumped from the window and escaped into a field. To this day, I can still smell the fragrance of the blossoming rye in which I hid and in which, from exhaustion, I fell asleep. Masses of thick, bluish blossoms waved above me, radiating warmth and beauty; every stalk of rye rose toward the sky like a small gnarled tree, every cornflower looked at me with blue eyes and long blue lashes. Maybe everything was not really like that, maybe I imagined all this loveliness later, many years later, or saw it in my dreams—I cannot tell you. I don't know. Next morning some countrywomen found me in the field and, for the first time in my life, I heard myself called 'little orphan.'" The doctor became silent and smiled wryly before he continued. "That year there was a good crop of orphans like me. In our small region alone, they gathered up thirty-five. Soon a Jewish charity brought us to America and we began life over again in an orphanage in Philadelphia.

"All orphanages are the same—in Russia as in England, in England as in America. The same clothes, the same beds, the same blankets, and the same smell in the rooms and corridors—orphan smell. But really, I have no right to complain. We were clothed, had shoes, were fed and taught. Step by step, little by little, we began to adjust. The fact that all of us shared the same homeland and now lived in another country forged a bond that could never be broken. I think no other children share that kind of bond. Not only as children—it was a bond that lasted all our lives—when we got older, our young men fell in love with our girls, and the girls preferred our young men to all others. In this way we mastered the new world. Every one of us graduated from high school and a good half graduated from university. Among the pogrom victims from our area alone there are several physicians, several engineers, one lawyer, and one famous journalist—whose articles, by the way, are still quoted today in Soviet newspapers.

"I still have to tell you how I returned to the Soviet Union. When I first came to America, the memories and melancholy didn't affect me. Only in rare moments would there flash across my mind a sudden picture of my father's forge. I could see the cold blue fire over which he worked, hear the sound of his hammer on the anvil and see the huge spray of sparks he created under his blows. I could smell the smell of coal and of the hot metal as it was plunged into cold water—and when I remembered and felt all that, it was as if someone had wrapped my heart in his hands and squeezed it too tightly. As the years progressed, the melancholy enveloped me more and more. I would be sad and tormented for days and weeks and think of nothing but returning. Of course, reading Soviet newspapers and magazines, listening to Communist speakers who lectured at Philadelphia clubs and, most of all, hearing the rumble of the first Five-Year Plan echoing across the ocean strengthened this resolve. It was as if each of us, each transplanted Russian, heard in our heads the sound of rebuilding. Shortly thereafter, I became convinced that my place was there—that is, here."

After saying all this, David Israilevich fell into a long silence. It seemed as if he were unwilling to speak further and wanted to bring his story to a close. Whether I was drunk or just trying to raise his spirits, I joked, "Here? You wanted to come here to the camp?" Confused, he replied "Here? No. No!" And only after saying these words did he realize I was trying to be funny and laughed. "For the nine years after I became a Soviet citizen I lived as a free cossack," he said—repeating his favorite expression—"and then I was arrested and accused of being a spy." "An American spy, of course," I prompted. Again the doctor laughed. "I don't remember exactly. It seems to me they threw in France and England, too."

3

The next day, David Israilevich was upset and concerned. His eyes avoided mine and, more often than usual, he would remove his glasses and clean them with a hesitant smile playing on his lips. It was plain that he regretted speaking so freely the previous night. "You know," he said, "it's necessary to drink on a regular basis or not to drink at all." Like all teetotalers, he had his own theories about alcoholism. "Drink without practice," he continued, "and you begin to speak nonsense. Please, forgive me and forget it."

Drink, talk, forget. Erase yesterday to exist tomorrow. Don't betray secrets, and you won't be betrayed. As if we made a pact, we never again referred to that conversation. Besides, it was not long afterward that an unexpected misfortune poisoned my few moments of leisure. Frankly speaking, I was too concerned about my own problems to think about the doctor's past.

Frightened of further persecution and longing to live near me during those difficult years, my wife left Moscow. Together with our five-year-old daughter, she moved to Siberia and settled in a small city within five miles of the camp. It was not only a mistaken move but a disastrous one. As an unescorted convict, I could sometimes steal an hour and visit them—but each meeting threw me into depression.

Imagine, if you will, the tiny dark room for which we paid an exorbitant rent, hung round with the owner's icons; my inadequate wages which were not even matched by those of my wife; the pale, pinched face of my small daughter; the poverty and extreme need they vainly tried to conceal from me; and my utter inability to help them. No, no, there was absolutely no reason for such martyrdom. Added to that my daughter Masha fell ill, fell ill so severely that local physicians could only shrug their shoulders, trying to guess: was it the

Siberian winter that harmed her or something else they didn't know about? I saw my child melting away.

In alarm, I told David Israilevich about my misfortune. He listened, humming as usual, and said, "Well, it would be helpful for me to see your daughter." Without thinking, I repeated these words to my wife. And, since my wife had already visited every physician in the area and not one of them could help her, she latched on to this suggestion with the fanatic strength found only in a mother frantic to save her child. The fact that David Israilevich was an American doctor and thus all-powerful, according to my wife's perception, also played its part. Within a short time I had to swear that David Israilevich would examine our child.

"Would examine." How? That which is simple when one is free is not at all simple when one is in prison. Sending a letter, for instance. Who among us would worry over such a thing? Write it, stamp it, drop it into the mailbox, and that's that. But not in prison. In a high-security camp one is permitted to send only one letter every six months. One sits down to write and agonizes over every sentence. It's as if a censor sits inside you and dictates each individual word. But that's not all. Once written, it must be left unsealed and placed in the camp letter box. From there it goes to the real censor, the camp censor. Now, what seemed harmless to one's internal censor can be totally unacceptable to the camp censor, who finds it full of hidden meaning. In the best case, the censor will call and suggest that the letter be rewritten. In the worst case, he will simply throw it into the fire. Not hearing from you, your family—who has already been anxious for six months—will now be convinced you are dead and will mourn you and bury you for another six months, until a later letter arrives.

How in God's name would it be possible for David Israilevich to examine my daughter? It goes without saying he would never be allowed to leave camp to see her in the city, even under guard. There was only one way—to bring Masha to the camp, despite the freezing cold, and somehow get permission for her to be examined at the checkpoint. But that was almost impossible as well. True, the camp commander was friendly to me—but so friendly as to violate camp rules? Knowing him, I doubted that very much. So I decided to go around him and to start, as people say, not from the head but the foot.

There was an old man of about sixty, who served as an overseer in our camp. He was rude and grumbling but was not actually a bad man. If there were no other guards at the checkpoint, he would check the food I brought back from the freedom and make remarks in a tone of voice that could not be mistaken. "Just imagine," he would say, "margarine! Just imagine, eggs!"—as if he were seeing these things for the first time in his life. Naturally, I always took the hint and would leave three eggs or a half pound of margarine on his desk. When I learned that this grumbler would be on duty the next day at the checkpoint, I spoke to him from my heart. As a result, the following morning my wife dressed Masha in all the warm clothing she had and brought her to camp in her sled. At the same time, David Israilevich and I managed to meet them at the checkpoint. "Don't mess around too long," the grumbler ordered.

Actually, the doctor worked quickly—but to my mind, he didn't really know how to speak to children. He spoke to Masha in a way that reminded me of a provincial photographer taking pictures of the very young. "And now I will show you something wonderful! Look here, Mashenka, now a bird will fly out of my sleeve." With that he put a teaspoon in her mouth. When she began to gag, he started to sing a child's song to her about a small goat. Suddenly, his eyes became terribly sad and his hands began to tremble.

After the examination, he looked at the prescriptions my wife brought with her and hissed disapprovingly through his teeth. To my wife's question, "Is it really the climate that is harmful to Masha's health?" he answered in a typical Jewish way. "Climate, shmimate," he said, "climate has nothing to do with it. The girl has worms, nothing more. I will tell you what to do, and from now on it's in your hands." Humming in his usual way, he wrote her a prescription. I will tell you right now that his diagnosis was absolutely correct, and he helped my daughter get back on her feet.

The overseer hurried us and, hastily saying goodbye to my wife and daughter, we returned from the checkpoint. The doctor lit a cigarette. I noticed that his hands were still shaking. "Imagine," he said gruffly, as if to hide his emotions. "I haven't seen children for twelve years—for twelve years—and I'm a pediatrician." The dangling cigarette prevented him from humming, so he spat it out. Without thinking I asked, "Did you have children of your own?" As if by reflex, he pulled off his glasses so sharply that he tore one ear and cursed rudely. After a moment, he replied, "Children? Children? No. I didn't!" and somehow he seemed upset.

4

Even in a situation as cursed as the one my family and I were in, happy moments could occur. Now I'm sitting in the small dark room with icons on the walls, and wood is crackling in the country stove. Masha, much less pale, is sitting on my lap, and my wife is nearby. It seems to me that my wife is now calm, her complexion is no longer sallow, and she feels content. How much does a human being need to forget his misfortune? My daughter is recovering, the fire is glowing—after all, aren't these supposedly trivial things the most valuable and important in life?

Alas, the happy moments disappear as quickly as they arrive. Suddenly, my wife looked out the window. Her face turned white, and fear distorted her eyes and lips. Whispering in a voice trembling with anxiety, she said "It is her again, and now there is someone with her!" Immediately, her anxiety was transferred to me. I didn't even know what she was talking about, but instantly I started to tremble. My heart began to pound. I began to realize that I had no right to be where I was, in this dark, dank room. At any moment I could be discovered. They would cancel my pass. They would exile my family even further to the north, to a frozen wasteland like Karaganda. Peering through the frosted glass, I also saw the women. In their heavy coats, with long scarves wound round their heads, they were standing next to our house and looking through our window. "See?" she whispered. "See?"

Almost unable to breathe from fear, she told me how, five days ago, after returning from the checkpoint with David Israilevich's prescription in her hand, she entered the pharmacy. The pharmacist was a woman. The moment she saw the prescription, she leaned out of the cubicle and asked insistently, "Where and from whom did you get this prescription?"

"I didn't lose my head," my wife assured me. "As if I were annoyed, I tore the prescription from her hand and began to leave. I left without looking back but, as if I could actually feel it, I knew the woman from the pharmacy was following me. I rushed home and, through the window, I could see that the woman—still wearing her white laboratory coat—was now standing near our house. My God, what a feeling went through me! I could picture what they would do to this convicted doctor! For about ten minutes the woman stood there. The day before yesterday, I saw her there again. And now she's here for the third time, and she's brought someone else with her! What should we do?"

"Nonsense," I said, "nonsense. Calm down." But I was far from being calm myself. A humiliating fear enveloped me. Who knew? Maybe there was a list of camp physicians in every pharmacy, and this vigilant employee discovered our David Israilevich had written a prescription for which he wasn't authorized. It was possible they were watching my wife constantly, too, and now she was caught red-handed—or maybe I was the one who was being watched. Those are only three of a dozen scenarios that flashed through my mind in an instant, and suddenly I was shaking. Oh, let it be damned, this fear that keeps us living like hunted animals! Pulling myself together, I asked, "Where is the prescription?" Turning her back to the curtained window, my wife took the paper from her handbag and, still whispering, told me she had gotten it filled at another pharmacy.

"And imagine," she said, "nobody there paid it any attention at all!"

I tore up the prescription and threw it into the fire. Then I put on my camp hat and hood and, without even saying good-bye, turned toward danger and left the house. I no longer cared. What happened happened. I was sick and tired of hiding all the time. I had nothing more to lose. Besides, it was ridiculous to try to pretend anymore. Believing that I had convinced myself of all this, I walked toward the women, rehearsing in my mind what I would ask them. "What are you doing here?" I would shout. And then the unexpected happened:

they were as fearful of me as I was of them. They whispered to each other and started to walk away. Then they began to run. Should I follow them? But who was I? I was a man deprived of all rights. As a prisoner, I was not even allowed to run. They could have me stopped, and then they'd discover I was in a place I was not allowed, engaged in activities that were forbidden. No, for a man in camp clothing, it would be ridiculous and dangerous for me to race after these women. Should I return to my wife and daughter? But perhaps someone else in another house was now watching. Better to get away and not beg for trouble. Slowly, I got control of myself and simply went about my camp business, thanking God that things seemed to be all right and misfortune had missed me at least another day. For the moment, I was safe.

Of course, I never mentioned a thing about these strange women to David Israilevich. Why make him nervous for nothing?

5

After that, three weeks passed. My daughter recovered completely and the mysterious pharmacist stopped appearing. To make the story short, everything returned to normal. Once, when visiting my wife, I even made fun of her fears. After all, when one looks at it, there is nothing surprising in the question "Where and from whom did you receive this prescription?" It is possible that, according to new rules, all pharmacies must list the name of the physician writing the prescription, and—like all doctors'—David Israilevich's handwriting was illegible. Then, with Masha as my biggest fan, I acted out how my wife had run from the pharmacy and the woman had followed her because she was certain my wife was stealing something. True, the pharmacist and her friend had also run. And what were they doing near our house? I had an answer for that, too. This pharmacist might have heard there was a room for rent in our neighborhood and had come to look at it. Why did she bring someone with her? Maybe she was a possible roommate. Now, suddenly, a fierce man came racing at them. It was nighttime, there was no one around—so it was natural for them to turn and run away. Masha laughed and applauded and my wife nodded her head, both believing and disbelieving me at the same time. Was she afraid? Yes, of course she was. For a long time now, fear had governed her whole life. "But you," she asked, "weren't you frightened?" She was so close to the truth that I didn't answer. Oh yes, I had been frightened. There was nothing funny at all in what had happened.

Three weeks is rather a long time and, as I mentioned before, we began to forget the event. Suddenly, the whole story was made clear. But now I have to introduce a new character, Raisa Markovna, because it was she who suddenly and unexpectedly burst into my wife's room. Before I could get a good look at her, I heard two sentences, each different in their meaning. The first was, "For God's sake, tell me, is Dr. Rivkin—is David Israilevich Rivkin alive?" The second was, "Oh my God, where am I?" and she covered her eyes. The first question was asked with such entreaty and despair that it wrenched my heart and, without listening to the second, I answered immediately. "Alive and healthy, I swear to you, David Israilevich is alive and healthy. I saw him today and I will see him tonight." It was my wife who answered her second question—"Where am I?"—because she guessed why it was asked. Pointing to the icons on the wall, she said, "Don't worry. These belong to the owner. Please sit down." The stranger didn't sit, she collapsed into the chair, and sobs tore through her whole body.

Even now, while I am telling this story, I hear those cries and see her bloodless face, her eyes—faded from years of weeping and full of tears even now—and the gray hair that shadowed a skin covered with wrinkles. She clutched her heart in pain and we gave her something to quiet her. Only then was she able to speak.

6

She interrupted herself frequently, leaping from past to present, and every time she stopped she would ask, "Is it true? Is David really healthy, is he really alive?" Each time I had to swear that I had spoken to our camp doctor just that morning. Was she comforted by my assurances? After several minutes, she would ask again, "This man, is he a very nearsighted man with a wonderful ear for music? Actually, he should have been a musician rather than a doctor, he has such a wonderful ear." Once she took a photograph from her handbag and, looking at it, I gasped. It was possible to recognize David Israilevich, though of course he had aged. But what had the years done to Raisa? In the picture, next to Rivkin, stood a beautiful young woman who resembled the present Raisa Markovna as a beautiful young girl resembles her grandmother.

As no doubt you've guessed, the appearance of Raisa Markovna was connected both to the frightening pharmacist and to the women who had stood outside the house where my family lived.

David Israilevich's wife had also been orphaned in a pogrom—in the most cruel one, in Kishinev. Unlike David Israilevich, from that terrible time she remembered only the icons with which the murderers entered the house. It's not difficult to explain why she had no memory at all of how her mother, father, sister, and brothers looked. She had blanked out the faces of the murderers as well, but the sunburned faces of the saints on the icons remained forever in her mind. That was why, when seeing the icons, she shrank away, covered her eyes, and cried, "Where am I?"

Meanwhile, her memory of the past did not prevent her from coming with her husband when he returned to the Soviet Union. She was a physician as well—indeed, that is how Raisa, after her exile, had met and become friends with the pharmacist near our camp. Together, the Rivkins worked in the children's hospital. They were both young, healthy, and hardworking—and the rigors of our life never bothered them. There was only one sorrow—their lack of children. But even this sorrow disappeared: three years before the arrest of her husband, Raisa delivered a daughter. The child was named after David Israilevich's murdered mother, Lyuba. When she reached that point, Raisa Markovna began feverishly searching in her handbag, so intently that she failed to notice or even care that her gray hair had again fallen over her face. "Here," she said, "here is a picture of our Lyuba. He, of course, won't recognize her. If you will really see him today, I beg you, please—please, give him the picture of our daughter.

He was such a good father, such a father! Tell him! Tell him, please. Tell him our daughter is alive!"

Later, when I walked to the checkpoint, I carried no alcohol or food. Somehow it seemed that the picture I carried to David Israilevich had to be carried alone. I thought of Raisa Markovna, now an old woman, and the doctor with his tired eyes and his humming, and their search for who knows what—from pogrom to America to a camp in Siberia and to Lyuba. So many years, so many lives, such a cost.

I looked at the dead trees that spring would not revive; at the vast, flat, frozen hell that surrounded me on all sides; at my breath, breaking into fine particles of ice through which I made my way.

Sooee

1

PEOPLE MY AGE remember the Chinese who slipped into Russia illegally in those years prior to the Revolution with no problem at all at the borders. There were so many that they spilled across the country in a wide stream. Some opened laundries, cheap cafés, or gaming houses where they could smoke opium. Others traded in muslin, cheap silk, toys, and paper fans—poor decorations for poor dwellings. Still others performed on the streets. Puzzling passersby with their tricks, they waved hands into which knives appeared that they threw in the air and caught; they opened their mouths and pulled out yards of splendid-colored ribbon and gossamer scarves; they blew their noses and fifty-kopeck coins flew out of each nostril, clinking and clattering into a waiting cap.

After the Revolution, the steady stream thinned into a trickle. Life had changed for both of us. Now those who crept in illegally were only the most desperate ones, desperate for food and work. New construction sites sometimes welcomed them, for the Chinese weren't afraid of manual labor. Willingly, they heaved huge loads on their backs and would carry them merely for bread.

In the thirties, though, the border was sealed tight. Still, despite harsh restrictions, hunger urged the strongest on. On dark nights, in storm and in rain, small numbers still appeared in our land. What was to be done with them? Inevitably, they were caught and shipped to far-off regions, where the work they were given demanded brute strength and unending days.

One of these was a certain Sooee. When Sooee tried to slip into our country, he was immediately seized by the border guards. To their credit, while they held him, the guards fed him bread and hot soup and he was able to exist. But after that they moved him to the middle of nowhere, to the desolate area of Komi. Who would have thought it but, to Sooee, Komi became paradise! With the money he earned from loading and unloading coal, he was able to buy as much soup and fresh bread as he wanted. He was even able to rent part of a room and, once a month, get drunk and visit the woman Maruska. To his continued amazement, his life flourished. Not even the war harmed this happiness. Because he worked even harder, he earned bonuses of bread and even extra broth which, though watery, was supplied in sufficient amounts.

But there, in paradise, several years after the war—when life began to get better—something happened. Was it the world in which we lived, or was it his destiny? Suddenly, after twelve years of living and thriving in the North, Sooee was arrested, chained to iron bars, tossed into a wagon, and carted to a big city.

2

I have to admit that I am somewhat embarrassed to begin this story about Sooee with so much emphasis on his smile. References to the ubiquitous Chinese smile have become clichéd. Nevertheless, the first thing we noticed when he entered the cell was his smile. It swam ahead of him, lit up the skin on his face, played on his cheekbones, and split his lips apart to reveal large yellow teeth. He did not seem to be entering a prison cell at all, but a festival where everyone eagerly awaited him—and, by flashing his brilliant smile, he apologized for being late. He first bowed his head to all of us and then to each person individually. As soon as the guard had gone, he introduced himself. Most Chinese names consist of three syllables, but we could remember only two: *Soo*-ee.

During his twelve years in the Soviet Union, probably because he was always working and spent little time with others, Sooee's way of life had done little to alleviate his illiteracy. He had learned practically none of our language, perhaps two or three dozen words. Immediately, we cell mates taught him several letters. Before long, much to his pleasure, he could read the brand name *Katusha* on a pack of cigarettes. "Kah-*too*-sha," he would read. Then, raising his shining eyes, he would smile at us meaningfully—as if he had just pronounced a word of great significance.

In the cell, Sooee soon began to miss his strenuous labor. It didn't trouble him that he sat under lock and key; the strict prison regime didn't trouble him, nor did the iron bars on the window, the brief thirty-minute walks, the endless clicks as the peeping "eye" in the door searched the cell. It didn't bother him that, in the cell, it was permissible to speak only in an undertone, for he himself preferred to be silent. Other prisoners would read books, play chess, checkers, or dominoes, speak quietly to each other, sometimes even quarrel quietly. Sooee would just sit, resting his coarse, work-worn hands on his knees—hands that still showed the traces and had the scent of coal dust. He would sit one, two, three hours—sit all day and far into the evening until bedtime was sounded. Who knew what went on in his soul?

With his hand on his knees, he simply sat—his face like a mask, his tongue locked in silence. Only later did we come to understand that he was aching for arduous activity. He had worked hard from his childhood. Work began and finished his day, gave him a voracious appetite and a good night's sleep, provided the sense and content of his life. Just to sit quietly was for him more difficult than the most exhausting labor. As he once explained to me—without work his back, ribs, muscles, and legs ached. For some reason, even his eyes watered, and there was a ringing in his ears.

All this stimulated him to search out as much work as he could find in the cell. Once found, he'd seize upon it with every worn finger and all the strength in his body. Mostly, I refer to all those tiresome tasks that convicts must undertake in concert—to bring out and wash the *parasha* (the communal chamber pot), to sweep, to move beds, to dust, to polish the floor to a mirror shine. By the third day he had already taken into his hands all these tasks, but even they couldn't fill his time, so he added more—he washed our handkerchiefs. That done, he helped us wash ourselves in the bath, rubbing each back to rosy redness.

In the cells there is an unwritten law: the poorer prisoners must receive a tenth or twentieth part of any supplies purchased in the canteen by the more fortunate. For Sooee the cigarettes, the gleaming fruit drops, sometimes an extra piece of bread or an unfinished bowl of thin soup merely served as embellishments on his real gift, "the work." Food was deliberately in short supply so, for a man accustomed to working with his body all day, it was obviously not enough. The additional crumbs that fell to Sooee were appreciated. Smiling his splendid smile, he ate them with the haste of a man who has become acquainted with hunger. Indeed, he cracked down on the hard fruit drops with such noise that the guards invariably slid back the "eye" and ordered us "not to engage in hooliganism."

3

One's first interrogation. I can't remember a single convict who returned from his first interrogation without a sense of shock and terror. For the first time the arrested one hears a long, fearful list of accusations. For the first time he realizes that liberty is a lost hope. For the first time he comes face to face with the person on whom all his fate depends.

But on that day, when Sooee returned, his beaming, childlike smile floated on the air toward each of us. Slowly he sat on the bed, leisurely lit a cigarette and then, as ten pairs of eyes watched anxiously, announced with pride, "Many, many wrote."

Even now I can hear the sound of his voice. He was astonished and awed by the fact that, while he simply sat at the small table doing nothing, an important personage sat with him writing page after page—and all about him, Sooee. "What did he write?" we asked. In an amazed and admiring voice the same answer came, "Many, many wrote. All, all wrote." Then, obviously sorry for the poverty of his vocabulary, he held up his forefinger, now stained with black ink. Yes, an important commander had written and covered not just one but many pages with writing—and all Sooee could do to help was to put his fingerprint on it—his fingerprint and nothing more. One of us, a severe old man with iron glasses who was always reading the same book, muttered, "He's speechless as an infant. Those monsters! They'll write him up for fair!"

Sooee nodded his head happily. Of all the words the old man spoke, only one phrase got through—"will write." And again, he radiated gratitude and admiration over the stream of pages the commander had devoted to him. He shook his head wonderingly from side to side and clucked his tongue. What could he do to repay the extraordinary effort of the investigator? Nothing! And over and over he'd show his ink-stained finger almost apologetically—as if ashamed that the only thing he could add to those marvelous pages was the mere mark of a finger.

As if to reward himself for the idle hours he had spent in the investigator's room, he threw himself even more ardently into whatever task he could find. He not only washed and cleaned the *parasha* but also worked on it with a brush. Forcibly, he found and pulled out many of our handkerchiefs and washed them. Soon suds and foam splashed in every direction.

4

In the course of further interrogation, Sooee began more and more to realize that his ignorance of the language posed a serious problem. In spite of all his efforts to cooperate, it was a problem he could not overcome. Freely, in response to all questions, he smiled and agreed. But this affability was not enough for the commander. It made his job too simple. His annoyance grew, he began to shout and beat his fist on the table. To Sooee's grief, now the investigator not so much "many, many wrote" as he "many, many swore."

It is not difficult to imagine. Here, at the scene of confrontation, sits a person who does nothing but agree. Tell him that he crossed the border with "malicious intent." He smiles and agrees. Tell him by so doing he was carrying out the treacherous orders of an "enemy country." He smiles and agrees. Tell him he is guilty of grave espionage on behalf of a "known state." He smiles and agrees.

True, during all of Stalin's tyranny, the worth of a denial was zero—but still the combat continued. In order to break the resistance of the accused, the investigator was expected to expend large amounts of energy. As a result of this struggle, the questioner could prove his importance, prove that his efforts exposed all the "criminal machinations" of such peril to the state. But in this case his efforts were futile; the complicated instrument of accusation failed to function because there was no resistance. Suddenly, a man used to hammering his fist forcefully on the head of his enemy merely smashes into thin air. Suddenly, the enemy assumes an unexpected character, he becomes unique. He exists, yet he doesn't exist. He becomes ephemeral. Besides, the criminal has a responsibility, too. Not only must he confess but he must also implicate others—two or three at the very least. He must also specify the amount of money he was paid for his treason. Now try to imagine the smiling face of the amiable Chinese who answers "yes, yes, yes" to every accusation. How is it possible to keep one's control, to keep from turning nasty and savage? And, most important, how is it possible to finish the case, to close it according to the rules?

Over and over, the interrogator asked Sooee the questions to which he needed replies. Over and over, Sooee tried to satisfy him by agreeing to words he could not understand. More and more, the investigator became angry. Sadder and sadder became Sooee each time he returned to the cell. So preoccupied was he that even a good meal failed to tempt him. Something had happened to the commander; the commander was very angry. But why, why? Sooee understood that it was somehow his fault, but what exactly was the nature of the fault? Unable to discern the problem, he was unable to make things right. With difficulty we drew forth the words needed for explanation and, in response to our efforts, he shrugged his shoulders, spread his hands, and smiled the sorry smile of a kind and simple soul.

Meanwhile, time passed and the case was supposed to be closed. Not only was it supposed to be closed but closed in the proper manner.

5

It is said that just before the patient dies he often feels better and believes he is going to get well. It is a pennyworth of mercy that opens the gate so the doomed may proceed to misfortune without fear or faltering. So it was with Sooee.

One day Sooee returned from the interrogation earlier than usual and in such high humor that we recalled his first happy days. What luck! The next day there would be an interpreter at his interrogation! Using mostly gestures, he made us understand and, once convinced that everything had been made clear, he flashed his old irradiating smile. It was impossible not to smile back.

Remember, it was near the end of 1949. None of us had any hope for ourselves, for we knew the road from the prison ran only one way—the way to the labor camp. Yet, for the smiling Chinaman, we dreamed of an exception. Certainly, the translator would manage to explain that Sooee had no connection whatsoever with a "known state." He couldn't have. Twelve years ago, desperately in search of food, he had come to us, and for twelve years he had honestly made his way. The translator would surely understand that from Sooee's first words. A brother in country and language, he would understand and explain that a terrible mistake had been made and that the Chinese man must be set free immediately. Waving our hands and acting it out in whispers, we showed Sooee how he would soon leave the prison and again handle a shovel and a load of coal. One of us staggered against the wall and then embraced another convict. Sooee guessed it was he—free. Having drunk some vodka, he was walking in Komi with his arm around Maruska. Happily, he smiled, showing his teeth. Then, shutting his eyes, he uttered several sentences in Chinese—no doubt explaining something to the interpreter he would see the next day. Possibly, it was the first time in twelve years he had begun a conversation in his own language. We listened carefully but, of course, did not understand a single word. From his face, however, we knew he was practicing a very convincing appeal to his brother for help in freeing him from the trap in which he'd been caught. Then quietly he staring into space, he listened to a silent voice, and nodded again and again. There was no doubt his comrade was responding in the same direct and friendly way.

6

The next day Sooee was recalled for questioning. Whispering, we assured him he would come back quickly with good news and then leave the cell finally and forever. In our minds, we walked with him through the long labyrinth of corridors; silently we were present at his interrogation. In a strong, clear voice Sooee explained about the mix-up and, by listening to the words of the interpreter, the big commander (as Sooee called him) decided to reconsider the case and expunge the foolish accusations. After all, how much was really needed to untangle this knot and establish the innocence of the wordless Chinese?

Occupied with our fancies, we returned to reality only when suddenly, way ahead of schedule, Sooee was once again thrust into the cell. Even in the dim room deprived of sun, we could see that his face was the color of clay and his eyes were focused inward. Unable to keep from speaking, he mumbled and muttered but could not find the words he needed. Finally, in a hoarse croak, he uttered one word, "Korea." It was the word for which he had been searching, and desperately he repeated it over and over. "Korea, Korea, Korea!" Then, seeing our puzzled, unhappy faces, he cried, "My China! She, Korea!"

It took us a while to fit together the pieces, to recreate the scene. Fool of happy hopes, Sooee had entered the inquisitor's room. He had not been there long before another man with the same black hair and shining brown eyes entered the room and sat next to the investigator. Sooee rose, bowed and, enraptured by the sound of his native language, repeated the words he had rehearsed in the cell the previous day. When the answer was spoken, Sooee thought he had gone mad—either that or he had forgotten how to speak Chinese. Not one syllable spoken in reply by the black-eyed man had he understood. Vainly, hoping that repetition would remove the problem, he began to speak again. Distinctly, slowly, he repeated his words of Chinese. Again, the translator replied in a completely foreign language. Finally, he fell back on Russian and said, "We, Korea." Forlornly, Sooee returned to Russian and said, "My, China."

At that point the investigator broke into the conversation impatiently. "Why bother with these scum?" he complained and, still trying to salvage the situation, demanded angrily, "Isn't it all the same?" Then he answered himself, "Of course, it's the same!"

No, it was not the same. The Korean didn't understand Chinese, the Chinese didn't understand Korean. Indignant, the investigator castigated them both as his cursing roared through the room. "This Chinaman is a pain in the ass!" Gladly he would have opened the door and knocked him out of the room. His position demanded, however, that he phone the prison instead and request someone to call for the prisoner in the room specified. Only after the guard arrived to remove Sooee did he give vent to his utter frustration. Unable to restrain himself another instant, he shouted, "Take the bastard away!"

7

For several days, Sooee was left alone in the cell. Gradually, the rest of us returned to normal. As usual, the arrow on the barometer of our expectations wrongly pointed to good weather. We actually made an exception of Sooee and built up our hopes, actually believed that fate would be merciful to him. Whether it was because the accusations against him were so ridiculous or because his unquestioning submissiveness had won our hearts, we truly believed that soon he would be sent back to Komi. "Let's go to Komi," we encouraged him and he understood and nodded in agreement.

On the fourth day, ninety minutes before the sleep signal, Sooee was called back to the investigator. He came back shortly before bedtime, so we couldn't discover many details of the conversation. Sooee's only answer to our questions was brief. It was "Sit." Not too long after, though most of us were half-asleep, we heard the lock turn, the door open, and a guard take Sooee away. During the night, we were awakened and led to the bath. The clock in the corridor showed 3:00 A.M.

Sooee was nowhere to be seen. When the sun rose, Sooee was brought back. Immediately, he was taken to the bath. On his return, he threw off his clothes and went to bed. The very next moment, the guard sounded the wake-up.

After that, the investigator began to call Sooee only at night. Why did he do that? What could the torture of sleeplessness add to Sooee's "confession?" Obviously the case was peculiar. Therefore, the investigator had to bring out his whole arsenal—to prove to his superiors that he had done everything possible. Thereafter, Sooee was taken for questioning several minutes after retreat was sounded. They sent him back in the middle of the night and, within half an hour, awakened him and kept him up until sunrise. Actually, he was subjected to no questioning at all. Sooee just sat at his table and the interrogators, replacing each other every few hours, made sure he didn't sleep. That was during the night. After sunrise the same procedure was repeated, but this time the guards carried it out.

For the first three days, Sooee bore his trial stoically. Every other moment, the guards clicked open the "eye" to make sure he wasn't asleep. Sometimes one would burst through the door and materialize in front of him. But, despite their excessive zeal, they couldn't catch him disobeying. He never once closed his eyes, or let his head droop, or leaned against the wall and, without realizing it, began to snore. Sooee, of course, had become noticeably thin, perspiration covered his forehead, his eyelids puffed up and became red. But he continued to cooperate and never gave in to weakness. Keeping his fingers close together, he kept his hands on his knees and sat as directed. His chiseled face remained motionless, masklike. Even his eyes stopped moving; he ceased to blink. If someone spoke to him, he acknowledged it, but mostly he was silent and almost stopped talking altogether. For four nights he was not allowed to sleep. Then the fourth day arrived.

8

Man is complicated, and it is indeed impossible to fathom what goes on inside him merely from his outward appearance. When did the change begin in Sooee? It seemed to me it began after that fourth night. When he came back from his ordeal, he seemed to enter the cell more slowly than usual, and he was pensive. A deep wrinkle creased his forehead. It was the first time I ever saw him in such a tense and introspective state. There was still about a half hour before we were supposed to rise, but he didn't even try to go to bed. At six o'clock we went, as usual, to the lavatory. Sooee was so immersed in thought that he hadn't even heard the guard order us to go. When we returned, the boiled water and bread had been brought. Despite all our efforts, Sooee touched neither. He was so sunk in thought his lips mouthed words as if they were prayers. Then suddenly, as if the words had been ripped from his soul, he began to speak. Pointing his long fingers toward his chest he asked, "Mine man?" Then he answered himself affirmatively in the same words, "Mine man!" It was as if, for the first time in his life, he had been forced to question his very essence and the answers had failed to come easily. Again, his gaze was directed within, again his long fingers turned toward his chest and tapped it. Again, he repeated the same words with increasing certitude. "Mine man. Mine man." Then, with the same conviction, he added, "Man sleep. Man sleep, sleep."

When tormented by lack of sleep, most convicts use several methods to distract the guard so they can seize a few moments of rest. Sooee descended to none of these. Like a rock in his realization that he was a man and a man needs sleep, he removed his high boots and lay down on his bed. He had hardly shut his eyes before the guard entered the cell and shouted at him to get up. Whether Sooee was asleep or not, I don't know, but he ignored the order. The guard then pushed him and suddenly Sooee shot up, clenched his teeth, and bared them. So fiercely did he snarl that at that moment he looked like a wild animal. "Mine man!" he said forcefully, "Man sleep, sleep!"

The guard was an old hand, but even he was confused. He could only say, "Sit as you should sit, or walk along the wall! But sleep is forbidden!" Sooee shook his head, and again stretched out on the bed. "Sleep, sleep," he managed to say before closing his eyes and turning his face to the wall. "Man sleep."

Without a word, the guard grabbed him by the shoulder and, shaking him, tried to lift him up. As before, stretched out with his back to the guard, Sooee wrapped strong hands around the iron bars on his bed and refused to move. They struggled only briefly—the forces were unequal. Sooee was too weak to resist. Again, like a wild animal, he bared his teeth and even wrinkled his nose. "Stand up!" shouted the guard, "Stand up and stay up!" The guard then moved Sooee's bed so it was visible through the "eye" from outside. Before the guard even reached the door, Sooee flung himself back on the bed, muttering "Sleep. Sleep."

Then, with all the strength he had left, he wound his arms and legs about the bars and prepared to fight for his right to sleep. The guard returned with two others to help him. The three of them threw Sooee out of his bed and removed it from the cell. As soon as they shut the door behind them, Sooee stretched out with his face against the floor. "Sleep, sleep," he murmured, "mine man."

The guards returned again; this time there were four of them. They kicked Sooee with their boots, trying to turn him on his back. For a long time, he refused to move. Finally, he sat up and, turning his head from side to side as if to bite, again bared his tightly clenched teeth. He looked so wild and ferocious that even the burly guards retreated. Growling, Sooee rose. Grabbing his meager ration of bread—his daily *pika*—he threw it at one of the guards. Then he reached for his cup of water but, before he could throw it, the men immobilized him. "Sleep, sleep," he roared like a wounded animal, "Man sleep!" They grabbed him from all sides and carried him from the cell.

We never saw him again.

The Flour and the Glass

"I WAS AN investigator at that time."

In such a way, during the long winter evening, the exiled Aleksey Ivanovich Kassyanov began his story. For ten years Kassyanov had been in a labor camp. In '49, just a year and a half after his release, he was arrested again and sent to a small remote village in northeast Siberia in Krasnoyarsky Kray. In this small village he met and became friends with fellow exiles.

One winter evening, sitting near a crackling stove as the fire cast long shadows on the long beard that covered his face, he began to tell us about himself. "I was an investigator at that time," he repeated. "My story belongs to those few weeks when Yezhov was replaced by another people's commissar and, for the first time, there was a brief respite between slaughters. In order to create the impression that the cruel methods of Yezhov would be discontinued, the new commissar fired many former investigators all over the country—some were even arrested. In such a way, the problem arose of how to replace the old ones with the new ones now required for duty.

"I don't know what they did in the capital, but in the region where I lived they did it very simply. One of the local party authorities looked through the list of possible candidates, culled the required number of suitable people, and there you were, my friends, in a new job.

"I had not worked in this city very long and had very few friends. Besides, the devil made me graduate from law school, so it's not surprising that I proved to be among the suitable. I was called to *Obkom,* the regional committee of the Communist party. There they said several words about the trust they were placing in me, casually reminded me that party discipline precluded my refusing the job, and my official papers were instantly signed, sealed, and delivered.

"So there I was, sitting at the investigator's table, flipping through the immense file left unfinished by my unlucky predecessor—which, if you'll permit me to use legal terminology, I had to start all over again from the stage of preliminary investigation.

"All right, so let it be from the beginning. But why was it necessary for me to read and study a file I already knew was worthless and had to be redone? To tell the truth, I looked only for the personal data of the convict with whom I had to deal. Last name: Korostelev. First name and patronymic: Nikolay Fedorovich. Age: 47. Education: Four grades and graduated from the Food Institute. Party member: since 1917. Position: Director of Regional State Mill No. 1. No history of party penalties, no convictions.

"Are you familiar with the special kind of dedicated civil-service official who dominated the country until 1936 or 1937? He devoted all his energy, all his time, all his talents to the job and was happy only if it ended up without reprimand or rebuke. He could chair a *kolkhoz,* head an institute or regulate state trade. He could open a small café or organize a market. Just say it's necessary and off he goes—to the sowing campaign, to grain procurement, or to villages where he sleeps on the floor in unheated barns and eats only bread and water—all just to report that the task was completed on time or even a little before. Whatever you can imagine, he is asked to do. He collects fuel. He pulls flax. He digs potatoes. He conducts campaigns. He is moved from one job to another, from one place to another, and fulfills uncomplainingly anything he is asked, one commission after another.

"According to the report, citizen Nikolay Fedorovich Korostelev was just that kind of person. And after I called for him and got to know him, I was satisfied that I had not generally been wrong. Imagine a broad-shouldered man with light hair and blue eyes—but my God, what had happened to him during five months of sitting in inner prison! These days, I am already accustomed to everything—I have seen so much that nothing surprises me any more. But, remember, this was my first convict and I could see how dramatically he had lost weight; his suit hung on him as if were not even his. I will forever remember the expression in his tired eyes, the fatigue on his unshaven face. I noticed his dirty, collarless shirt; I noticed the unlaced shoes required of prisoners, I smelled the special convict smell—a combination of unwashed body and rotten, badly digested food—a smell to which I fortunately became inured long ago.

"The conversation with Korostelev (after the first dozen official questions such as where was he born, where was he baptized, and so on, and so on) I began by announcing that now, since I was his new investigator, I would like him to tell me his story from the very beginning—truthfully and sincerely.

"My announcement had a stunning effect on him—stunning. It was obvious that his heart had been damaged in prison, since he began to pant and to breathe with an open mouth. His eyes darkened, his nose became waxy, as in death. It took him a long time to get control of himself and even to speak in a relatively steady voice.

"'I admit'—in this way he began his testimony—'I admit that I committed the most severe crime against party, government, and people. The mill under my control supplies the military department with flour. In order to undermine the power of the country and annihilate thousands of Soviet soldiers, I systematically threw glass into the grain elevator. The bread baked from the flour, mixed with glass dust, doomed Red Army soldiers to much torment and inevitable death . . .'

"After that followed many details I omit because they are not important to my story.

"In all honesty, I was overwhelmed with horror at his confession and continued to write only with difficulty.

"The year 1937, the peak of our repression, was already behind us. Many months had passed, and I already knew the many tricks of my predecessors. I already knew the pleasure each took in devising plots like an amateur Sherlock Holmes. But here, seated before me is a solid man who is seeing me for the first time in his life. I didn't threaten him. Quite the opposite—in a calm, quiet voice I announced that I was his new investigator and asked him to tell me his story honestly. And, without any pressure from my side, look at what he blurts out!—he admits he is guilty one hundred percent. Not only guilty but also a monster, a cannibal, a Satan. Contrasting that with his decent appearance, I was not only surprised but shocked. I remember that, confused, I asked him the silliest question: 'What can you add to what you have already said?' The response I heard was 'Nothing. I have said everything. I freely admit my guilt.'

"Yes, with that we separated that day. I now leafed through the unfinished Korostelev case with new attentiveness and read all the reports filed by his former investigator. The same story was repeated on numerous pages—not very literate but still very impressive: 'Flour—glass—death.'

"For ten days I let Korostelev sit in his cell but, during that time, I worked no less than fifteen hours a day. Among other things, I studied several heavy books on the flour-grinding business, which I can remember to this moment. I remember all the centrifugal sieves, the grain brushes, the flour spinners, and the spindles. That I wanted to discover the truth goes without saying, but I also wanted to solve the psychological puzzle. A relatively young man at that time, I trusted my first impressions—and I have to admit that Korostelev made a good impression on me. How could it be that such a straightforward fellow is able to commit such cruel, senseless, mass murder? How many souls—not hundreds but thousands—had he sent to the other world, this devourer of human beings?

"As you can see, the questions were not trivial and demanded direct and categorical answers, so I decided to visit the remote region of Mill No. 1. The entire week I lived in the 'best' room in the House of Collective Farmers, with the ubiquitous carafe of yellow bleach-disinfected water. In the mill I met Korostelev's replacement, the temporary director. He was a specialist engineer—raised before the Revolution—an old man with a wedge-shaped beard and tortoiseshell glasses. He was a dying breed, but you know the type—on one hand, he had swallowed the Soviet way of speaking and, on the other, he still lapsed into the courtesies of the court. I had a talk with him in Korostelev's former office, and here—I must confess—I made a mistake. I announced at the very beginning that I was the investigator on Korostelev's case. As I remember, I even showed him my official papers.

"The old man listened to me, removed his glasses, then pulled a checked handkerchief from his pocket and polished the lenses. 'Who could imagine?' he said, looking at me with grief-stricken eyes. 'Who could imagine? Of course, if I may be permitted to say so, the guilt must fall on me personally. The enemy was standing next to me, yet I trusted him.' His repentant speech, interrupted by deep sighs and long pauses, was rather long. I listened to his every word and every breath, and then we began to examine the mill. It was natural that we begin the examination as I suggested—that we begin with the grain elevator. Near the elevator stood a soldier, holding a rifle.

"'You put a guard on now, after the event?' I asked the old man. My question surprised him.

"'Lord help me, how could you even think that? We work for the military department. Armed guards are here all the time!'

"'Does it ever happen that this elevator remains without a guard?'

"'We work all day and all night, and every day and every night a comrade with a rifle stands near the elevator—and not only near the elevator. Perhaps you would like to speak with the commander of the guards?'

"'I would,' and so a new person appeared to give me information. A participant in the Civil War, he was a short man of about forty—one of those whom, even if they live to be a hundred, will never remove his uniform; a fat, round man who introduced himself with every military formality. Carefully, he explained to me how the guard system worked. He showed me and proved that nowhere in the mill was there a single place—even for a single moment—that was not seen by the eyes of at least one soldier.

"'Well, and if, let's say, some employee or worker in the mill would like to throw something into the grain elevator—let's say poison. Could he do it?' I asked.

"He looked at me as if I had, straight to his face, insulted the whole military defense service of the entire Soviet Union. Without thinking even a moment, he shrugged his shoulders and said, 'Why should I try to justify myself, comrade investigator?' From his pocket he took a small iron screw and handed it to me. 'Let me leave. You try to throw this into the grain or flour anywhere in the mill. If you are not detained and brought to me, I will give you my six-month salary.' Then, thinking a moment longer, he added, 'and I will put my party membership card on the table with it.'

"With him as well, I spoke about Korostelev, and he too shook his head, with grief. Spreading his arms in wonder, he said, 'Live a century, study a century, and you still die knowing nothing. Who would think this could happen with such a person—a party member with a solid record, a serious, diligent worker with so many friends?' He fell silent and, after a long pause, finished decisively, 'As you can see, he proved to be a scoundrel.'

"Involuntarily, I blurted out, 'How do you know?'

"'Forgive me, it is a fact. We had a general meeting of the workers and we were told. This degenerate was labeled a violent enemy of the people.' Ah, I thought, so everyone already knew—knew he was guilty and had already labeled him.

"Then I went to the laboratory chief. The young man was made very nervous by my arrival. He knit his brows and stammered. With shaking hands, he showed the book containing all the flour analyses from the past several years. He proved conclusively that during all those years the mill had produced and sent only the highest quality flour.

"'So why was the director arrested?' I asked.

"He gave my question no consideration. 'If he was arrested, there was a reason.' Then he repeated definitely, 'There was a reason.'

"Still not satisfied with the material I had collected, I sent an official request to the military department to provide more exact information concerning the medical history of the whole incident. I received a report that not one case of disease connected with glass dust—certainly no fatal ones—had ever been registered.

"All this searching, as I have already told you, took me ten working days. Only on the eleventh did I call Korostelev again. How to begin our talk? Not having thought about it, I decided to try subterfuge. 'I didn't record your previous testimony entirely, citizen Korostelev,' I said, when I greeted him and sat in my place, 'so once again I ask you to tell me your story with every detail and without rushing. I warn you that absolute preciseness and truthfulness are necessary. Understand?' He nodded, waited until I had spread my papers, and began: 'As I did last time, I admit freely and honestly the crime I have committed.'

"And again, I heard the story about the glass. In this story, there were details. After all, I had asked for them. For instance, there was the story about how he got the sheet of glass, how he drove to different regions around the area for it, and then how, unnoticed, he threw the piece of glass into the grain elevator. He didn't forget to tell me how he kept those criminal activities secret from his wife, children, neighbors, and employees of the mill. I listened and listened and then interrupted him at the high point of his story.

"'Listen, Nikolay Fedorovich,' I said, 'why are you telling me all this nonsense?'

"'You asked,' he answered.

"'I asked you to tell me the truth, not fairy tales.'

"'What fairy tales?'

"'Let's not make fools of ourselves. Now I will tell you the real story, comrade Korostelev, and you will listen.'

"Yes, I called him 'comrade,' and with the free and easy familiarity of an apprentice showing off his new knowledge of the flour business, I recited all the details of my visit to Mill No. 1. There was only one thing I decided not to repeat. I didn't tell him how his former friends felt toward him. Why upset him for nothing?

"While telling the story, I watched his face attentively. I expected it would suddenly light with joy, that his eyes would begin to sparkle or—and I have to admit my fond hope—that his head would droop, and tears of gratitude would stream down the heavy growth on his sallow cheeks. Nothing like that happened. Korostelev changed very little. To be more precise, he did not change at all. Neither joy nor sparkle nor tears—nothing happened. And, after I fell silent, he muttered indistinctly and started to repeat the same nonsensical story. Then, unable to stand any more, I took out my case, opened it, and showed him the official medical report I had received from the department.

"And here what I had expected earlier happened—though in a different way. Struggling to control himself—breathing heavily through his nose and covering his eyes with his hand—his body suddenly heaved with sobs and he burst out crying. Yes, this large man sat there and sobbed and, looking at him, I could say nothing. I just stood and waited. After a while, he finally calmed down, and only then did I offer him a glass of water and a chance to take a break.

"'No, no. I don't need anything,' he apologized, 'I cry like a woman.'

"'So let us continue our talk,' I said. 'Are you able?'

"'Yes,' he answered. 'Now I believe you. Only now, at this very instant, do I begin to believe you.'

"'And before?'

"He waved his hand. 'You are my third investigator,' he said. 'Do you understand? The third. With the first one I fought for four months. Should I bother to explain to you how the investigation was carried out? It was a fight that cost me years of my life and finally broke my health completely. Before, I had always been in perfect condition. So for four months I fought. Then I was put in the cage and, to put it briefly, experienced everything. Someone once said very wisely—God forbid that a man should experience all he can endure. After that, and only after, did I "admit my guilt." After, led by the investigator, I testified to everything I testified to you. One devil is the same as another, so why be tortured for nothing? And in reality, it seemed as if the torment had come to an end. No torture, no sleepless nights, no cage—nothing of that kind. Whatever the investigator directed, I did. I fabricated and dictated, and he wrote everything down. But finally, when the investigation was all over and all my testimony was given, I was called to the very same office and, in the very same place where my first investigator sat and you sit now, a new and different investigator sat. He introduced himself. He said my previous testimony no longer existed and—forgive me—he asked, just as you did, that I tell the "truth."

"'Overcome with joy, filled with hope—I don't know how else to describe my state—I began with a description of my previous investigator. I said it was my deep belief he was a fascist degenerate, a fervent enemy of our state. In detail, I told what methods he had used from the very beginning to force me to incriminate myself. The new man listened attentively, wrote down exactly what I said, then asked if I had anything either to add or correct. I swore that now everything was exact, and that my testimony needed neither addition nor correction. I was then asked to sign my name. I did so and was returned to my cell, where I could not fall asleep. All night I was awake, I was so anxious and excited. What was I thinking about?' He continued after a short break. 'The sleepless night always seems endless. It's impossible to remember all the thoughts that race through one's mind, why try to restore them? Naturally, I now dreamed of how I would be set free, how all this horror would come to an end.

"'Impatiently, I waited for morning, then I began to wait for dinnertime, then for the evening. Still I wasn't called. They were the most agonizing, excruciating, and endless hours of my life. Naturally, I searched for and found explanation for the delay. I imagined that, first of all, my new investigator had to inform his superiors about my changed testimony, that they had to erase everything that had gone before. Then, they had to decide about bringing my first investigator to trial. In short, I tried to fill the time and comfort myself and, in this way, three days went by. Finally, I was called. I thought, thank God, the long-awaited hour has come. Atheist that I am, I kept repeating to myself that the old people are right when they say, "God sees the truth, but doesn't say it right away." And the guard knocks on the now familiar door. I am taken in. And who do you think I see? Both investigators. In a pompous, important way the first one is turning over the pages of my testimony, and says, "So? You believe

I am a fascist degenerate?" I sat, silent. What could I say? I was silent until they both began the torment all over again.'"

* * *

At that point, Aleksey Ivanovich finished his story.

"So what happened?" asked his friends. "You, of course, released your Korostelev?"

Kassyanov took a long puff on his cigarette before answering.

"No," he said, "I didn't release him. I had no time. In several days the brief respite came to an end, and the new people's commissar got better at his job. Everything became as before. From the investigator's office, I was moved to a cell and, simply, imprisoned properly—for ten years.

"And the flourmaker?"

"Well, naturally, the flourmaker remained in prison. I believe he suffered the same sentence I did."

How We Return Home

LONG BEFORE THEIR release, most prisoners begin to worry about how they will look, what impression they will make when they get back home. How can one possibly show up in front of family and friends wearing camp issue—a short shabby coat; prisoner pants; and *portyanki,* the dirty, smelly rags we used in place of socks, which always showed over our cheap, worn-out boots? Top that off with a frayed camp hat that has earflaps wildly flying in the wind. That alone would frighten people away! Indeed, how could anyone recognize a father, husband, or friend under such ragged, dirty, peculiar clothing? There are innumerable variations, all on the same old story—the story of how a prisoner finally returns home.

Now he comes home, the former convict, comes home and, with fingers shaking beyond control, tries to push the doorbell. A young girl appears who was born several months after her father's arrest. Naturally, she's frightened and slams the door on the stranger, calling, "There is a beggar trying to get in!" Because he had no chance to warn her, his wife doesn't recognize him either. Inevitably, though, all this is followed by the exclamations, tears, sentimental scenes, and happy endings for which—as is well known—most prisoners long.

My story was different. I was in my good suit, which was as fresh and well-ironed, as usual. Equally fresh were the shirt and tie. I was wearing an old hat that had maintained its fashionable shape. Draped over my arm was a new spring coat, carefully folded so the elegant silk lining was displayed. My wife and Dasha, my daughter, were both at home. With loud cries they greeted my return. Hugs, kisses, and laughter followed with such joy it was as if we had previously agreed that this reunion would be without emotional pain. As is usual, after these initial ecstatic moments of happiness, an awkward silence falls. That happened with us as well, but evaporated as soon as it appeared. What was necessary was to return to normal as soon as possible, and this we did without difficulty. My wife started to prepare breakfast. Dasha kept staring at me as if she couldn't tear her eyes away—eyes that were pretty, trusting, and a bit sad. And I, as if I had just returned from a wonderful trip, filled the conversation with light laughter and trivialities.

In the midst of all this, the bell rang and Dasha went to open the door. Without explanation, I knew who was there. In a flash, my head began to pound, and there was a whistling in my ears. My hands were paralyzed, it was impossible to move my feet, and my heart was cold. My face must have looked strange because my wife asked, "Are you all right? Is something wrong?" I was silent and could only shrug my shoulders. I would have said, if I could, "It's nothing, you're mistaken," but not even my tongue could move. Women have to have a definite explanation for everything, so my wife said, "You've probably forgotten how the ring of a doorbell sounds." Then she repeated what all wives eventually say when their husbands return from prison, "Oh, my poor dear, your nerves are shattered." My silence continued. I was unable to speak. And, even if I could, how could I possibly admit that I had had a premonition of exactly what was happening? I had foreseen that Tonya would appear—I knew it was she who had rung the bell—and I knew exactly what would happen in this apartment today.

Still, Tonya's entrance startled me. For a man used to living under normal conditions, it's difficult to imagine how many different emotions can race through the prisoner's mind in a single instant. For a long time—for a very long time—I had imagined this meeting. I still hoped it would be possible for me to playact, to pretend I was the same carefree, joyful person who had been seated at the table with my family just a few moments before. In my mind, I was choosing the gestures I would use, the words I would recite. Meanwhile, Dasha had opened the door and was chattering with the newcomer. I didn't have to listen; I already knew what they were saying. My wife told me unnecessarily, "Oh, it's Tonya. She must have heard about your arrival and rushed here to see you." As before, I was silent. While Tonya was removing her coat in the corridor, I continued to plan my performance. Miserable man that I was, I didn't realize that any control I'd ever had disappeared completely. I was broken and beaten—but the one thing I wanted was to prevent her from ever seeing what had really happened to me. And, in truth, she didn't see a thing.

Oh, how sincerely overjoyed Tonya seemed in greeting me—it was immediately apparent. A lovely scent wafted into the room with her. Despite being slightly heavy, Tonya was light and graceful in her movements. Her plump cheeks were rosy, her eyes were clear and sparkling. In other words, she hadn't changed at all. Smiling openly, she kissed and embraced my wife, then kissed and embraced me. Strangely, I responded. The touch of her lips on my cheek brought me back to life, and I was suddenly myself again.

I heard Tonya explain her appearance in almost the same way in which my wife had a few moments before: " . . . just learned that you returned and couldn't help but rush to see you." I gathered that, after my disappearance, she had often visited my wife. Her exact words were irrelevant. The important thing was that her visit had been preordained. As if inspired, I began to lie and invent stories about how good life had been "there," in that place. I even reproached those who spread lies about the terrible life in prison. "They're just slanderers," I said, openly exaggerating. "Believe me, convicts can read what they want, exercise as much as they want, meet their acquaintances, visit their friends." I remember even saying that I hadn't lost anything by being in prison—quite the opposite. "I finally had time to think about things and really understand them." I heard myself going on and on and knew why, but neither cared nor wanted to stop. Once Tonya interrupted me, "Listen to him. It sounds as though he's trying to sell everyone on going to prison!" I looked at her. How firmly she believed that she was impervious to all harm, that she was protected by some kind of armor. I think our ancestors believed that way in an all-powerful God. Wasn't He always with them? Didn't He always defend them? Who could doubt, who would dare to doubt Him?

My eyes were fastened on her longer than I intended. Our eyes met. But what could she learn from any look when she had not the slightest doubt that she was safe? I decided to change my tactics. Quickly and sharply, I did a complete about-face, with an explanation ready should anyone ask why I was changing my story.

No one asked anything.

"The door opens unexpectedly. You don't hear the guard reaching it," I said. "All you hear is the click and the guard appears, entering the cell. Silently, he studies a piece of paper, on which a single name is written. He lifts his head and looks slowly at each one of us—all twelve convicts. It lasts forever—time stops. I believe that at that moment all twelve feel the same as one who is doomed to die feels when they come to take him to be shot. Which one of us is now doomed to the torture of interrogation? Everyone is waiting. Time no longer moves. You feel nauseated, as if you will throw up blood and bile. All twelve are standing, the wait is interminable, nervousness eats up the air. But it's beyond nervousness. Twelve men are teetering on the brink of insanity—and the line is so ephemeral, so arbitrary that many may have crossed it long ago. The guard looks from right to left, from left to right, looks at each of us—looks long, as if for eternity. Then, scrutinizing the paper again, he asks each prisoner to identify himself. Thus begins the ultimate psychological tolerance test. I can assure you that anyone who passes this test several times (and prisoners are usually given it more than once), that anyone who passes this test can never be considered normal again. Slowly the guard raises his hand and points to you, asking you to repeat your name. You answer, then wait. For all my life I will remember that waiting. May it be eternally cursed! Sometimes, the guard will ask several convicts their names over and over. They are almost lucky—it shocks them into such numbness they no longer feel the terror. At last, the victim is identified: his last name matches the one on the paper. But this is not the end of it. Now the guard prolongs the grisly game. The prisoner must give his first name, then his patronymic. Then he must spell them. Finally, the first name and the patronymic are acceptable. Then the guard says to the victim, 'Get ready for the investigator,' and vanishes.

"A large collective sigh of relief bursts from the breasts of eleven convicts—but that word is totally inadequate. Yes, the convicts feel a release—but what kind of release? It's a change in the blood, a pang, a throbbing ache and a heaviness in your chest; it's the beginning of an untreatable disease. And the man whose fate has been determined? The one who has to be 'ready'? Look at him . . . "

But here my wife broke in. "Stop, please stop," she pleaded. Her face was distorted with pain. But I couldn't stop. I glared at her. I hated her at that moment. I wanted to continue. "Consider Dasha," she cried, "look at her."

Only a pure young heart could weep with such feeling. I paused. Though the story was still unfinished, it was impossible to be silent. I turned to Tonya, "For you, and only for you, I must finish. Let's go." My words came out as an order, not a request. Had she recognized this? No, she was comfortable in her armor and trusted in its impenetrability. She answered, "Yes, yes. Let's go." Immediately, we found ourselves in a room that was strange to me. It was brightly lit with fluorescent tubes, about which I had heard only while I was away. Neither the room nor its strange light surprised me. It was as if I knew that everything destined to happen was destined to happen here.

At this point, I have to admit that I had done something suspect. I had stolen something, but I will go into more about that later. Finally, Tonya settled herself in the chair and I continued. "In misfortune, in unrelenting calamity, man is always alone. Alone he is ill, alone he loses sanity, alone he dies. And when he is carried to the cemetery, and his head wobbles on the coffin pillow, he is alone. You, his closest friend, can only follow the hearse. Now it is misfortune that separates the twelfth person from the other eleven prisoners.

Twenty-two eyes follow his every move. He makes a pitiful attempt to pretend that nothing out of the ordinary has happened—he's simply been called for questioning, that's all, and he even allows a faint smile to hover on his lips. Now he must get himself ready—as he has done over and over in his life—when he went to work, when he went on a date, when he went to visit friends. Now he is just getting ready again, 'preparing,' as the guard put it. He pulls on his shirt, his socks, his shoes. Then he goes to the *parasha* and, holding the lid as a protective shield, he urinates. Sometimes, unable to ignore the demands of his body, he sits on the *parasha* and his bowels turn to water. But I'm only describing the outward picture. It is only a weak and incomplete suggestion of what is really going on inside the twelfth person. And what is going on inside him?"

I asked that question and then fell silent. Unwillingly, I remembered how many times I myself had been separated from eleven others—I remembered my getting ready, saw myself with that shield in my hand—and I could not utter another word, my lips could only twitch. Then, unwillingly, as I remembered these things, I began to weep. Not because I was sorry for myself. At that moment I saw all humanity as that one unhappy man, and I wept for his fate and the fact that he was doomed. I wept because the road to death had been made so unbearably difficult—and I wept because, even if he survived, his life was now over. Why? Why should I have had to experience all this?

Meanwhile, Tonya just sat there. Not only was her body impervious but also her conscience. Fury swept over me, and I turned red from rage. Then suddenly I lost all interest in continuing. Why had I confessed all this? I had humiliated myself. Did I really think I could "improve" her character? And the word "improve," for some reason, enraged me even more.

What should I do next? I sensed only one thing for certain—that my time was limited and I had to act quickly. Tonya was sitting on the chair waiting, not for the inevitable, but for the rest of my story. She was still protected by her invulnerability.

I became thoughtful. Is it really so important that the person sentenced to death must listen to the prosecutor explain the reasons why? That was old-fashioned, a thing of the past: the trial, the testimony of the witnesses, the accusations of the prosecutor, the excuses of the defense attorney, the deliberation. Modern mankind no longer felt the need. If sometimes they still practiced this travesty, it was from inertia and not a sense of justice. Rarely is the person sentenced to death told that this is the moment when he will die. "To the investigator," he is told and, accompanied by the guards, he is led through the maze of corridors, taken down and down and down the staircase, and then, in the basement, they simply put a bullet in his head.

While I was thinking about that, something that a fellow inmate had told me in camp flashed across my mind, a story about so-called repentant thieves slashing a nonrepentant one. They slashed him meticulously for two hours—they made thirty cuts. Their aim was not to kill him, just to prolong the torment as long as possible. Had I become like those murderers? Again, I had the realization that time was short; I had only a few seconds left. And, like a man who is readying himself to leap over an abyss, I asked, "Why did you do it?" I rose and, as soon as I did, my theft was revealed—the knife I had stolen fell out of my pocket.

Now did she understand? Now did she guess? No. With her quiet, level voice she answered my question with a question. "What are you talking about, my dear?" She even had the nerve to call me "my dear"! That's how secure she was in the strength of her protection. Of what importance was my question or the knife that fell from my pocket if she was absolutely convinced her betrayal would never be discovered. I didn't respond immediately and she asked again, "What are you talking about, my dear?" The knife waited on the floor. I didn't pick it up. I knew it was not a trial, with prosecutors and attorneys, but I had to tell her. I knew my time was almost up—I didn't know why—and I had to rush. Still I asked, "What devil ruined me? Is it ever possible to grant forgiveness?" I didn't look at her—I couldn't bear to see her. She answered, "That's the point, my dear. One never finds out." Her voice was serene and steady, her self-confidence never wavered. Again, I fought tears—my wife was right, my nerves were shattered. My God, how easily we learn to betray, with what perfidy—and how easily we adjust to it. A whole army exists—a whole army of traitors, informers, betrayers—and they live among us without any feelings of guilt. From day to day they walk the streets, visit our homes, sit at our tables, maintain friendships for years—all for one thing, for the one time they will denounce us. And they always do it peacefully and quietly, with a completely clear conscience. "My God," I thought, and this time I could no longer hold back the tears, "Why is it soldiers in this army so seldom commit suicide? Do they ever hang, poison, or shoot themselves?" No. I had never heard of a single one. Look. Here is an example. One is sitting here right in front of me and she looks at me with wide eyes radiating innocence.

Her mouth moved, but I was unable to make out the words. Stuttering, racing against time, I told her how I had discovered her treachery. My interrogator was young and inexperienced. He repeated word for word things I had told only to her, to Tonya, only to her. Once he even said her name. Of course, it was an unpardonable mistake, but even a perfect machine sometimes fails to run properly. I didn't even look at her, or listen to her response—it was essential to rush and some force was pounding on my back saying, "Faster, faster, faster." I didn't use the knife. I put my hands around her neck and began to squeeze and squeeze, to choke her. Suddenly my hands were covered with blood. Something heavy hit me on the head.

* * *

His forehead hit the edge of the table, and his book fell to the floor. The jagged keys on the jailer's ring scraped his knuckles. He remembered his hands were covered with blood and tried to hide them. The guard was in the cell, standing before him. "You were sleeping," he accused. The prisoner mumbled something. "You were sleeping," the guard repeated. "You deliberately tried to deceive me by holding a book in front of you. Three minutes ago you were sitting as you are supposed to and I thought you were reading. Now I warn you for the last time!"

"For the last time," the convict promised—and only after saying these words did he finally wake.

Single Combat

1

NEWCOMERS ARRIVING AT Kacha camp would take one look at Kropnik and be unable to take their eyes away. I remember that I, too, had been amazed at his appearance when I first saw him. I had stared so long and been so stunned that I was practically mesmerized.

Many convicts in camp are gaunt and emaciated to the utmost degree, but even among those, Kropnik stood out—with transparent skin the color of parchment, feverishly bright eyes, cheeks sunken like a skeleton's, and pants that appeared to be empty because they were entirely bereft of buttocks.

Recognizing a campnik is usually easy—if not by the prison-issue pea coat, then by the canvas boots or visored cap or cotton drawstring pants. Kropnik, however, wore only his own clothing. Since he was now serving his fifteenth year and received no help from any of his family (they had all been sentenced and sent to scattered sites throughout the country), it is not difficult to imagine what his things looked like. He had to patch them every day. Add also that those same clothes served as his bedding—he had neither a straw mattress nor a pillow stuffed with wood shavings or hay. He didn't even have one of those filthy flannel blankets we prized, in such dreadful condition that they could only be found in prison camp or some derelict shelter for the disabled.

What had Kropnik done? Why had he been singled out for such bizarre punishment? But that's the point. The truth was that Kropnik was not being punished by anyone. The truth was that Kropnik flatly refused to recognize camp authority; so it was he himself who had refused its clothes and bedding.

I will tell you more. From the hands of camp authority Kropnik had never taken anything. He had never gone to breakfast; he had never gone to dinner; he had never gone to supper. Whenever bread was brought to the barrack, as is customary in camp, his bunk mate accepted Kropnik's daily *pika* and passed it to him. The same with sugar. During all the years of his confinement, all fifteen of them, Kropnik had taken no other provisions. Also living in the barrack were former peasants who had been driven to utter poverty by Stalin's anti-landowner campaign. Few ever received parcels from home—and fewer still had a rusk to share with him. Dinner cereal? Watered-down soup? You must be joking! Kropnik wouldn't even take camp tea. Nor would he take water from prison barrels. During the Second World War, Kacha camp had produced earthenware crockery. A few prisoners had supplied Kropnik with several pots and some small pitchers. These he was still using at the time of our arrival. In the pots he kept water which he carried from the well himself. In the pitchers he steeped small portions of his daily ration of yeast bread. This soon became *kvass,* the cider he drank for sustenance and strength.

Kropnik lived on the upper berth of the bunk bed. This is not a slip of the pen—he actually lived there. He descended only to drink water or attend to his physical needs. At no time did he ever come down to do any work but, during my time, command endured his actions silently. How could they not, when Kropnik was only a skeleton papered with parchment? One other thing command endured—whenever they came to the barrack and sounded "Attention!" and everyone jumped to stand in place, Kropnik would stay on his upper berth. If he was praying on his knees, he would continue to cross himself and bow. If he was mending his clothes, he would continue to sit, the needle flashing through his fingers.

About twice a year we were inspected by high command from area headquarters or even Moscow. Ah, those inspections! That the top brass was about to descend on us had been divulged to the administration a good fortnight before their arrival. That's when the torture began. Our camp was always in neglected condition, so it was necessary to give it God's own shape immediately. Even the invalids—who ordinarily worked only four or five hours a day—were forced into duty from dawn to dusk. We cleaned the slit trenches in the toilet next door, we redug and leveled forbidden buffer zones—pulling every plant up by its root so that no footprint would go unseen on the barren earth. We raked up all the trash and burned it, producing a low fog that loomed over everything. We washed and scrubbed the barracks. We whitewashed the buildings, fences, and watchtowers. Finally, the entire prison population was herded into the square where they cut our hair en masse, as if they were shearing sheep. Even the criminals had their fancy forelocks cropped. In other words, utter chaos ensued with enough extra, totally unnecessary, and tiresome ado that we cursed the generals who came to visit. Devil take them! Let them stay and sit in their headquarters! Even without them we were sick!

Now what made me bring all this up? Kropnik, of course. Because, even for high commanders, Kropnik made no exception. Not only did he disregard our forced endeavors but he didn't descend from his bunk—not even at the very last moment when the generals and their escorts would strut before us and we all had to stand at attention. But what about the high commanders themselves? Many had heard of Kropnik, whose name was as bizarre as he was, but they had passed him by as if he were invisible. Only once did an important general stop, glance up, catch sight of Kropnik's flat back and bare heels and ask, "What's that?" As usual, he was on his knees facing the wall. The camp commander leaned over and began to whisper. He whispered a long time. Finally, the general shrugged his shoulders and that was that.

For the most part, on his upper berth, Kropnik prayed. Were someone to wake during the night and see a shadow racing across the ceiling, he would realize it was Kropnik, kneeling and bowing. In the same position—exposing his parchment heels—he prayed at dawn, during the day, and in the evening. He would come down from his bunk only tentatively and unwillingly—in much the same way as an unskilled swimmer dips into icy water. Hopping like a hunted animal—totally exhausted, flat as a wall, with a beard as sparse as that of Ivan the Terrible—he would step high and look from side to side with feverish eyes. He would dart in and out of the toilet, then attend to his pots. (During the summer he lined them up in the bushes outside so he could drink some *kvass,* then hop back to his perch.)

At that time Kropnik was in his fifties. He had been born and had lived in Volyn, where he grew small grains. He was serving his second term under Article 58, the political catch-all for anti-Soviet activity.

With these words it should be possible to finish Kropnik's story—an obscure ripple of resistance in a sea of senseless cruelty. But then Shushkin, the new overseer, was assigned to Kacha camp.

2

Four years before Shushkin's arrival, a certain captain had been serving in a facility far to the north of us. Deputy camp commander and censor, he was a gallant and a womanizer with a voluptuous grin constantly playing on his thin lips. The whole camp was informed of, and feasted on, Borodulin's love affairs. Naturally, as is usually the case in such situations, there were more than a few exaggerations—but it was generally accepted that the captain had enjoyed most of his co-workers' wives, all of whom were living in the settlement nearby.

And so it went until a new guard showed up with his delectable eighteen-year-old bride. It was Shushkin. I saw her years after the story I'm telling you now. She was splendid. There's nothing more difficult than describing a woman's beauty, so I'll restrict myself to that one word—splendid.

Captain Borodulin began to woo her, as he did all the wives. But, despite his experience and persistence, he met with no success. A simple daughter of the taiga, she maintained a fidelity that was practically foreign in our midst. How did her sergeant husband react to Borodulin? Stupid and shortsighted, he was flattered by the fact that the captain would visit from time to time, bringing vodka and snacks.

The details of this drama came to me through the words of other people—from prisoners who had lived there at that time. To the amazement of all, Borodulin's courtship continued for over a year. Only then did Shushkina agree to leave the sergeant and be Borodulin's wife. Carrying just a small bundle of clothing and some bedding, she moved in with him.

I realize I'm relating these events in a matter-of-fact way, but that is the way I first heard them. I was given only facts. It's not without regret, therefore, that I must deny my desire to delve into every detail. For instance, what was the reason for Borodulin's overwhelming passion? I do not know. Nor do I know what finally convinced the girl to succumb. Was it his persistence? Did she suddenly respond? Had she simply seen a way to better herself? Or was it a moment's caprice? One thing I do know and that is how the sergeant reacted to his wife's desertion. Never indifferent to wine, he now began to drink more and more. The captain took delight in showing off his pretty plaything and clothed her in elegant gowns. Shushkin, slipping into the captain's apartment when no one was there, took scissors to every dress. A furious Borodulin threatened to take him to court, but the sergeant refused to calm down. Pain, insult, and shame engulfed him. Once, when drunk, he attempted suicide. He went to the railway and lay across the tracks. Fortunately, it was during the day. The engineer saw him and managed to stop the train just in time.

His suicide attempt was, of course, reported to area administration headquarters. The area commander at that time, not without basis, decided it best to separate the charmer's two husbands—former and current. Shortly thereafter, Borodulin was transferred to our Kacha camp to an important but slightly lesser position. He was in command of the overseers.

How did it happen that, contrary to the wise decision of the area commander, Shushkin was later transferred to the same place? Even worse! How did it happen that he was placed directly under Borodulin's authority?

The answer is simple. Three years is a long time. During that time the area commander had retired and his assistants were assigned to other places. Briefly speaking, no one familiar with the love story was left. So—such is the irony of fate—Shushkin, too, was transferred to Kacha camp.

3

One wonders how Shushkin, now fat, flabby and pathologically suspicious, felt when he saw his former rival again. Knowing Borodulin, I can imagine with what malice he gloated as the sergeant stepped into his office. He might have asked him several innocuous questions—for instance, how did he feel, what did he do with his time off, was he happy, did he plan to start a new family? I doubt, however, whether the captain would have been that generous to his wife's former husband. Even conquerors of generous spirit are seldom sympathetic to their vanquished foes.

It is probable that the more his superior humiliated him, the gloomier the sergeant grew. Standing straight at attention as the captain lounged comfortably in his chair, Shushkin gave monosyllabic replies. The sergeant realized that it was going to be hard for him in Kacha camp. Borodulin would now take revenge for the cut-up clothing, the scandals, and the simple fact that he, Shushkin, had once been the husband of the captain's wife. Grimly, the sergeant realized it was perfectly possible that he could be expelled from Kacha region, losing both his job and rank. For what? It didn't matter. Couldn't a supervisor discharge a subordinate for nothing at all? Of course! So go and look for justice! And the chance that he would never find it but would simply bring disaster on himself the sergeant knew very well. That must have been the way their first meeting went, in Kacha. It lasted no longer than fifteen minutes. Finally, Borodulin checked the schedule beneath the glass on his desk and said Shushkin's first task would be to take the head count in our barrack, the invalid barrack. In this way Shushkin took his leave, thoroughly convinced that from that moment on he would be completely under the iron hand of a captain intent on revenge—a captain who would take advantage of any infraction that could give him reason to dismiss his subordinate.

4

A new overseer! That is a big event in camp where so few events occur. Quickly, as soon as the signal clanged on the metal post, we gathered outside the barrack and fell into formation. Intently, we looked at Shushkin as he approached. His head hung down, his gait was slow, and his glowering face boded little good. The prisoner-foreman read from the wooden tablet that substituted in camp for a notebook. Crying "Attention!" and enunciating more clearly than usual, he reported that living in the barrack were a certain number of convicts—that right now, were so many in the workshop, so many in the kitchen, and two inside the barrack—an orderly who was sweeping and a Kropnik.

"At ease," Shushkin ordered. Then, just as the general before him had done, he asked, "A Kropnik? What's that?"

Laughter resounded. Somebody said, "God man." Scowling and hunching his shoulders, Shushkin looked at the prisoner-foreman and asked, "This whatever-you-call-him—is he also sweeping?"

The prisoner-foreman loved to play up to his superiors and knew how to do it well. Loquaciously, he launched into a long tirade, in a complaining tone of voice. "A willful tormentor and a pain in the neck, a real devil! That's what a Kropnik is! What would it cost him on a beautiful May day to step out of the barrack for ten minutes and form up? But, as you see, he doesn't want to. He doesn't want anything! He doesn't give a damn about anything or anybody! He would like to spit on all of us! If you are a convict, you have to obey the law, how else can it be?" In this way, the prisoner-foreman spoke and the more he went on, the darker Shushkin's face became. Somebody laughed. Someone else tried to be funny. The sergeant ground his foot impatiently into the earth. Then, turning to the prisoner-foreman, he said, "Let's go inside!"

Shushkin had not yet made up his mind. He had merely been alarmed. Stepping into the barrack, he strode past the long rows of two-tier bunks. Then, craning his neck, he stopped. On his knees, on an upper berth, was Kropnik—flat as a board, bowing and straightening. As usual, Kropnik was facing the wall, and his dirty heels seemed to stare at the sergeant darkly and blindly. Shushkin saw only strange clothing covered with patches; a scrawny neck sticking out of a wide collar on a homemade shirt; a wild torrent of hair that had not been cut at camp. Yes. Something was strange. What did it mean?

The moment the question flashed into Shushkin's mind, it was accompanied by paranoid suspicion. He was not green. In all his years as a guard he had nowhere, ever, seen a convict like this. A convict who didn't obey rules? No overseer-commander would ever permit it. Of course not! This whole comedy had been contrived by the captain. Shushkin had been purposely sent to the invalid barrack. The scoundrel's clothing had been purposely changed—he had purposely been ordered not to form up and not to obey the guard. Why? The reason was clear. To humiliate Shushkin in front of the prisoners and then, using that as an excuse, to fire him.

By this time, practically psychotic, Shushkin glared at the prisoner-foreman. He was convinced that not only was the prisoner-foreman in on it but also every prisoner. They hadn't laughed for nothing when Kropnik's name came up. Yes. They were all in league with Borodulin. Was there any other way to explain their snickering and snide remarks?

"He will fail. Nothing will come of this," Shushkin said aloud, but the prisoner-foreman interpreted the words in his own way.

"No," he warned, "if he doesn't want to, that's it. You won't be able to do anything with him."

Shushkin didn't even hear the prisoner-foreman. His forehead was furrowed and his whole appearance had darkened. This matter could affect not only his current life but also his future existence. He had been pushed to the brink of disaster. Borodulin would learn this very day if Shushkin allowed some delinquent to ignore him and not form up for head count. A report would fly to headquarters without a moment's notice. And, besides, Borodulin didn't even need to write; Shushkin wasn't that high up. The captain could throw him out and discharge him on his own. It was good he'd caught on in time. No! Shushkin would never permit anyone to dupe him or destroy him again.

"Hey, you!" The sergeant shouted at Kropnik. "You there! Face me!"

There was no answer.

"I'm talking to you, devil! Are you deaf?"

Kropnik continued in silence. Bending his back, he bowed and straightened, and his right elbow moved as he crossed himself.

"You see, citizen overseer? That's the way he is," the prisoner-foreman said sympathetically, "Forgive me, but he'd just as soon spit on you."

Threateningly, Shushkin shouted, "I'll show him who'll spit." Throwing off his greatcoat, he began to climb to the upper bunk.

Looking up, the prisoner-foreman saw the guard shoving Kropnik. Moving away on his knees, not even looking at Shushkin, Kropnik continued to pray. The guard grabbed him by the arm and began pulling him toward the edge of the bunk. Kropnik resisted by not resisting. ("It was as if he were a sack," the prisoner-foreman would later describe it, "a sack of flour or sand.") Then suddenly he broke away and flew down to the floor. It seemed he had been hurt badly, he lay flat and still. But as soon as Shushkin came down, the convict crawled under the lower berth with unexpected speed. Shushkin crawled after him. From under the berth the sounds of heavy breathing and blows could be heard, as the guard pushed and beat him. In several minutes, Kropnik crawled out. His shirt was ripped. With catlike agility he jumped to his feet and leaped back up to his usual place. Once there, he sat back on his heels and began bending and straightening, bowing and crossing himself.

The duel lasted a good half hour, repeating over and over in every detail. As before, neither resisting nor submitting, Kropnik was like a sack. After a silent struggle, Shushkin would throw Kropnik out of his berth. The convict would fall and lay motionless. Then, as soon as Shushkin climbed down from the berth, Kropnik crawled under the bunk. Shushkin would follow. Panting. Blows. Then Kropnik would break free and clambered back up to pray with his usual silent devotion.

Once, in falling, Kropnik cracked his head and his whole body was covered with blood. (Incidentally, never on that day or any subsequent day did he ask the camp doctors for aid. After all, they were part of camp authority, too.) The convicts could only peer inside and wonder, "Where in God's name does he get his strength? He is too weak even to keep his soul in his body!"

The calmer Kropnik was, the more frenzied Shushkin became. He bit the convict, shouted at him, cursed him in the foulest language. He even blasphemed God. "I will kill you," he roared as if possessed. "I will kill you, and nothing will happen to me." And, actually, had overseers been allowed to carry loaded guns at inspection, he would have done so on the spot.

In the midst of this, as the struggle continued, the time allotted for inspection came to an end. The fall-out signal clanged on the metal post outside the overseer's office. Timidly, at first one by one and then more and more boldly in groups, the convicts began to drift back inside. Soon they had all entered the building.

It was only then that Shushkin came to his senses. Now a different danger threatened him—one that was much more real. He had violated a direct order. He had not made the evening check. He had failed on the very first day of duty! In a moment, the convicts would all disperse since they would be free after the second signal.

The instant Shushkin rose and stood on his feet, Kropnik also rose. Naked to the waist, wet with sweat, bloody with open wounds and bruises, he leaped back up to his bunk. There he continued to bow and straighten.

Shushkin didn't look well, either. There is always dirt under the bunks, and the sergeant was gray with it—it covered his hair, shirt, pants, and boots. One of the shoulder stripes on his tunic had been torn away, and he hurried to hide the fact by putting on his coat. He covered his hair with his cap.

"Go out and form up," he hissed.

The prisoner-foreman echoed the order. "Go out! Go out! Form up!"

The convicts left immediately. As before, only two people remained in the barrack—the orderly, sweeping with his broom, and Kropnik.

On his knees, with his heels pointing into the room, Kropnik resumed his prayers—bending and bowing, bending and crossing himself. And only by looking closely could one see how his movements had slowed and how, after bending down, he had to help with his hands to straighten back up. Only then could one see how weary the struggle had made him.

Vasily Vasilyevich

1

IN THE EVENING—when the barrack was smoke-filled, stuffy, and dark, and his head was throbbing from the sobbing accordions and the funereal psalms sung by the Baptists—Igor Shevelev, a former student from Moscow, would visit Vasily Vasilyevich.

While he was still being held in interrogation prison, his cell mates had celebrated his eighteenth birthday. Now, in camp, it seemed not months but years since then. "God, how silly and naive I was," he would deride himself. Just remembering his former foolishness aggravated him and made him angry.

The more unbearable life in Lubyanka became, the more convinced he was that he would never be free, the more rustic and charming he would imagine the frozen north for which he was destined. Words like "Siberia," "a warming hut in the squatting," and "taiga" he could pronounce only with a sentimental catch in his throat. From prison camp he would, of course, run away. After all, people used to escape in the olden days—even from the fabled Schlisselburg Fortress. He would escape and wander from village to village where, as in the celebrated song, "a wanderer would always be given tobacco." And even in prison camp, no one could force him to sit with his arms folded. He would always find something to do.

It wasn't very long before nothing remained of his adolescent imaginings. In the past two years only two criminals had tried to escape. One was caught by the guards the same day. The day after, workers from the hunting cooperative trapped the other one exactly where Igor had pictured himself—a warming hut in the squatting.

His barrack mates were dull—for the most part uneducated and unimaginative peasants. To Shevelev they reacted with disdain, referring to him as "the infant." One of them—a sarcastic fuzzy-headed hater, often remarked that Igor should never have been put in prison, just spanked and thrown in the snow. It was only Vasily Vasilyevich to whom he could relate—and whom he liked more and more after each conversation. Only Vasily Vasilyevich consoled him and kept his waning hopes alive.

Prior to his arrest, Vasily Vasilyevich had been chief fireman for an enormous region. He had been in charge of dozens of men and supervised several fire trucks. Always generous, Vasily Vasilyevich would often loan trucks to his superiors. As it turned out, they were in league with the truck drivers and smuggling kolkhozniks to market so they could sell their goods. For this they were charging indiscriminate amounts of money. When the fraud was finally uncovered, they framed Vasily Vasilyevich and he was sentenced to eighteen years.

"That case, I thank it!" he would tell Shevelev. "That case opened my eyes and set my mind straight. So! This is what life is going to be like! I had better understand and adapt to it."

Today, as usual, Vasily Vasilyevich welcomed his young friend warmly. "Hello, Igor Mikhailovich," he called in his deep husky voice, addressing Igor as an adult and not a boy. His eyes, quick and bright as a fox's, were framed by blond hair and white skin—yet his lips were negroid and his whole face seemed somehow African.

"I am very glad to see you, take off your coat. Sit! I am dying for a cup of tea."

Vasily Vasilyevich lived separately in a semibasement closet that served as a wardrobe. Hanging in it were the costumes used in camp productions for reeducation. That Vasily Vasilyevich was "very glad to see him" Igor had heard many times, but it always made him feel better, as it did today.

"Do I come too often? Are you sick and tired of me?"

His host gestured for Igor to sit on the folding bed. The closet was very low and very damp. Lifting one's hand while seated, one could touch the ceiling. The smell of wet earth and wet brick seeped into everything. Above the bed, on the opposite wall, the costumes hung. Mostly, they were soldier's tunics with insignia. The rest were blue full-dress uniforms with crude, brightly painted swastikas on the shoulder stripes. Khaki tunics and blue German uniforms all blended together in one dark gray mass that made the small shabby room look as though it were covered with mold. Fake revolvers, painted black and gray with dust, were piled up in one corner next to a prop machine gun standing on tiny wheels. Near the bed, a paper shade covered a bare bulb that hung over a rickety round table made for one of the sets.

Shevelev basked in the silence. After the barrack, the wardrobe seemed like paradise, a precious oasis in a perilous world. Ducking his head and narrowing his eyes, Vasily Vasilyevich peered into Igor's face, first subtly and then more directly.

"Are we sad again?" he asked. "Confess. Are you upset?"

In all honesty, Shevelev had been increasingly depressed during the past few weeks and came constantly to Vasily Vasilyevich for words of comfort. He needed them more and more, but was too proud to admit it openly. His lips curving in a weak smile, he said, "Today there was nothing to do so I counted how many days I have left to serve. Not many at all—2,961."

He would have liked to say more—to say that even after an endless term he would never be allowed to return to Moscow; that he would never be allowed to graduate; that his mother—about whom he felt overwhelming guilt—was old and sick, and most likely he would never see her again. And all this because of a case against him and his classmates that had been fabricated from whole cloth! In truth, mostly by inference and by his weak smile, he had already spoken, and he knew Vasily Vasilyevich would not approve—he ridiculed such complaints. But, realizing that his voice would tremble and betray him, Shevelev drifted into silence.

"You are teasing me," smiled Vasily Vasilyevich. "Admit it."

"What makes you so sure? There were, after all, a lot of people before us who sat out their whole term—sat for ten or fifteen years. And even those who managed to survive are still suffering in exile."

"You are teasing me," laughed Vasily Vasilyevich in a husky, cheerful voice, as he tried to allay Shevelev's anxiety.

"What makes you so sure?" Shevelev repeated, although it occurred to him that perhaps he was overdoing it just to be comforted. "What makes you so sure?"

"*You* make me sure," Vasily Vasilyevich went on. "Oh, you're so inexperienced. You should be happy they caught you now and not five years ago. Happy and proud. Take me, for instance. I am more than three times your age, and I was not taken for political reasons. But still, believe me, I am happy and proud to be sitting here. Eighteen years? No, my friend, I'm not the kind of fool to make myself miserable over nothing. I won't agree to even eighteen months, won't agree at all. Would you like to bet?"

"Bet what?" asked Shevelev, guessing what Vasily Vasilyevich was going to say.

"In one year—and that's the outside—the gates will be thrown open and you—an innocent man—will be carried out like a hero. And when that happens, young man, you will owe me supper in the best restaurant in the city, and I will order whatever I want—and I want the most expensive things on the menu. Nor will you get rid of me with cheap wine, either!"

Listening to Vasily Vasilyevich's confident tone, Shevelev began to believe that, of course, one couldn't compare the 1950s with what had happened before. He pictured how the gates would clang open and he would be lifted high in triumph, seeing it so clearly it practically hurt his eyes. Then he had a disquieting thought. Wasn't it just that way the gates had been opened and the prisoners who had been captured in Germany were carried? Prisoners who were now in prison for having been taken prisoner? He was also reminded of the dark, sardonic old men next to him who had been sitting in prison since the twenties—since their lands had been taken during collectivization. Hastily trying to subdue his alarming second thoughts, he said, "So! You want to bet me!"

"Yes, I do. But I pity your lack of money, dear student. If, in a year, we are still here, I will pay you one thousand rubles. Make it even more! I can promise you two thousand, or even three, because I won't lose. It is you who will lose and have to treat me to supper."

Vasily Vasilyevich's prediction cheered Shevelev. And in truth, he reproached himself. He shouldn't give up, he ought not to let himself go. He should stand more firmly on his own two feet.

"You see, Igor Mikhailovich, you feel the way you do because you don't know real people," Vasily Vasilyevich continued emphatically. "You have never lived in the provinces, in a simple unspoiled region like our taiga. In Moscow what kind of people do you have? Only bureaucrats! All they know is how to get Stalin Awards—how to grab luxuries because they have learned how to grovel!"

Shevelev realized that what Vasily Vasilyevich said was true—that he didn't understand most people at all—and of course it had not been the decent people, the common people, who had betrayed the convict in the squatting, but some local scum. Then, mocking himself, and in order to amuse Vasily Vasilyevich, he said, "I know the common people very well. During the war my mother and I were evacuated and lived on a *kolkhoz* in Uzbekistan. Of course, I was only ten at the time!" They laughed, Shevelev boyishly throwing back his head and Vasily Vasilyevich with heaving guffaws, interrupted only by his emphysema. Then, unexpectedly, Vasily Vasilyevich made an announcement.

"I have decided to quit my job in the wardrobe and go back to the barrack. If I am an invalid, I shouldn't have to work. You arrested me, you sentenced me, period! Now leave me alone and do not expect me to wear myself out—especially if you do not pay me. Listen, I am not a fool. I refuse to sit in the dark here, like an ancient owl."

Shevelev heard his words with apprehension. The little closet was the only place where he could speak to his clever, experienced friend—where they could sit alone and he could seek solace. "Why do you have to move?" he asked, still troubled. "Invalid or not, they will bother you in the same way they do the rest of us. We have to chop all the logs and load them. If the commander is coming, we have to sweep the grounds and whitewash the barracks. They drive us hours to dig up potatoes. All the potatoes used in camp are dug up by the invalids."

"It is not so easy to wipe the floor with me. I know how to protect myself."

"But Vasily Vasilyevich, it's much better here than in the barrack."

"Nonsense," said Vasily Vasilyevich. "It's just too bad we can't be together. Since I am not political, they'll put me in with criminals and felons and, unfortunately, there is nothing we can do about it. Besides, there is not long to wait."

"But why? Why? Why do you have to leave this wardrobe?" Shevelev continued to implore.

Narrowing his eyes, Vasily Vasilyevich looked at Shevelev in a new way. In the dim light of the bulb, one could see only the pupils of his eyes—and they looked bottomless.

"You cannot guess?"

"Not exactly, no."

"Can you partially guess?" Suddenly, Vasily Vasilyevich's face simmered with fury. Red spots burned on his high cheekbones. "Let them go to the devil," he wheezed, hitting his fist on the table. "I will not serve them, even in this wardrobe. It's a matter of principle. Why should I? They throw me out of life, roll me in shit, and then tell me to guard their belongings. Guard their belongings? No thank you! Enough!"

"Please. Think it over," pleaded Shevelev. "It's so quiet and calm here."

"I don't want to think," growled Vasily Vasilyevich. "They convicted me, labeled me an enemy. So? I will be an enemy! Period." Then he began to boil again. "My time will come. I will find my so-called friends in high places. Only a wet spot will be left of them!"

2

Several days passed and Vasily Vasilyevich actually left the wardrobe. Aside from his lung problems, he had large varicose veins on his legs that looked as if they were ready to burst. Prior to leaving the damp closet, he consulted with the medical service and got its approval.

From then on Shevelev was deprived of his meetings with Vasily Vasilyevich in the cramped closet he thought so cozy. Worse, he could no longer count on him for hope. Only during short walks was he sometimes able to bare his soul to Vasily Vasilyevich. But, as ill luck would have it, the rain came like a wall of water, and there were fewer and fewer times when they could meet.

In the criminal barrack to which Vasily Vasilyevich had been moved it was more unsightly and even darker than in the political one. Everything vanished into thick clouds of cheap cigarette smoke; smokers hacked then spat on the floor with staccato pings; domino players slammed their tiles on the table with such blows that they deafened Shevelev like shots whenever he went to visit.

The worst of it was the thieves for whom Shevelev couldn't disguise his disgust. Naked to the waist, they looked as if someone had written on them with smudged ink, scribbling obscene tattoos from head to toe. Glancing constantly over their shoulders so as not to be seen by the guards, cursing without stopping, they played cards with deadly intent. And Vasily Vasilyevich? He noticed nothing—neither the dirt, nor the stench, nor the noise, nor the inconvenience. Joyfully looking around, squinting his eyes against the smoke, he sat on his bunk and pulled on his pipe or played checkers with a neighbor. As always, he greeted Shevelev warmly, but now they couldn't really talk, they could discuss only trivialities—because in camp even the walls have ears. Every so often though, Vasily Vasilyevich would remind his young friend of their bet and boastfully imply that he would win.

"Do you really think so?" Shevelev would ask eagerly. Even the playful hint revived his spirits, for his mother grew more and more miserable. He could not read her letters without grieving.

"And you stop worrying!" ordered Vasily Vasilyevich, laughing his guttural laugh. "Take me for example. I, personally, never worry—just on principle."

But here, as often happens, sudden misfortune arrived and Vasily Vasilyevich was forced to forget his own advice.

One morning several overseers arrived at his barrack door with a commandant named Sasha. "Everybody out!" shouted Sasha. A giant man of great strength, he had round birdlike eyes that were always open and a constant grin on his rosy face. "Everybody out to load bricks. The trucks are waiting!"

"Let them wait," the convicts muttered inaudibly. They both hated and feared the commandant, a repentant thief and killer. Behind his back they called him "Cain." "Let them wait," they grumbled, "nothing's burning."

Massive, rolling from side to side like a sailor and admiring himself, Sasha stalked through the narrow aisles rushing everyone. Since the weather was at its worst, the convicts took their time and dressed slowly. Suddenly, the commandant stopped before Vasily Vasilyevich. Sitting on his bunk, he was slowly sipping tea from an iron cup.

"And what about you?" asked Sasha, stroking his stylish mustache. "Are you waiting for a special invitation?"

Instead of answering, Vasily Vasilyevich pulled off his felt boots and displayed his legs. Varicose veins, looking like earthworms, wrapped around them as if they were purple ropes.

"So what?" Since Sasha didn't raise his voice, one couldn't tell if he were angry. "So what? They probably won't kill you, so get dressed."

Without answering, Vasily Vasilyevich lifted his bare feet and once again touched his tea. But he had no time to bring it to his lips. With an iron blow, still smiling, Sasha knocked the cup from his hands. Swiftly, giving Vasily Vasilyevich no opportunity to comply, he grabbed his shirt collar and pulled him to the barrack door.

"We didn't want to put on our shoes, didn't want to get dressed, so we'll go as we are," he said softly, as if speaking to a child. And, while the other convicts were forming up, Sasha dragged Vasily Vasilyevich over the rock-strewn ground and down the dirty, mud-filled road.

"Didn't want? Didn't want?"

Even the thieves, who contributed more than their share of bestiality, tried not to look at the miserable man. Practically knocked senseless, with eyes almost falling out of their sockets, he was cut and covered with mud from foot to face. Vainly, Vasily Vasilyevich tried to stop the commandant, tried to escape from his hands.

Finally, his voice weak and broken, he managed to wheeze, "I will bring charges! You will be held responsible, citizen overseer. I am the chief fireman. I am myself a captain of the MVD. Everyone here will testify, everyone here will be my witness!"

But the performance was not yet finished and Sasha refused to release his victim. With one hand, he tried to brush at his highly polished boots, now spattered with soft, rain-soaked earth. As he did, he glanced surreptitiously at the convicts standing in formation. How were they reacting to all this? But it was becoming more and more difficult every minute to drag Vasily Vasilyevich around and only when, with a weak pitiful moan, Vasily Vasilyevich dropped his face in the mud from exhaustion, did Sasha let him loose.

"Go! Go, the rest of you!" Sasha called, recovering his breath and laughing self-consciously. "If a person cannot work, it means he is sick. Let him rest on the soft bed out here."

3

The politicals, too, had been taken for work that day, so Shevelev learned only hours later what had happened. The story had spread all over camp and the tale was embroidered on each time it was told. Some said that Vasily Vasilyevich was so maimed he would never survive. Others claimed that he had been killed. Shocked and soaking wet, Shevelev rushed to Vasily Vasilyevich—to his barrack where he was told that his older friend was in the hospital.

It was true. Vasily Vasilyevich was in a dirty white ward with two rows of identical beds covered with identical black blankets and the cursed smell of carbolic acid and urine permeating everything. Among the many exhausted faces hiding behind stubble, he was finally able to spot his fallen friend. Vasily Vasilyevich's weakened condition and overly red color disturbed Shevelev to the point where he tried with difficulty to stop his heart from pounding. But Vasily Vasilyevich smiled warmly. Leaning an elbow on the crackling straw pillow, he tried to lift himself and sit.

"They worked me over a little," he said. "It doesn't matter. I just wish I didn't have pneumonia."

Judging from his color, it was obvious Vasily Vasilyevich was running a high fever. "How dreadful to die in such circumstances," thought Shevelev, turning cold at the idea.

"Do you need anything?" he asked compassionately. "Mama sent jam. I will bring it to you. Please, don't get up. Please! Lie back down!"

"Nonsense, my friend, nonsense. I'm still full of gunpowder—I can defend myself." Resting his head back on the pillow and pulling his blanket up to his chin, Vasily Vasilyevich wheezed. "I need a favor from you, Igor Mikhailovich. It is necessary to teach that bastard and all the rest of them a lesson. You, brother, must write an appeal for me to the camp commander. As soon as I recover, I will request an audience. Do you know the details? I will tell you, and you must write the complaint as it should be."

He was ready to start immediately, and it was only with difficulty that Shevelev managed to calm him.

"Don't worry," he assured Vasily Vasilyevich with tears in his eyes. He was touched that the older man had appealed to him with such trust and affection. "I will write it, I promise, as soon as you get better. You'll tell me every detail, and I will write them all down. It's impossible to keep quiet about this matter."

"Keep quiet?" Vasily Vasilyevich roared, getting excited all over again. "I will show them how to beat convicts. I will teach the overseers as well as the commandant. I know the rules and regulations better than any of them!"

"Please! Please calm down!"

Vasily Vasilyevich took a deep breath and snapped a salute, laughing. "And you, my dear Igor Mikhailovich, please come and visit—do not forget me."

Shevelev flushed with pleasure at his friend's request. "How can you doubt it? I will arrange it with the orderly; I will visit you every day."

And indeed, every day and often twice a day he went to the ward. Vasily Vasilyevich grew substantially stronger, and his fever subsided. In a short time, without getting too excited, he was able to recount every detail of his run-in with the commandant. Most important, he was able to explain in detail the fine points of writing a complaint.

Naturally, it would be helpful to send a copy to a public prosecutor—or perhaps even directly to Moscow—but command would never allow it to go out. Here the mail box hung, sealed with wax, where one could put an envelope addressed to the chairman of the Supreme Soviet himself—but what was the use? Written or not, the complaint would never see freedom. But writing to the camp commander was essential and had to be done. Dozens of people had seen how abusive Sasha had been, had witnessed everything. No one would be able to defend him. No one! Under the regulations, the administration would be forced to give him ten days and ten nights in solitary confinement. And then—this would be Sasha's final blow—command would have no choice but to fire him.

"You must write as forcefully as possible," Vasily Vasilyevich directed Shevelev. "Dig to the roots! Get angry! But why am I telling you? You, after all, are the scholar."

Already outraged, Shevelev began to write the very next day. It was not difficult to imagine how sadistically Sasha had acted, how he had pulled Vasily Vasilyevich along the muck-filled road, scraping his bare body against the rocks. Anger built up and grew in him until he was filled with fury and suffocated with hatred for the whole system. And suddenly, imperceptibly, he was no longer just a helpless, homesick boy. Suddenly, he was filled with pride and satisfaction and even power. And, in that moment, he mourned the fact that he had not been near his friend, that they had not stood together and been able to fight side by side. And, in that moment, he knew with certainty that one day they would.

The Correct Man

SOMEHOW, IN PUBLIC places, people have a tendency to speak more freely. Somehow, on trains, or ships, or in hotels people disclose more to casual traveling companions than to a circle of close friends. Perhaps that's because they are strangers whom one meets for the first time and, most probably, the last—perhaps that is the reason one talks so openly.

For convicts, a transfer prison becomes the substitute for public places—a substitute for the train compartment, the ship's deck, or the hotel lounge.

You were sentenced in Odessa. To serve your term you are sent to desolate Irkutsk and, before ever arriving, you will visit dozens of transfer prisons. For instance, in Bobruysk a man—with whom once you were briefly connected—is arrested. For interrogation and confrontation you will be transported from Magadan to Byelorussia and—since no one is in any hurry to get you there—you will live in transfer prisons. Or say command authority has decided to move you from one camp to another. Again, you can't avoid transfer prisons. Then, finally, after completing your term, you're exiled to a remote region to live the rest of your life. Again, you can't avoid transfer prisons.

Now imagine a long winter night. It darkens at four and the signal for sleep sounds much later, at ten. Those six hours seem endless. Under a dim light in the cell, one not only feels dizzy from cheap tobacco smoke but also has the impression the prison is swimming, floating, or drifting—that it is rocking slightly on waves. To keep their sanity, convicts will often recite aloud. It is more than pleasant to pronounce words to which others will listen, it is also necessary. And if, by chance, a storyteller turns up among them, then God has sent a blessing.

Just such a man surfaced at a Ural transfer prison, one winter evening in '49. For the time being, Varnashin—as he was called— was silent, listening to what the other convicts were saying. Their conversation concerned the huge number of informants that had multiplied throughout the country. Speak out on any subject, talk in a small group, mention that in such-and-such state store slightly damp sugar was being sold or that the millet reeked of kerosene and, on that very day, whatever you said would be known by "who has to know," and a mark would be made against your name. Friends you thought decent until the last day turned out to be spies. One man stated authoritatively that, if all of Stalin's secret files were made public, they would reveal fifty million informers in the country—one for every four people.

"You must be counting not only the old but the children as well," argued one of the convicts.

"Yes, children. Children!" was the passionate answer. "I knew one third-grader, ten years old, who systematically informed not only on his classmates—that would be pardonable—but on their parents as well. On the conscience of that one little monster there are more than a dozen victims."

"You must be exaggerating!"

Sitting cross-legged and still silent, Varnashin continued to listen. He was a big man, about fifty. He had a broad, large chin and a big mouth with crooked lips that made him look as if he were always smiling. Finally, he spoke.

"It's astounding how driven you are to search for and find someone else to take the blame. Listening to you, one gets the impression he is in the society of innocent maidens. But, let us be truthful. Each of us must admit he is guilty."

Such an opinion was hardly met with favor. Every voice in the room resounded.

"You, of course, are judging from your own example."

"Naturally, you see it from your own standpoint."

"If we ourselves believe we're criminals, how can we blame our commanders?"

When all the voices fell silent, Varnashin—on whom obviously the comments had no effect—continued.

"I have been kept in this transfer prison for more than a month and, from your own mouths, I know many of your cases. Please don't be insulted and don't interrupt me. After all, I received a full spool myself—twenty-five years—so there is no reason to curse me or compare me to the commanders. Several days ago, for instance, one man told how, demobilized from the front, he arrived back at his native *kolkhoz.* He had seen much. He had fought through half of Germany and joined in the fall of Berlin. Naturally, the farm women surrounded him and plied him with questions. Among the most diligent were the cow women, and that was understandable— before the war he had been their dairy chief. 'So, Uncle Vasya? How are the cows there? Are they bigger or smaller?' And Uncle Vasya, who prided himself on being an expert, replied that not only were cows in Germany a bit larger than ours but also every cow in the same herd was the same color."

Here Uncle Vasya interrupted him indignantly, flushed with fury.

"And for that I deserve ten years?"

"That's beside the point. Possibly your term was a bit generous," the narrator continued. And, because it always seemed that he smiled, one couldn't tell if he were serious or not. "Or, for that matter, take another comrade," he went on. "Who forced him, three years after the war was over—after an entire three years—to broadcast that American planes, which he filled with the same gasoline as he did ours, that American planes were better than those we put in the air?"

"And what if they really were better?" protested the victim. "After all, I'm a military technician. It was not from the blue I came to that conclusion. So, first appoint a commission. Prove that I speak falsely and that I slander our equipment. Only after that take me to prison."

But, as if he had neither heard nor noticed, Varnashin continued. "One soldier is here because his investigator believed that, having been captured, he should have committed suicide. Another remained in an occupied city and 'weakened our cause' by working in a brewery. A third 'deliberately, without resisting and trying to kill his captors, allowed himself' to be shipped to Germany as slave labor. So, in answer to the question 'Are you guilty?' each of us must answer 'Yes!'"

"All right!" exclaimed the former dairy chief. "So sentence me to just one or two months and, afterwards, I will tell all my friends and even my enemies to keep their mouths shut!"

"I, too, would settle for such a term," smiled Varnashin. "But that's not what I'm talking about. I simply say that it is not only possible to be careful, it is essential. And, to prove it, I'd like to tell you a story about a man who understood that, who actually managed to do it. A real man, who was careful and correct."

Intrigued, the inmates urged him on.

"Osadchy is his last name. I will call him by his first name, Nikolay, because I've known him half my life."

Thus, Varnashin began his story.

"Up to a certain point, Nikolay was no different than anyone else in our land. He was a typical Soviet citizen with a typical background. He never served in the Tsar's army; he was too young—and he joined the Red Army at the beginning, around 1918. He fought against the Tsar's Denikin, fought with Wrangel and almost occupied Warsaw. Then he was demobilized and, in a dirty greatcoat he had already outgrown, he returned to Moscow. As you can see, nothing out of the ordinary. And, furthermore, in his whole life you would never see anything out of the ordinary. Nikolay wasn't one of those so-called heroes who broke into the social service office shouting, 'What did we fight for?'—who, after hitting the light bulb with a crutch or sometimes hitting an employee, pounded on the floor apoplectically and disappeared only after getting what he wanted. No, my friend Nikolay wasn't like that. But he wasn't a helpless lamb either. He knew what he had coming to him and managed to get it.

In such a way he soon secured a room and a job and provided himself with an excellent iron bed, a kerosene stove, a pot, and other essential accessories. After adjusting to his new state and feeling a secure base under his feet, he began to study again.

"Before the army, Nikolay had had no time to graduate, so he enrolled in the Workers' College first, then went on to an institute connected with the fishing industry—he studied either breeding or canning, I'm not sure. In his time, he studied women, as well—girls from the college dressed in floppy hats and short fur coats made from young horses. I used to meet him with them all the time. 'Let me introduce you to my little wifey,' he'd say, and then, in a year, a new 'wifey' would appear with the same button nose and the same textbooks under her arm. Everything, as you can see, was completely ordinary.

"Frankly, by that time, I would meet him only infrequently and by chance. In fact, for several years he disappeared from sight—simply disappeared, and that was that. Then, suddenly, he appeared again and seemed an absolutely different person—one might almost say transformed."

"It was, of course, 1937," interjected one of the comrades, who was ready to divide the whole history of humanity into after the peak of Stalin's repression and before.

"Somewhere around there," agreed Varnashin. "But when this change took place and how it came about I cannot say because, I repeat, I hadn't seen him that often. The previous year, I hadn't seen him at all. Then I ran into him on a train near Kuybyshev. He was on fish business, of course. Naturally, I was very glad to see him, and he—or so he said—was equally glad to see me.

"So there we were, sharing a compartment. Notice, there were only the two of us. We were talking when the train came to an abrupt stop. I looked through the window at a small station, located in the wilderness—surrounded by rugged steppes and unmowed meadows. The wind was whipping the rain and lashing it against everything in sight. The scene was not a pretty one. On the track next to us there was a long train loaded with guns and light equipment—some of it was covered, some was not. At that point, since we had exhausted all small talk, there was nothing to prevent our looking outside—at the weapons, at the soldiers with their tent raincoats, and at the loading platforms marked with numbers to disguise their final destination. Naturally, I stared. And, can you imagine, Nikolay put his hand on my shoulder and said, 'Better not look. After all, the cargo is strategic—military—so why should we stare at it?' I must tell you, I didn't understand him at first. 'Why not?' I asked.

"'I'm telling you,' he repeated. 'The cargo is military. We'd do better to turn away. Why look and—if something should happen—find ourselves in a difficult position? It's much better to be able to say, 'I saw nothing and I know nothing.'"

"What a juggler," laughed one of the listeners. Then, the person who was ready to divide all history into before and after 1937, said, "Clearly, he wanted to trap you, to hook you."

"Nonsense," scoffed Varnashin. "It was something completely different. By some special gift, some genius for prediction, or just plain instinct—I don't know exactly what—Osadchy understood that Stalin was planning a great test for many of us, and he began preparing for it in advance. So there I am, just looking at him. And before me is this stranger, wearing an expensive coat with a fur collar. He has a respectable appearance, a steady voice, clear eyes, and a long chin like a pike."

"Projecting, so to speak, a professional image?" joked one of the listeners.

"You happen to be right. There was something fishy about him that I had never noticed before."

"And, had you been more observant," continued the humorist, "you'd have discovered that his blood was cold and that he had a fish brain, too—something wrong in the head."

"Are you implying he was mentally disturbed?" Varnashin asked. "No, I can assure you that Nikolay Osadchy was absolutely normal—as normal as any of us during Stalin's time—you, me, and millions of others. No, as I told you, it was that special instinct—warning him it would soon be necessary to endure one of the greatest ordeals in history.

"It was not until several years later, in Moscow, that we met again. He was in a hurry and spoke in whispers, constantly looking about. What was happening? It turned out he was squirreling away documents about every year of his past so there could be no question concerning his loyalty to the current regime. Because everything was disorganized, it wasn't easy to do. Nevertheless, he managed. He discovered that church records had survived unscathed, and for three rubles he got a paper that verified his birth—the day, the month, the year—and that he had really been baptized Nikolay at such and such a place. By some lucky chance his school documents were also available and verified that he had only been in fifth grade during the old regime. Of our own time, it goes without saying: his old division verified his service, the Workers' College verified his attendance and the institute verified his graduation."

"And what kind of life does your Nikolay live?" asked the former technician. "Does he have a wife? Children? Or did all those Workers' College wives disappear and leave him all alone?"

Varnashin shook his head disapprovingly. "Oh, comrades, how quickly you jump to conclusions—how quickly you try to wrap everything in a neat package. Now you have your hearts set on his being mad, living like a monk and finally ending up in an asylum. No, Nikolay will never end up in an asylum. And in no way does he resemble the image you've created. He's a good employee, a specialist with a good position, a good—if demanding—husband, a good father and—as I've told you over and over again—an inordinately ordinary man. A man, in fact, such as you—before being imprisoned—met every day, shook hands with, and asked 'How are you?' But I haven't finished my story.

"As I have said, my meetings with Nikolay were always of a casual nature. I didn't, in fact, know where he lived. I only knew that he worked at the Commissariat of the Fishing Industry. Once—for a reason I no longer remember—it was necessary for me to contact him, so I dropped by the Commissariat and asked if he would see me. As we walked along the corridor, discussing business, I apologized to him. 'Forgive me, Nikolay,' I said, 'for coming to your office, but I don't know your home address.' And he answered, 'I receive no one at home.'

"Being a sinner myself, I decided that he probably had problems with his wife—fighting, divorcing, who knows? At his age, though, it was already time to calm down. 'Why?' I asked him.

"'I receive no one at home,' he repeated. 'The house manager, even he knows that during the past year no one—except him—no one has ever visited my apartment.'"

And here Varnashin added an interesting detail. It seemed that Nikolay had a brother—a professor—who lived in Rostov. That professor had come to Moscow for a meeting and naturally wanted to visit Nikolay. And what did Nikolay do? Nikolay met him in Theater Square and, for an hour and a half, just walked the streets with him."

"Now that's going too far," sputtered Uncle Vasya.

"There are other interesting things," Varnashin continued. "I learned of them by chance. With none of his friends did he correspond, and he handled business only at his office. In his home, he kept not a single printed piece of paper. (After reading a newspaper, for instance, he would destroy it immediately. After all, what excuse can there be for saving old newspapers?) As for books, he had none but the poet Nekrasov. Somehow, he loved Nekrasov and believed him acceptable under any circumstances."

"There is a major contradiction in your story," interrupted the military technician. "What kind of scientist can be employed by the commissariat who reads nothing but books by Nekrasov?"

"I meant political and literary books," Varnashin clarified. "Of course, he read books pertaining to his profession, but only those and nothing else."

At this time the narrator was interrupted by a young Georgian. Infuriated, he could no longer contain himself. Stamping his feet, so red with anger that it made his large black eyes seem even larger, he exploded. "To hell with the cowardly son of a bitch! To be afraid to talk; to be afraid of people, books and newspapers; to be afraid to invite your own brother to your house; always to be anticipating an answer should you be taken to the investigator. No! It's impossible!

Better a uniform with a number on your back, the strictest camp, the hardest labor, the worst food—better any prison for life than living the life of a mole! Of what use is liberty to such a person, of what use is freedom?"

Varnashin waited until the Georgian simmered down.

"Did I ever say Nikolay Osadchy was free?" he asked. "I simply promised to tell you a story about a correct man and to prove it's true that God helps those who help themselves. Until 1949 nobody touched my friend Nikolay—but then, of course, he was taken as well. Now, keeping in mind that all his papers were in perfect order, that he had no black marks at his place of business and that, in his house, they could find no letters and no books other than Nekrasov and some scientific material; keeping in mind that the house manager actually testified that no one ever visited Osadchy's apartment, and that Nikolay—as all the evidence proved—was guilty of nothing; keeping all this in mind, Stalin's judges gave him the best treatment possible.

"They gave him only five years."

The Prophet

"JUST WHAT WE need," sneered Aleksey Vasilyevich, who loved to remind everyone that he was the namesake of the famous people's poet Kol'tsov. "It is only a prophet we are missing from our Noah's Ark," he continued caustically. "We have Vlasov's soldiers, Bandera supporters, cossacks from the Don, cossacks from the Kuban, prisoners who served under Hitler, murderers, thieves, pretend cripples, policemen, and pederasts. We even have a young gallant who used to be a grave digger and stole clothing from the corpses. The only thing we do not have is a prophet. But don't be despondent, my friends; very soon we will add one to our collection."

We laughed because we all knew what he was talking about. In the far north a camp had been liquidated. Little by little, the prisoners there had been transferred to us. It was they who told of a certain Trifon Nikolayevich who was due to arrive very soon. As it should be—or so it was related by those who ought to know—the power of prophecy had been handed down to him by his father, and to his father by his father, and to his father's father by his father, and so on.

And though every thinking person knew these so-called prophets were simply frauds, they swore Trifon Nikolayevich had never been mistaken—not in a single thing. Take, for instance, the sadistic commander who had been sent to their camp and dealt savagely with the prisoners.

"Wait, brothers, don't be too upset," Trifon Nikolayevich had said, lending hope to his listeners. "A month won't even pass before he's gone—but whether he will be brought to justice, just reprimanded, or something else is not our concern."

What had happened? An unscheduled inspection committee had flown in, and the dear enemy simply disappeared. And, just recently, Trifon Nikolayevich had announced that the northern camp would be closed. As ordained, it had been shut down.

"What idiocy! Oh, my God, what drivel," scoffed a professor Babayan, interrupting one of the Trifon worshippers.

He was immediately upbraided, not only by the storyteller but also by the prophet's other followers. "Our Trifon, God grant him health, doesn't speak drivel."

Finally, with the delivery of the very last party of prisoners, the famous Trifon Nikolayevich arrived. We old inmates could only lift our hands in disbelief. This was a prophet? A person so unprepossessing that even honoring him with a patronymic seemed laughable? Silent and skinny, he was shy as a girl—constantly tugging, perhaps from timidity, on a wheat-colored mustache so sparse it was barely outlined. He had been arrested in Moldavia after predicting the bad harvest of '46, and had been sentenced to a full spool of twenty-five years—and that was all we were able to divine from his disciples. So what about the prophecies? Day followed day, but the so-called prophet was silent. We had just decided the northern prisoners had made fools of us when, about twenty days after his arrival, Trifon Nikolayevich started to speak.

What prompted Trifon Nikolayevich to resume his predictions? Perhaps his northern friends suggested it. Perhaps the rest of us were beginning to sneer, so he decided to take the step. Did he really possess supernatural powers? Or had he once, in the north, only accidentally hit on something that had actually come true and, in so doing, had convinced himself he was gifted? Or maybe the first few weeks in March '53 had turned his head.

At any rate, until then we had no answers to those questions. We knew just what his followers had told us—that Trifon made predictions only when they came to him.

So, without warning, Trifon began to speak. With lowered eyes, surrounded by listeners, he sat outside on a bench near the barrack and, as was his habit, tugged at his mustache. Then, softly and slowly, he started to speak—as if he were talking to himself.

"So then—in the Kremlin—there will soon be an event. An important commander will vanish and, because of that, a great release will come for us. Be waiting."

That, as I recall, was the gist of it. For those who learned only later that something had come to him, he repeated his prophecy. But when he was asked to which important commander he was referring, he answered in the same thoughtful way.

"The approximate date is known—soon—and the fact that he is important is also known. But who he is, what his name is, has not been revealed to me. I do not know."

That is how he referred to it, "has not been revealed." Kol'tsov's namesake—who by chance was there—told me about it in his usual acrimonious manner.

"The prophet, as you can see, expresses himself in ordinary terms, without obscurity—as if the subject were ordinary, too. Just one thing—he's a little bit late, this Trifon the wonderful. Had he made this prediction at the end of February, before Stalin's death . . . " He grinned knowingly. Then he added with real concern, "But he should never, even during this transitional time, have made such a prediction so openly, before so many people. Something could happen to him."

Alas, that time it was Alexsey Vasilyevich who proved to be the prophet. The camp commander learned immediately what Trifon Nikolayevich had said and demanded his presence late that very night.

After March '53 there was not a single corner in camp where secrets could hide. By early next morning, two convicts were already acting out the conversation that had taken place between the commander and the Moldavian.

The prophet was asked sternly, "Convict Trifon Makushkin, did you talk about events in the Kremlin?"

"I did."

"So! You admit it. And do you know the punishment awaiting you for provocation? More time, plus a permanently locked cell."

"I understand," Trifon Nikolayevich replied, "but there was no provocation."

"What do you mean, no provocation? You said, 'Soon in the Kremlin.' That is what you said, wasn't it?"

"I don't deny it. I do not deny it at all; I confess it completely. And everything will be as I said. You have only to wait a little while. Then, if nothing happens, I have no excuse. If nothing happens, give me a longer term and a locked cell."

Cunning. Clever. So that had been the decision, and the prophet had been granted a brief postponement. From that moment on, the conversation between Trifon and our top commander became the main topic in camp. Everyone talked about it. The prophet's people were noticeably worried; some were even depressed. What if Trifon had not been mistaken but had simply erred in his calculations and come up with the wrong date? With commanders you can't make mistakes! This one would wait only a short while and then the poor man would be punished.

The whole camp was on edge, awaiting the final outcome. Some were curious, others just laughed, the rest were nervous and afraid—but we all knew the prophet's time was short.

In this way, eleven days went by. Then, on the twelfth day, the radio blared and when we heard the event already known to everyone in Moscow. Beria had been arrested and was now in prison.

The elated northerners reveled in their victory. To each comrade they called, "Didn't we tell you? Didn't we tell you Trifon Nikolayevich should never be doubted?"

And what about the prophet himself, about Trifon Nikolayevich? As usual, as he had been before the announcement from Moscow, he was quiet and shy, walking with eyes lowered. But now, even to the chronic disbelievers, his demeanor seemed different. Now his shyness and simplicity seemed significant, full of mystery. And the guards, whenever we pelted them with the inevitable question—How soon will the politicals be released?—invariably replied, "Why ask us? You have your own expert. Ask him!"

Understandably, our camp commander no longer plagued the politically suspect prophet. In fact, as the sharp-tongued Aleksey Vasilyevich assured us, from time to time he began not to summon but to "invite" Trifon Nikolayevich to visit. Not to interrogate him, of course, and not to threaten him with a locked cell. Not at all. Each time the stern commander would ply the prophet with the same question: "I beg of you, don't be afraid. I ask you only as a private person. What does the future hold? How will all this turn out? Beria has been arrested and will, of course, be liquidated. But what then? What is the future?"

To all that, or so Aleksey Vasilyevich assured us, the prophet would lower his eyes and, as ever, tug at his wheat-colored mustache. Then he would answer in the same shy way.

"I do not know. What has not been revealed to me, I do not know."

In the Late Hour

HE HAD ARRIVED in the morning but took the place next to Voronov just a short time before lights out. Setting an overstuffed bag where a pillow should have been, he placed his jacket on the floor and, grunting as he lowered his long body, asked, "I'm not bothering you, am I?"

Voronov looked at him and thought, I don't understand. Why do so many of them have beards? And this one isn't even old. (Voronov was fifty-five. People near his own age he never considered old.) The newcomer's face was overgrown with thickly matted hair—curly, wiry, and red. In the dim light of the transfer prison, one could barely make out his snub nose and shifting eyes.

After lights out, the stranger stretched on his back and avidly inhaled a cigarette. Only when the room had quieted did he turn toward Voronov. "You, too, cannot sleep?"

Voronov had no desire to speak to the red giant. "As you can see."

"I heard you addressed as Mikhail Pavlovich. Are you originally from Zanivye?"

Voronov sat up. Taking out cigarettes, as if to smoke, he struck a match so he could better inspect his neighbor. The red giant understood and smiled.

"You won't recognize me and, if you do, you won't want to speak to me."

Now Voronov was curious. "Do you intend to speak in riddles very long?"

"Not at all. Just one question interests me, and I want you to answer it honestly. How, I wonder, would you welcome a soldier with whom you fought in Zanivye in January 1918, thirty-two years ago. It is not possible you would forget."

"Wait! Wait! You are talking about—what was his name—Grishka Dolgoruky?"

"Dolgoruky was a nickname given him by his grandfather. His real name was Konbasyev, Grigory Maximovich Konbasyev. But you didn't answer me. How would you welcome that Dolgoruky?"

"In other words, you," murmured Voronov. "Here. Throw away that cheap cigarette and take a good one. So. How would I welcome him? First of all," he held out his hand, "I would say good evening, and then I would say I am glad to see you."

Suddenly, he was eager to learn if the house in Zanivye still stood and how his village looked. Had the church near the cemetery survived? But Voronov had no time to ask anything.

"It's hard to believe," said the red giant softly, as if speaking to himself. "It's the same with me. I am actually glad to see you, too. And, comrade Voronov, I considered you my archenemy. For years, to tell the truth, I could not forgive myself for letting you go and not killing you. I was so ready to take your life that my hand would not even have trembled."

"Thank you for your honesty," said Voronov grimly.

"Yet this morning," Konbasyev continued, "the moment I heard your name, it was as if I were drawn to you by magnets. I ached to speak to you, but there was no hatred—quite the opposite—only joy, as you said, and gladness. I cautioned myself, though: Take it easy. There are a lot of Voronovs in this world. Then I heard someone address you by your patronymic. The probability that it was you had now increased and, oh, how I longed not to be mistaken! It was unwise to inquire in front of the others, so I decided to rest near you, and ask when it was dark. But what then? What if you didn't want to speak to me and sent me away?"

"Honesty deserves honesty," said Voronov. "It was because of you that I fled from Zanivye forever. And it was because of you I determined to join Denikin's army and fight the Reds, so I sneaked away to the south. There, as an officer of the White Guard, I fantasized about meeting you on the field of battle, comrade Dolgoruky—excuse me, Konbasyev. I was convinced that, since you were in the Red Army, it was inevitable we would meet. I will meet him, I thought, and with exquisite pleasure I will put a bullet through his brain. It was naive and ridiculous, but there is nothing to hide. What was, was. Didn't someone write a story like that?—about a White brother who meets his Red brother and shoots him?"

They both laughed sadly. Then, as usually happens after a long separation, each tried to find the answer to as many questions as he could. Finally, taking advantage of a pause, Voronov asked what he had wanted to ask but couldn't bring himself to ask before. "How is my house, in Zanivye? And what did they do to my village, did they turn it into a *kolkhoz?* The church, of course, was probably ruined."

Each question he asked, however, was met with Konbasyev asking one of his own. "I don't understand. Why did you return to your estate that time? And, most important, wearing a uniform with your insignia as an officer of the Tsar?"

"If you remember, it was you who tore off my insignia. In retrospect, I should thank you. At least you didn't nail them to my body, as happened to others."

He continued ruefully.

"Why did I return to my estate? What a rich name for such a poor place! Only 150 acres on rather mediocre land, with a dilapidated cottage that only had five rooms. Until last year I lived abroad and, you have to believe me, in France and even in what used to be Latvia, the average farmer lived in a better home and had more money."

"Now I don't doubt you at all," Konbasyev assured him, "but to Grishka Dolgoruky your dilapidated place seemed like a palace. When you arrived as the landowner-heir to the late mistress, I saw you only as a gold-decorated bastard who symbolized the worst kind of counterrevolutionary. Forgive me, but I thought of you as a man-eating shark and every blasphemy I could think of."

"Why did I return to Zanivye?" mused Voronov, hardly hearing him. "Ah, my dear comrade, who can say why we do or don't do certain things? At one time, fighting the kaiser during the war, I was so weary I thought I would lose my mind. My nerves were shattered, and I could no longer deal with either the world or the hatred I met every day from my own troops. I kept asking myself: Why on earth do you need this officer business? Why do you need that St. George on your chest and those gold stripes on your shoulders? You need them as much as you need the snow from last winter. That's when I should have ended the whole thing, thrown away my uniform and ridden the roof of a cargo train to St. Petersburg, where I could have graduated in history and linguistics. But that's where my memories trapped me. That's the way it is with memories, you see—they trap you when the soul is most disturbed and desperately needs rest. So instead I returned to Zanivye." Suddenly shaking his head from side to side as his face distorted with pain, he cried angrily, "Memories, memories! They lie to you, damn them, and ruin everything! The moment I thought of home, my eyes misted over and my throat choked up. That entrance, upholstered in ripped oil cloth, seemed to me the gates of paradise. The blue room with the peeling wallpaper that permeated the air with mustiness—I remembered it as precious, the only place in the world. And how did I picture the cherry orchard—actually only a dozen old rheumatic trees—and the wheat fields that grew to the porch? As pearls. To be honest, it's difficult even now to speak of them. But you haven't yet answered me. What about this palace with its torn oil cloth, is it still standing? Or, with the help of God, has it finally fallen down?"

"I don't know. I cannot lie to you. I myself have not been to Zanivye since 1921," Konbasyev replied.

"But what happened? If I remember correctly, you were chairman of the soviet council there."

"I was. That is true," answered Konbasyev. "But then I decided to grow—and I grew and grew and grew, and by 1931 I had already graduated from Lomonosov University and become an engineer."

"I am amazed!" said Voronov in admiration.

"It's nothing so surprising," Konbasyev continued. "When I was in Workers' College, I remember, I wrote a composition on 'Anna Karenina, as a Product of a Rotting Nobility.' Other students wrote other compositions, and all of them were about 'products,' too—Onegin as a product of something, Bazarov as a product of something. It was a veritable food store of compositions. But the truth is, I was a 'product' myself—a product of the Revolution—and I tell you this in all seriousness. In his youth, the sainted Lomonosov first arrived in Moscow with his fellow fishermen. In the same way, in the first year of the Revolution, hundreds and thousands of other future scientists—soldiers, workers, peasants, all the formerly downtrodden—they all dragged to the big city 'to gnaw or nibble on the hard rock of science,' as people used to say at the time. On all the entrance papers that year, applicants used to write, 'I was a herdsman,' or, at least, 'my father was a herdsman.' Nowadays, such biographies are no longer an advantage and students have stopped writing them. But I, you must not forget, had truly been a herdsman. And, although I didn't tend the cows of the Voronovs—because your mother had only five or six—I did take care of all the other cows in the village."

Regretfully, he looked at the end of his cigarette and took one last puff. "He will smoke himself into oblivion," Voronov observed and offered him another. Aloud he said, "I'm afraid that's something I never accomplished—I mean, finishing college. But tell me more. For what sins have you been sentenced?"

"It's a long story," the red giant sighed. "For several years I worked in a plant in Moscow and I delivered one-hundred percent, as a dedicated Bolshevik should. Don't doubt that for a moment, comrade Voronov, it's absolutely true. I submerged myself in the party without a moment's hesitation, without the slightest deviation, zero. I'll give you an example. Somewhere around 1926 my nephew

Vanya Maltsev, a boy of no more than twelve, came to visit me from Zanivye. He had decided to follow in his uncle's footsteps and study. So, as it should be, I took him in. I shared my room, I fed him, I helped him find work, I arranged for him to study, and I educated him. The boy wasn't bad—quite the opposite—he tried to work and to study at the same time. Then, at the right age, he joined Komsomol, the Young Communist League. In 1932, when he was eighteen, they were trying to mobilize young communists to build the city of Magnitogorsk in Siberia. So, since it was my duty as a party member, I tried to educate him to his responsibilities. After I went into the whys and wherefores, we both agreed he had to volunteer. Of course, it was clear that similar political sessions were taking place at the factory where he worked and in the school he attended; I just added an extra push. So among several thousand other young people, he left for Magnitogorsk, sent off gloriously with music and speeches. Six months passed and suddenly Vanya returned. I remember it as if it were today, how we embraced and kissed each other. 'What brought you here? Have you come on a business trip?' The answer proved to be no. My Vanya had run away. 'It was unbearable,' he wept. 'There was nothing to eat and I almost starved. And we lived in an unheated tent all the terrible winter. I caught pneumonia.' I took him by the collar and threw him out without a word. To be more exact, there were words as he tried to escape from me. I thundered, 'Lout! Bumpkin!' Then I threw him to the floor and began to stamp on him. Honestly, just stamp! Fortunately, I lived in a communal flat. Twenty residents ran to us and tried to grab Vanya away from me; otherwise I might have killed him. And you know, I really loved that boy. I would have given him my last piece of bread. But in this situation, I neither knew nor wanted to know mercy. It could not be! My nephew—a member of Komsomol—a deserter? It was unthinkable! That was the only way I could see the situation at that time."

"You threw him out?" asked Voronov softly.

"Not only did I throw him out but, with the help of Komsomol—this time without music and speeches—I forced him to go back and die. And you ask what sins I was sent here for? No, when it came to my beloved party, I never sinned once."

"But since then?"

"Since, indeed," he went on. "Since I've begun, and since I've already smoked most of your cigarettes without a single pang of conscience, I will tell you my story to the end. In 1935 I was sent to Germany as a trade representative to purchase electric locomotives. I had a family by that time, a wife and two children. Together we spent a year and a half in that nest of fascists. And again, never doubt it, I worked night and day, not out of fear but out of party loyalty. And my devotion to the party grew even stronger!"

Konbasyev stopped speaking for several minutes, and both men were silent. "No," he began again, "you can never understand how it was. There is no way you can understand. When did you say you returned to the Soviet Union? In '49? No, it is impossible for you to understand. Three months before they arrested me, the party organization in the plant expelled me. Why? I thought, later, that I had lived abroad, and so they no longer trusted me, but it doesn't matter—it absolutely doesn't matter. In all honesty it was for nothing. And it was for nothing, afterwards, that they put me in jail. They started by accusing me of having purchased the wrong locomotives. Then they said I had disgraced myself as a trade representative and, like Judas, I had befriended people who later proved to be our enemies. They finished up, in the GPU, by accusing me of espionage and being a traitor. But I am running ahead of myself. For three months, they let me keep my job and my apartment. They also let me remain with my family and paid my salary, but those three months during which I was expelled from my beloved party were the worst I will ever know. Here I am only telling you about it—merely recalling the details—and my heart is pounding and my hands are shaking. Three months. A sick, insane three months. With the way it affected my mind, at the time, I would have preferred that they cut off my arms and my legs—I would have suffered less. It was as if they had stripped my body of its skin. One cannot compare any torture to that which I experienced. Since then, twelve years have passed, but I will never forget the pain. None of the tortures that came later erased it. I suffered at the plant—it seemed that everybody stared at me, accused me, hated and despised me. I suffered on my way home from the plant. I remember

I wouldn't even walk on the sidewalk, I would walk in the middle of the road, so as not to meet anyone! Even on the tram, I would stand by myself on the back platform. And I suffered at home, because it was there I gave way to my despair. But in what a way! Basically, you see, I am a simple peasant from Zanivye, so I began to drink and to beat and torture my wife and kids. The kids are screaming, the wife is sobbing, the neighbors are trying to separate us—the house was an asylum! When they finally came and took me away, I actually felt at peace. Can you believe it? It seems it is much more painful to beat oneself than to be beaten by others. In fact, others can beat you and sometimes it does you good—they knock the nonsense out of you."

He laughed and took another cigarette from Voronov. But now he was calm and his hands no longer trembled. Even his voice was steady. "No, you will never understand it—nor will you understand why it took me so long to change my political views, as it did all those other 'products' of the October Revolution. People who are younger—who joined the party, for instance, during the war or after—the moment they were arrested, they changed like lightning. But for us the conversion was agony, yet when it came it was complete. I recall how just last year, after serving ten years in prison and one year in exile, I was taken again. I was in prison with a former Red commander—a commander of a mobile unit—a commandeer who had been at the front lines. There was another prisoner, a former White activist. He had been captured in Czechoslovakia, given to us, and sentenced to twenty-five. The former front-liner fell on him. 'You,' he raged, 'you're a spineless good-for-nothing!' he cried, 'and all your White activity was good for nothing. You just slept, while you were abroad, and did nothing but talk. It was necessary to *do* something, but all you did was talk!' The former White activist was confused. 'Wait a minute,' he interrupted, 'Do I understand you correctly? You are not blaming me because I fought against you, you are blaming me for not winning?' And the former front-liner replied with fury, 'Correct! You understand me correctly!'"

Forgetting where they were, the two laughed uproariously. Several prisoners lifted their heads and peered at them with surprise.

"A spineless good-for-nothing," repeated Voronov, after the others had settled down and gone back to sleep. "The judgment was an angry but a good one. It was enough simply to proclaim, 'The motherland is waiting for you, forget the past, it no longer exists,' and thousands of White activists—maybe not real activists, but common ordinary emigrés who had already spent thirty years abroad were pulled home."

"And you among them, Mikhail Pavlovich?"

"And I among them, comrade Konbasyev. I won't boast, because I was certainly not wealthy, but I did well enough. I drove a taxi in splendid Paris, and I owned my own cab. I fed my wife and son. Why, I ask you, did I return? To lose my family, to lose twenty-five years, to be sent to unknown camps in Siberia? One cannot explain. And even if one tried to explain, you are right—it would be impossible to make any sense out of all those tangled, mixed-up emotions. But yet I can understand why you were distraught after being betrayed by your comrades and what destroyed your convictions so completely."

"Then please explain something else to me," Konbasyev asked. "From where did it come, and to where did it disappear, this fury that overwhelmed us—this feral hatred toward you and toward people like you—hatred that consumed not only me, but hundreds and thousands of people like me—and you as well? From where did it come and to where did it vanish, that flaming rhetoric, all those words and the dogma drummed into our heads? You, for instance, you laughed just now about the Red brother who met the White brother and killed him. But it happened, it happened. And how did all those passions simply evaporate? An old man, a Baptist I met in camp, once told me a parable. There were, once upon a time, three brothers. One became a White, and the Revolution killed him. The second brother stood apart and took no side, and the Revolution killed him. The third one plunged completely into the Revolution—and it killed him."

"A bitter message," said Voronov. "But now, my dear countryman, you sing from another aria and croon a different tune. It is interesting, true, but it is still different, and it is late. It is time to sleep. Tomorrow, perhaps, we will be transported to another prison."

"True, comrade Voronov, the hour is late—but our conversation has comforted me. And who knows? Perhaps we will even land in the same place."

"Perhaps, perhaps. It is possible. That would be good."

"Then, my friend, let us continue to hope."

In June of '53

OVERSEER MATUSOV WADDLED his way to the invalid barrack. A good-natured veteran, he was overweight and red-faced, with fat feminine cheeks. The wooden walkway outside the guard's building had washed away in high-water season, but Stalin had died that March and the spring had been busy. It was remembered only in June. Now they had to find a convict who would work a few hours with a shovel and axe.

As spring and summer surfaced, peasants in the invalid barrack would pine for planting, pulled by the lure of the soil. As soon as Matusov began to speak, those who longed for labor leaped at the opportunity.

One of them was Nefedov. Calling out, as he climbed down from his upper berth, he urged, "Let's go! Let's go!" Adroitly airing his foot bindings, he began to wrap them around his feet. "For such a business it's not a sin to work," he apologized to his comrades. Continuing, as he laced up his boots, he said, "Long ago this platform should have been repaired." His implied criticism would have been unheard of before the scent of impending freedom permeated the air.

Now Nefedov worked—slowly, as if feasting his senses and savoring every moment. Each stroke of his axe was sustained with a vocal beat. "Hock!" then hit. "Hock!" then hit. Spitting on his palms, he lifted the shovel with relish, cocked his head to one side and squinted to take better aim. With each squint, he would look at the hot sun and smile. At what? The beneficial day? The satisfying work? Or his own thoughts?

Near him was the portly, perspiring Matusov—who shifted from one foot to the other, pretending to be busy. He had already encircled Nefedov several times. Several times he had loudly and musically yawned. Twice he had adjusted his boots and his service cap. Then, spreading his legs apart, he straightened his boot tops—bending so low to tie them that he could see, through the triangle where his trousers met, a clear vista: a sliver of blue from the sky and green from a small tree. Pulling himself up, he plopped wearily on the porch of the overseer's office and, from a small tin that had once held American sausage, removed some tobacco and began to roll a cigarette.

"Smoke if you want," he called to Nefedov.

The convict nodded. With one easy toss, he parked his axe in a utility pole supporting the transmission wire buzzing overhead. Swinging his shovel as if it were a cane, he strolled toward the guard. Then, at the same lazy pace with which he worked, he took out his cheap tobacco, shaped a cigarette carefully, wet the end in his mouth, spat out a few loose crumbs, and sat on the lowest step. Finally, he stretched his legs and lit up—drinking in the dense, foul-smelling smoke with deep appetite.

"Now," he pronounced, "this is good—especially for a person with troubles, like you."

"What are you talking about?" demanded the overseer.

"About this tobacco," Nefedov hastened to explain. Peering at his cigarette, he inhaled again. "About this poor tobacco. One puff, breathe deeply, and the soul no longer suffers."

Matusov removed his military cap, wiped his brow, and agreed. "Exactly," he said.

Then, unaccountably, Nefedov chose to deny his own words. "Wait a minute. What do you mean 'exactly?' Maybe the head will become easier and begin to swim. But the soul will continue to suffer, to be sick. And, by your appearance, I can see how worried you are and that there is no way out for you."

Several moments passed before Matusov, moving his lips as if he were mouthing the convict's words mentally, felt compelled to ask, "Why should I be worried?"

Craning his neck, Nefedov stared at Matusov with surprise. Taking two fingers, he snuffed the end of his cigarette and tucked it behind one ear. "That's a strange thing to ask. Who else should be worried, if not you?"

Again, there was a long silence. Again—because who knows who knows what in camp—the overseer asked, "Why should I worry?"

The convict grinned. "Oh, you're just pretending not to be upset," he said firmly, "just pretending. How many barracks are empty already?"

"Seven," Matusov answered immediately. "Last week we nailed up the seventh."

"Aha!" said Nefedov. "And why are they nailed up?"

Now it was the guard's turn to grin. He loved conversation, loved both to pontificate and to listen—but the question was so silly he spoke as if to an idiot, "They read the newspaper to you, the radio in the barrack blares the whole day, and—during cultural sessions—they explain everything by writing on the blackboard and holding up cards, and still you ask, 'Why? Why?' For the last time, if you were a thief or a swindler or made off with less than fifty thousand rubles, you got amnesty. That was the order, straight from Moscow. You yourself know that in May all their papers were prepared. They got their money, their daily ration—and it was go as you please, go without guards right to the station, get tickets, and go wherever you want. Count them yourself, how many left. So? If people are pardoned and the barracks are empty, the buildings are boarded up."

"Precisely," agreed the convict, suppressing his hope before it suffused his face. "And what will happen next? What will happen to the politicals?"

Over and over, during the past few weeks, Matusov had heard this same question. Everyone was asked—the camp commander, the assistant commander, the commander of reeducation in the cultural division, and every guard. The directive had not yet been received, so one could only surmise—even the officers were at a loss. For instance, the reeducation commander had stated that for 58s there would be no relief. As they were sitting, so they would remain sitting, from arrest to release. No one had been surprised by the usual answer, then something happened and—for the past ten days—the prisoners could talk of nothing else. It seemed the camp commander had received a message from Moscow, after which he called in reeducation and castigated them for a good hour. It turned out the reeducation commander had no right to say what he had said; there had even been the rumor he would be fired. So? Go figure!

For Matusov, it was safe to answer only that which was allowed. "It's no concern of mine," he stated positively. "As Moscow orders, so it will be done!"

"Yes, yes," agreed Nefedov. "That's the official line, of course. But everyone knows the decision has already been made. Soon every barrack will be boarded up, and the whole camp will be shut down."

"So? Let it be," the overseer answered automatically. "What's that got to with me?"

Nefedov replied in a soft singsong, as if he were speaking to a child. "You-ou-ou?" He stared at Matusov through eyes that had now become slits. One would have thought, except it was unthinkable, that he was being insolent. "If you want to know, you are the main person it has to do with. The barracks will be boarded up, the camp will be closed, and—if he's lucky—maybe one guard will be allowed to remain. But even one guard is too many—who needs empty barracks in the taiga? What need is there to guard them? And you, it's sad to ask, what will happen to you? For you, it's the comma and the period!"

Matusov stirred in irritation. Again this stupid nonsense. His son-in-law, that empty-headed skirt chaser, he and the other young guards talked like that. The camp would be closed, and all the officers and overseers would be out of work. It was irritating nonsense. After all, Matusov wasn't green; this wasn't his first year serving in a camp. No one was ever discharged! Well, sometimes, because of old age.

Move you, yes, they could move you—Matusov had been moved three times from camp to camp—but that was it!

It was in this way that Matusov meant to answer Nefedov, but now it seemed that Nefedov had not quite finished.

"What will you do?" he inquired solicitously. "What, so to say, *can* you do?"

In the convict's questions, and in the odd way he asked them, Matusov sensed an undercurrent. Was it insult? Abruptly, he changed his mind and said something completely different from what he had planned. "I, of course, can go wherever I want, and good manpower is needed everywhere—in Kansk, Achinsk, Minusinsk, and even Krasnoyarsk. I was told that the climate is very good in Minusinsk."

The convict seemed to challenge him. "Good manpower? Forgive me, but what kind of manpower are you? You count the convicts and scratch the number on some wood to show that everyone is there. Is that good manpower? In Krasnoyarsk, in Kansk, in a plant, for instance, it's necessary to work hard. You can't just walk around with a wooden tablet in your hand. And again, forgive me, but it may be impossible for you and your brother guards to work hard—perhaps you've forgotten or never knew how in the first place. You, for instance. Judge yourself. You are sitting on a bench doing nothing and yet you perspire . . ." He didn't finish his sentence.

Matusov was annoyed. Too many questions! Too many words! And then he blinked at what he was seeing. The convict had actually made himself comfortable, had even put his leg on the bench and was resting in a relaxed position. Nefedov remained silent but Matusov knew it would not be for long. It was necessary to take charge, to assert his position—so in the same challenging way that Nefedov had spoken to him, he answered, "I, of course, will not go to any of those places. I will go to a *kolkhoz*."

"To a *kolkho-o-oz?*" the convict sang. "Don't even think of it! At a *kolkhoz* they don't keep you for only a 'thank you.' They have enough parasites as it is. Besides, keep in mind—on a *kolkhoz* there is no salary, no free food or uniform, no boots, and no generous rations. Just work. Hard work, and that's it. And with the way you're used to working, you may not earn even a pound of grain a day. Take my word for it, just put that one out of your mind." Rising, he returned to his work. "No," he repeated, spitting on his palm to start, "you're in a bad position, no matter which way you look at it." Nefedov smiled. "The worst." Then, energetically, as if there were no longer anything to discuss, he resumed his digging.

Matusov looked at the skinny bones pushing out of the convict's shirt and anger swept over him. He wanted to curse Nefedov, to say something usual like, "What? You don't like Soviet authority?" and subject him to punishment. But the words were inappropriate—and suddenly it struck him that maybe now was not the time to be saying such things. Meanwhile, it was necessary to respond. Still in a high temper, he snapped, "Why did you come here? To agitate? I don't need your agitation. You came to work. So work!"

Slyly, Nefedov remained silent, but his victory made him glow. With a smile in every wrinkle on his face, he swayed to the sound of his joyous thoughts, lifted his arms, and aimed his axe. Several times he called "Hock! Hock!" and it seemed as though those words, too, were filled with sarcasm.

Matusov sat on the porch. The sun crept closer and scorched him with its midday power but he didn't notice. He was thoughtful.

The Murderers

1

THE PRISON CARS—the infamous Stolypin trucks—were six or seven hundred kilometers from Moscow when the train halted momentarily, and two new prisoners were thrust into the jail compartment. To judge from their appearance, they had been detained only recently but, despite that, they radiated an air of unconcern. Healthy, tanned, and round-faced, the pair looked almost like brothers. Adapting immediately to our cramped quarters, they clambered high into the third tier of berths and, from their perch above, began to speak to me.

"Have you been in the lockup long, father?" asked one of them.

When I replied, giving them details not only about the length of my term but also about the reason for my presence on the train, they nodded their heads approvingly—liking the fact that an experienced convict was with them. Even more, they liked the fact that, beginning with the fall of '53, I had begun a rigorous campaign to get my sentence reviewed—that, over the months, I had virtually bombarded headquarters with dozens of complaints to bring my case to their attention. The result? The original decision sentencing me to ten years had now been revoked, and the case was currently up for reconsideration. That was the reason they were transporting me to Moscow.

"Who scrawled the complaints? You yourself?"

"Are you up on the laws?"

I told them, yes, that I had written all the complaints myself and, yes, I knew something about the law. Lying prone on their bunks, with heads hanging over the side, they stared at me long and attentively, hardly blinking. And, although they had full faces that seemed as genial and well-fed as teenagers, their eyes were black as coal. I realized that even if they looked young, they must have been in their mid-twenties.

"Hey, father, is it true a law can't be retroactive?"

I had no sooner nodded my head in acquiescence than both of them leaped to the floor with such joyful shouts that the convoy guard came to the cell immediately. Looking through the small barred opening, he stared at us for a good minute.

I, too, stared at the young men. Their vocabulary was so limited, so riddled with inaccuracies, that I was amazed at their sophisticated reference to laws that were not "retroactive."

Suddenly, I was eager to learn more about them.

"Yes," I spoke further. "In principle, a law cannot be retroactive. But the court always takes extenuating circumstances into consideration."

"Extending? What extending? Where do you get extending? If it's not retroactive, it's not. Period!"

Their attitude toward me had changed instantly. Now it was disapproving, almost threatening—as if, in the course of making the law clear, I had maliciously placed obstacles in their path—obstacles they were not yet sure they could overcome. Quietly and in detail, but in a way that might make them more comfortable concerning my advice, I tried to explain the meaning of "extenuating circumstances."

My plan was successful. Soon, stumbling over each other's words in their haste to make sure I knew every detail, they began to tell me what happened.

"You'll see for yourself. There are no circumstances here at all."

Just eight days ago, they had been free as free. There was another pal, too—Petya—"a great guy!" Together, the three of them had been living like a king on his birthday. One day they went for a spin and, in Saratov, saw a ship and decided to go aboard. They bought the cheapest seats, then sneaked into third class and began to play "twenty-one" with, to tell the truth, an absolute idiot. Nobody asked him, he pushed his way in. At first, the friends were slightly in the hole but, with luck, they soon began to win a lot and were really taking the idiot for a ride. So they threw in their cards, treated the idiot to a little beer, and left for the buffet in the bar upstairs, where they each bought a tumbler full of vodka. But the appetizers were rotten, just dry old sandwiches.

"So old, the sausage had turned blue!"

"They were standing at the bar, laughing and trying to decide whether to have more vodka or quit, when suddenly a man came in from third-class. He said the idiot who lost was crying and complaining that the swindlers—meaning us—had stolen his watch and that his wallet had disappeared, too, and they—meaning us—were crooks and professional card sharps. As soon as we docked, this idiot threatens, he's getting the water militia to arrest us. Meanwhile, he was going to come up to the buffet and demand his stuff back."

"Now that was an insult," said one.

"Yeah. We got insulted," said the other, "so we decided all right, if that's how he wants to play."

"On the way back down, I lifted a fire-axe off the wall, just in case. My friend here had nothing to defend himself with, so he picked up a small trashcan—which was okay because it was made of metal. Only poor Petya had nothing. So here we are, walking toward the idiot, who is still moaning and whining and kicking his feet around.

"'You!' he cries, 'Swindlers!' he cries, and tosses a mug of beer into Petya's face."

"That was the final straw, we'd had it! So right then, Petya grabs him around the chest. Why? Because, if he'd shut up, we might have let him alone. But he keeps yelling and accusing us, and now we hear the ship is docking and the idiot actually tries to break away and get to the water militia. Well, by this time there was a crowd around us. True, they weren't making trouble, but I had a feeling we were headed for disaster so—very lightly—I bopped him with the fire-axe and my friend here—to make sure he gets the message—gives him a slight tap with the trashcan. And what does the idiot do? He falls down and begins to bleed all over the bench. Thank God Petya gives us a signal.

"'Beat it!' he yells and starts to run, with us following right on his heels."

"Well, most people don't get involved, but the dummies blocking the exit didn't know anything yet, so they didn't budge— just herded together like sheep. Finally, we're able to push through and we take off—us in one direction and Petya in the other. Then we look back and see we're being followed—by the cops and a bunch of bastards from the freedom or maybe the ship—a big storm cloud of them against only two guys. Of course, they got us, just cut us off, the sons of bitches. Petya managed to disappear. They told us he got away. What else they told us was that the idiot had croaked, right in third class where he was sitting. The cops searched us, of course, but for what? All we had on us were a few pennies of our own!"

The excitement of reliving the experience stimulated them, and the prisoners recited their story with relish. Afterwards, they stared at me with their cold eyes and waited for my response.

"This is a serious matter," I said. "There is a new law now, perhaps you know—I heard about it just recently in Sverdlovsk, in transfer prison. With the new law, there's no appeal. If you're guilty of murder, you're shot."

My companions grinned.

"But we knocked off the idiot two days before the law. We learned about the new law, too, when we were booked. We asked when it was going into effect, and they told us—but our little matter took place two days before the law went through. And you said yourself, the law isn't retroactive. So that's the circumstances. Is that enough for you, father?" they challenged. "Satisfied?"

They were obviously not interested in hearing further from me, and we were silent for a long time. Then one of them said, "It'd be too bad if they grabbed Petya."

"You'd be sorry for him?" I asked.

"Oh, naturally, but Petya's too smart—they'd never find the stuff on him, not a single watch or wallet."

Then I said, "What if they do grab him, and he talks?"

One of the killers said, "Why should he talk? There's nothing in it for him. There's not one violation stamped on our papers, they're absolutely clean. If Petya talks, they'll just begin to poke and pull and it'll finally come out that all three of us were released during the amnesty after Stalin died."

"Don't worry," I assured them, "they'll find that out without Petya."

"You think so?"

"I'm sure."

They were distressed only briefly. Then, deciding I was mistaken, they smiled confidently and said, "You can't tell a thing from our passports, they're clear as glass. So why would they inquire?"

At that, with the same monkey-like agility with which they rolled down, the pair climbed back up to the third tier. There they tossed and turned from side to side and from back to belly, chewing automatically on their prison ration of bread.

2

Somewhere near ten in the evening (we were supposed to arrive in Moscow by dawn the next day), a shriveled old man with metal eyeglasses was squeezed into our compartment. Thin, short, and dressed in cheap clothing, he was wearing boots so old the leather had turned green. Cylindrical lenses magnified his eyes. Taking a few short steps inside, he turned after the door clanged shut and pressed his face to the bars as if he were stuck to them. In one hand, he carried all his belongings wrapped in a large square handkerchief.

"One can see nothing," he said, in a flat voice. "One can see nothing, one cannot see the platform from here."

Above, the light bulb was burning—it too was confined behind iron bars, just like our compartment and the entire car. The little old man took off his spectacles, turned a bit, put his bag on the bench, and began to wipe his glasses with the hem of his jacket. It was then I noticed his face was so drenched with tears that even his white mustache was wet.

"What did you want to see, my friend?"

"The daughter and son-in-law are on the platform." His voice trembled and, controlling it only with difficulty, he added, "I wanted to see them, for the last time."

"Why the last?" I asked compassionately. "God permit, you will return."

Wringing his hands, he sank down on the bench.

"The son-in-law said, 'I will ask the commander for a vacation. I will come to Moscow myself and find you a lawyer. I promise,' he said."

"There. You see?"

The old man wrung his hands again and, making a small fist, began to rub the tears from his eyes awkwardly, like a small child.

"Of what use to me is a lawyer? It is only a waste of money. It was I who killed the boy."

From above there came a whistle of approval. "Now that's a grandpa for you!"

The old man didn't answer. Craning his neck, he looked up—only then noticing the young prisoners.

For several seconds, no one said a word. Suddenly, as silently as it had stopped, the train started up again—we heard neither ring nor locomotive whistle. The old man jumped to his feet in agitation. Shifting from foot to foot, he began pacing up and down in the cramped compartment. Several times he sobbed uncontrollably. Annoyed with his lack of control, he shook his head from side to side.

"I am not sorry for myself. I have lived long enough," he said a bit later. "I am sorry for the boy, he was only fourteen. So life-like he lay there—as if, at any moment, he would jump up and run—except that he was white. All white!"

"Why did you kill the kid?" the top ones asked.

Exhausted, breathing heavily, the old man sat down. Stricken with grief and remorse, he was ready to talk about his tragedy to anyone—to the top two, even to the convoy guard who paused outside the bars and listened attentively.

"I alone am guilty. There is no one else to blame," the old man began. "I live with the daughter and son-in-law. They respect me, they are very good to me, so what else do I need? But no. One day, people from the local cooperative come to our place. They are looking to hire a guard for the summer. They have an orchard nearby, and need someone to stop the neighborhood boys from climbing the trees and stealing the apples. My pension is small, and I am ashamed I must eat off the daughter and son-in-law. Besides, the guard salary is a good one, four hundred rubles a month. I am thinking, eight hundred rubles! I would be able to give the daughter and son-in-law eight hundred rubles! Let them throw it away on themselves and enjoy it. So I go, and I get the job."

He became silent, as if absorbing his own words. Then, with shaking hands, he began to slap each pocket of his shabby jacket—finally finding a box of cheap cigarettes and some matches.

"Have a smoke, citizen," he said, offering me the box.

"Thank you, I do not smoke."

"We do, grandpa. Treat us!" called the top two, and hung down their hands.

"From that moment on, the misfortune begins," the old man continued after inhaling deeply several times. The smoke from his cigarette rose to the ceiling where, drifting through their hair, it almost created a halo around the heads of the two young killers.

"I am given a shotgun and some dummy pellets—a few live ones, but all the rest are filled with salt—to frighten the children away. During the day, I sleep in a tent, sleep as much as I want. At night, I just walk up and down. Once in a while I fire off a shot, only to let the mischief-makers know I am around; so let them beware. Every day, the daughter comes and brings me a hot meal. Every day, as if she senses something, she tries to convince me, 'Papa, quit this business. What if you get sciatica, sleeping in a drafty tent?' 'What sciatica?' I ask her. 'All this fresh air does me good!' and I laugh."

"That might have been your last laugh, grandpa" came from aloft, the two enjoying their own joke.

The old man sobbed, as if he hadn't heard, and smoked with trembling hands.

"My health, of that she was afraid," he went on. "But it wasn't my health that was the problem. In two weeks the apples begin to ripen, and not a night passes but the children sneak in. And I, of course, fire a few shots every once in a while because they are afraid of the gun. But my eyesight is good for nothing and the day before yesterday—what devil confused me?—I take a wrong pellet. I take a real one! Without even aiming—why would I aim, with my eyesight?—I shoot it off. Suddenly, I hear sobs and screaming. I run up to them. The night is clear, light blue, and the moon is shining. I see a boy, stretched out on the ground. His face is peaceful but pure white. Well, I am thinking, he is pretending. Any minute now he'll jump up and run away. I begin turning him and then I begin to shake him out of fear, but he is cold. And now my poor eyes see clearly—I have hit him directly in the stomach."

"The day before yesterday? That's too bad, grandpa, that's the end of you. Bang, bang!" said one of the uppers. The other, bending way over the berth, caught my eye and said, "Now there you are, father. A real 'circumstances' for you!"

After that, no one said anything. The old man sat folded over—large-eyed, with loose-hanging clothes.

"They pity me," he said suddenly. "The daughter and son-in-law pity me. They come to the train station, bring me some sausage, buy several French rolls and candy and cigarettes." He stopped speaking. Evidently, his history had ended and he had nothing more to say.

Shaking his head in sympathy, the convoy guard moved away from the bars. Immediately, as soon as the guard disappeared, the young prisoners swooped down. In an instant, they grabbed the old man's bundle and shot back up with the same speed at which they had shot down.

"Don't get upset, grandpa," one of them whispered. Leaning his head over the side of the berth, he put his finger to his lips, warning the old man to be quiet. With a full mouth, still chewing, the other added indistinctly, "This is the way it is in prison, we criminals must stick together. We have to share."

Generously, from above, they returned the handkerchief to the doomed man. We watched as it floated down to the floor.

II

In the Freedom

1

JUDGING FROM LETTERS, there was a shortage of food in the freedom. Toward the end of his term, Juravlev began to collect the remains of his bread and bake them into rusks. He also began to cure fish. The morning he devoted to his work as an orderly. In the afternoon, he heated the oven. In the evening, by the time the convicts returned to the barrack, there was not only the smell of baking bread but, hung like garlands over the oven, there were small, chip-like pieces of cod. These, too, had the aroma of "home."

How many days left? It was an unnecessary question, asked every evening by his comrades. Juravlev always answered, "Including to-day?" "No, today we don't count." Everyone had questions, everyone gave advice—those imprisoned for years, those who had just arrived. It was necessary for Juravlev to go to the commander's office and ask directly—would he be allowed to return home, or would he be assigned a new place to live?

"Ask."

"They won't tell you in advance."

"They have their own ways."

The same discussion always arose and, as usual in camp, always moved to a quarrel and grew into abuse. Juravlev would always listen in silence, something dull and indifferent appearing in his transparent eyes—eyes in wide-boned cheeks that became very noticeable after he'd shaved his beard. And when, following a long argument or quarrel, someone finally asked his opinion, he would invariably answer as if speaking about a stranger, "It will be seen."

There was even further furor: would he really be allowed to go free, or would they sew a new case onto his old one—add a longer, additional term? Such things happened all the time! But even to that Juravlev paid little attention. It was as if the closer it came to his release, the more difficult it was for him to function, the more difficult it was to think. He became absentminded in his duties, cleaned the barrack perfunctorily, went less often for water. Sitting near the window, he mended his clothes almost mindlessly—putting one patch on top of another on his jacket or cotton pants, or rechecking the worthless belongings in his trunk.

A week and a half before his release—on a nonworking Sunday—Vassyok, the messenger from the office, ran in. Bent over and quavering, he shouted Juravlev's name and called him to the photographer. Then, smirking slyly, for the hundredth time he began to boast and brag about his career as a thief. As usual, the convicts ignored him. So, it looks like Juravlev will be released in term and without delay! Comrades resting on their backs near the oven or playing dominoes and checkers began to rush their orderly. They called 'go, go without delay!' And Juravlev? He scrubbed interminably at the wash bowl, dressed slowly, dragged a comb over and over through his short hair—then twisted and untwisted his mustache. Indifferent to the advice, ignoring the urgent admonitions, he walked out of the barrack without interest and with a wavering gait. Looking at his back, it was hard to believe he was not yet fifty.

Had he at least slept that night? No one cared and no one knew. On the day of departure, he had risen with everyone else. His duties he had distributed to other prisoners on the previous evening and, in order to avoid unnecessary delay, had removed his blanket, pillowcase, and sheet. Some of his comrades, saying good-bye that morning, nudged him or knocked on his head or just shook hands. They then left for the canteen and from there went to work, felling trees in the forest. The new orderly had already gone to clear the road of snow. Juravlev was left alone in the barrack. He sat on the stripped bunk. To his right was a small green trunk with his lock on it; to his left was a long, narrow bag stuffed with rusks and dried fish. There was nothing to do. After a while he rearranged the slats on the bunk again, opened and closed the trunk again. March was coming to an end. The day was frosty and, with that blinding brightness that happens only in Siberia, a cold sun sparkled through the window. Judging by the hour, the office staff would already be at work. As usual, gray with dust, the omnipresent radio—tuned forever to one station and played from dawn to dusk—was just enough off-frequency that nothing could ever be quite understood.

At about eleven, Vassyok appeared. "Run to the office. Get your release papers," he directed and sat on the neighboring bunk. "Ask for Kherson. What a life there! Tell them that's where your woman lives." Juravlev didn't answer and Vassyok continued. "I forgot. You're an Article 58—you won't be allowed to go to Kherson."

"Before, I got two tickets a year—'go wherever you want,'" Yuravlev said unexpectedly in a low voice.

"Before, before," mimicked Vassyok, "before I had maybe fifteen suits and I sold them all on the Kherson black market. So go! Don't linger!"

But he had to linger. Interminably. In the barrack until the new orderly returned, at the checkpoint where the guard on duty never bothered to open the door. Shifting from one foot to the other, and actually seeing nothing, Juravlev stared at his surroundings. All his term, all ten years without counting the five months he sat in interrogation prison, he had spent in one camp. During all this time, the camp hadn't changed at all. True, the post fence had been replaced with barbed wire, and a few barracks had been built, but mostly it was the same. Behind the high fence the taiga still stretched—during winter, dark green and smothered in snow; in summer, alive with a swarm of sounds and colors. And, beyond, it was still possible to glimpse the thatched roofs of the settlement nearby.

The office was located beyond the work zone. Juravlev passed the vacant brick plant,. then passed the shrieking, yelping, gnashing sewing machines where the criminals now worked. Finally, inhaling nervously, he steadied himself on the slippery steps and climbed up to the porch. Inside, they checked his record quickly and just as quickly gave him his release papers—but in order to collect the proper signatures, Juravlev had to return to both the work and the residential zones—tramping for hours in the half-dark corridors, waiting for each commander to sign his clearance. When he finally reached the checkpoint again, where he could collect his certificate and money for the trip, he reached it just in time to see the sun set over the toothed peaks of the giant cedar trees in the distance. The snow had begun to turn blue.

2

Beyond the gate, beyond the barbed wire fence, everything looked strange. It was as if he were seeing a world unknown to him.

How odd it seemed that having allowed him to pass the checkpoint, no overseer followed him. Even though he had been released, even though he was free of them forever, Juravlev kept checking—frequently looking from side to side. But one thing was clear. During the past ten years the settlement had grown. From every window he passed, he could be watched; from every door a person could appear and demand his papers. In camp, like all the other convicts, Juravlev had no papers, no certificate. Now he kept touching his pocket. Were they lost? No. Were they written as they should be? Were they signed properly? The thought that he was being followed and that every second he could be detained drove him forward even faster—forced him to rush, made him careless.

Near the last house Juravlev stopped, finally realizing it was not possible to travel further, not possible to leave at such a late hour. There were still twenty-five kilometers to the place he had to go to get his passport, twelve to the nearest village, and the road went through the taiga. During the night, in the forest, he could be both robbed and killed. There was no doubt about it, he would have to spend the night in the settlement. Meanwhile, the snow was turning more and more blue. In contrast, the remote houses with their lit-up yellow windows radiated a look that was cheerful and cozy. Somehow it reminded him of the village where long ago, leaving his railway caboose, he had to collect kerosene, salt and matches. And suddenly—as though she were a memory come to life—a girl of about eight, wearing a long coat that looked as if it belonged to someone else, came out of the house swinging a kerosene bottle.

The appearance of a real child seemed miraculous—something beyond possibility. He stared at how she shifted her legs in the shapeless boots and how she swung the bottle around on its rope. Now she'll be frightened and run, he thought with alarm, immediately trying to put a cheerful expression on his face. Slowing her steps, the girl neared him. "Hello, little beauty. Where are you going?" he asked as gently as possible.

She looked at him with surprise. Directing her mittened hand toward the side of the settlement, she answered, "To the small store."

"Will you let me spend the night?" Juravlev blurted out, then immediately regretted having spoken—not in such a way, not so quickly, and especially not with her should he be talking about a night's lodging. "The house is shut with a small lock and you won't be able to find the key," she said simply. "Wait until I come back. I won't be long."

In fact, after a very short time, she did return. Now she held the filled kerosene bottle by the neck, extending the opening away from her face. As if he were an old acquaintance, she beckoned him in.

A good half of the whitewashed room was occupied by a high alcove where a large stove stood. Juravlev noticed only later the small pantry next to it concealed by a cotton curtain. A shade made of colored paper covered the electric bulb hanging over the table—a bulb which, like those at camp, appeared to burn at only half capacity. On the bed there were four pillows—one large, one medium and two small. Over the bed there hung Christmas and New Year's cards, spread in fan-shaped patterns. Directly across the room small pictures, cut from magazines, were displayed. Displayed also was a large piece of paper on which were drawn huge black targets, perfectly punctured by shots that had been fired at them. Wafting through the whole room was the smell of something strong and fragrant—whether it was toilet soap or some special seasoning, Juravlev couldn't tell.

Now, thought Juravlev, was a good time to polish his conversational skills with children. Reaching for his trunk, he drew out a small bag with several fruit drops and two honey cakes. "Here then, bite into these," he said, holding them out.

It almost seemed as if the girl hadn't heard. With the concentration of an adult she removed her coat, hung it on a hook, unwound her headkerchief, and then, peering into the mirror, arranged her hair—not forgetting to comb the bangs. After that, throwing off her boots, she pulled on woolen socks and paced up and down on the painted floor. He was about to repeat his invitation when she came to the table. Picking up a honey cake, she took a taste, scrutinized it and asked, "Are these the ones for 8,00 rubles or 9,60?" From then on her childish chatter was so incessant it was impossible for unaccustomed ears to listen to, let alone to follow, what she was saying. For what seemed forever she went on in minute detail about the neighbor's pig who had eaten her own piglets. Straining to hear, trying to follow the thread of her story, Juravlev asked whether she had finally been speared. The girl burst out laughing in a high clear voice. "No. It's true he beat her, but stab her with a knife? No, he didn't."

Only then did he realize that she had finished with the pigs and had now turned her attention to a certain Mikhail Nikolayevich who, when drunk, struck his wife and once almost put out her eye.

All the while she told her story, the girl kept looking constantly at the clock, as if distracted. Juravlev couldn't help but notice. "What is it?" he asked. "Is it bedtime already?" No, but she needed help in finishing her homework. Yawning, she untied a cloth bundle. Removing the workbook, she handed it to him.

Immersed in the peaceful problems—surrounded by all the apples, the boxes of tea, and the green and blue fabric—Juravlev felt the stir of sad memories he preferred to forget and shook his head to clear them. But it was pleasant to sit in the chair under the paper shade, chewing on a pencil and working out the figures. So pleasant was the ringing silence, in fact, that when a sudden sharp knock sounded at the door, he leaped in fear and surprise—then looked at the girl questioningly.

Springing up, she glanced at the time and said, "Right on the button!"

3

Juravlev suddenly realized how strange it was that he had never thought or even asked about the owners of the house. He couldn't have assumed that the girl lived alone. Uneasy, with eyes lowering under his brows, he sat and waited. His uneasiness intensified as a ruddy-cheeked sergeant entered the room and, as convicts do, he shot to attention. He could see only bright black eyes and beet-colored cheeks. The upper part of the face was completely concealed by a heavy woolen cap pulled down to the eyes and ear flaps tied under the chin. Lifted over mouth and nose was a large gray lambskin collar. An icy gust of cold air rolled into the room along with the sergeant. It emanated from boots turned into stone by the cold and rime, already condensing into frost on the big brass buckle cinching the waist. With stiff clumsy fingers the newcomer untied the chin flaps, jerked off the hat, and threw it onto the bench, revealing a large tumble of brown curls. Glancing into the room, she laughed and, with a voice still hoarse from the cold, said, "Oh, Nadyusha is entertaining an admirer. What a grown-up girl she is."

Still standing, unaware that he was stiff at attention, Juravlev explained, "I'm . . . I asked . . ." He wanted to say he had asked for a night's lodging but decided against it. "I asked for respite from the cold. I was released today, but it's already late . . . dark."

While he spoke she managed to scrutinize him carefully.

"Understandable," she said. "Please be seated." As her body warmed, her cheeks became less red and her voice became softer, less rough. She had a turned-up nose, thin fashionable eyebrows and small full lips which she habitually licked to keep warm. She threw off the sheepskin coat. Underneath it was her uniform—a shirt with epaulets, worn over thick padded pants. She called "Nadyusha" and the girl, without even asking, braced one hand on her mother's chest and pulled off the boots with the other. The sergeant's stripes on her red epaulets made Juravlev freeze in place, and he continued to stand at attention. Recalcitrant curls fell wildly over the woman's forehead and cheeks. In such a way, with lifted arms and untied foot bindings, she disappeared behind the cotton curtain of the pantry.

Nadyusha parroted her mother's words. "Please be seated."

Something had changed, however, with the overseer's arrival. It was as if the light had become dimmer. Slowly, Juravlev sank back into place. As if dazed, he looked at the pencil still in his hand, at the textbook, and the now unpleasantly blank piece of paper. He tried to decipher the sounds emanating from behind the curtain, rippling in response to the movement behind it. They echoed softly and quietly. Once, something fell and the woman swore. Then suddenly she reappeared, changed to such an extent that Juravlev momentarily mistook her for someone else. She was wearing an attractive pink blouse, a short black skirt and dressy short boots. Her pretty face was powdered and she had managed to put on some makeup. The pleasant aroma he had been unable to identify earlier had now became keener and more provocative. Approaching Juravlev, she held out a small hard shovel of a hand with a silver band on the index finger. "Olga," she said firmly. Juravlev, too, gave his name.

He continued to stare, looking at her with surprise. Her full lips smiled cheerfully. She adjusted her blouse and, throwing back her head, tossed the tumbling locks from her face. She now looked like she was entertaining at a party. Juravlev remembered there was something he had to tell her. It had come to him, just as she disappeared into the pantry. Now, recalling it, he spoke with difficulty—searching for the proper words. "I was under Article 58, ten years from arrest to release."

He blurted it out and immediately regretted having spoken. Now, when it was completely dark and only dogs were walking in the settlement, he would have to leave and look for lodgings in a different place. Frowning, her fashionable eyebrows drawn together in a crease, she bit her lip. "Because you couldn't keep your mouth shut. Right?" She had guessed immediately the reason for his sentence. Without waiting for an answer, she continued quickly. "They grab and grab.

For nothing Stalin grabbed people. Soon there won't be any more room in Siberia."

Juravlev's eyes opened even further. From a woman's mouth, from anyone's mouth, such words might have caused no surprise—but not from the mouth of a sergeant! Yet so genuine was her vexation, so sincere her voice, that he couldn't help asking, "And you guard them?"

Now it was her turn to look surprised, so much so that she forgot to brush back the hair that fell onto her forehead. "Naturally. When people are put in prison, it's necessary to guard them, isn't it?" Somewhat abashed, Juravlev had to agree.

She continued, as if her thoughts were not completed and he had not understood a word she had been saying. "Think for a moment. You. You were released. Now where are you supposed to go? To a *kolkhoz?*"

"Let's assume that," Juravlev replied. His statement encouraged her to go on. "Exactly! And what is life like now, with so many living on such collective farms? My mother lives on a *kolkhoz*. She's an old woman, but still she must work. So every month I have to send her thirty rubles—or rusks of dried bread, if I have any leftovers."

"I am also taking dried bread," he said, pointing to his bag.

"How long do you think they will last?" she asked, then burst into laughter. "Better be careful. They say if a man eats only dry bread, his children will be born without brains."

Her manner was suddenly arch and slyly inquisitive. Laughing, she tossed back her head. Juravlev laughed as well—noticing how her breasts moved and how her bare neck seemed to be blushing. Again, uneasily, he grinned and became silent. Then, as suddenly as she had laughed, she became sad and angry. "If we keep talking like this, I will forget my housework. The cow is neither milked nor fed," she said, with peevish discontent. He remembered her arrival, recalling her hoarse voice and her sergeant's epaulets. Grabbing her hat, she jammed it on her head and dragged the heavy lambskin coat across the floor as she put it on one arm at a time. Finally, lifting a bucket, she left—slamming the door loudly behind her.

A moment later, Juravlev left to follow.

4

The sky was covered with countless stars. Here and there a few fell, fluttering with iridescent punctuation. The light in the stable was so weak that Juravlev could hardly see it through the chinks in the gate. Opening the door, he saw Olga had thrown the last of the hay from the loft and was already climbing down the ladder, carefully clutching the crossbars. In the narrow stall—everything was narrow in the shed—a big-bellied cow with plum eyes turned her head toward the light. Scooping up a huge armful of the pungent hay, Juravlev squeezed into the cubicle.

"Ah, a good master," the woman said. "You'll find plenty to keep you busy once you get home."

Pushing past him in the crowded stall, she squatted onto a small bench and put the pail between her legs. Then, quickly washing the udder, she began to work her hands diligently as milk spurted into the pail.

"Do you have a cow?"

"I don't know," Juravlev replied.

"Now there's a fine farmer!" she said sarcastically.

"To tell the truth, I'm not a farmer."

"But you said . . . "

"My specialty is the railroad. I was a switchman, hut number 673. Perhaps you've heard of the Semenovka station in the Chernigov area? From the Semenovka station mine was the ninth kilometer."

"So you are going to your ninth again?"

"That's the point. No!" he said passionately. "They will not allow me to return to the railway. It's not permitted, they say. I'm an Article 58."

"That's true," she concurred. "With politicals they won't permit it."

"That's the point," Juravlev repeated. He had evidently thought of his situation with those same words and now repeated them. "That's the point. My family. Yes, my family lives on a *kolkhoz* now. And, if you want to know, during the last five years I haven't heard a word from them—no letters, no news. With the war, I began to think they weren't even alive. And hard as it is for me to believe, I myself haven't written for a whole year."

"Do you have children?"

"One girl, a little older than yours."

Olga sighed and said, not even thinking, "You're all the same. You produce the children, then do what you want—you have no interest, even the wish to write."

"Wait," he interrupted heatedly. "What is there to write? I, if you are interested, don't know her at all. She was one-and-a-half when I was taken. I tried writing, even last year I tried writing. 'Good morning,' or 'Good evening, daughter Zina,' I would say. Then what? Sometimes I thought it would be best to send just an empty sheet. Here, for instance, when I met your daughter. 'Hello, little beauty,' I said and couldn't for the life of me think of what to say next. I have grown away from children, I have grown away from people. And the same is true of my wife. I have grown away from her as well. I'm not talking about the physical part, that she could have had an affair with someone else. That's not the point. But it's been ten years. Think about that. Ten years! She is a stranger to me now."

Again, the woman sighed and sank into thought. Sadly and dramatically, her face changed before his eyes. Looking down at her, he saw the youth and animation fade. Sharp wrinkles appeared at the corners of her mouth. How old is she? he wondered. Thirty? Forty-five? Instead, he asked, "And what about your man?"

"I do not have a man," she said after a brief silence. "He was at the front. He was killed before my eyes."

"Does that mean you were at the front, too?"

"Yes. I am not a native here, either. I studied for six years in lower school, then left to work for the post office. The Komsomol drafted me and sent me to the front—to a field post service." She told him about her husband. After his death, when she discovered she was pregnant, she was permitted to leave. But there was no place to go. For one year she worked as a civilian employee and then got her job as an overseer at the prison camp. It wasn't hard just to stand on a watch tower. "And that's the way I live," she finished. "And here my daughter grows."

Her story made them equal. From that moment, there was just a woman before him to whom he, a man, could speak—not a former prisoner and his former guard.

"So-o-o," he drew out the word and joked in spite of himself. "So, if only you could find at least a temporary man for yourself."

Lifting her gaze, she looked at him with irony. "Without men, one feels pain—and with men, one feels pain."

"And why so?" asked Juravlev.

Although the cow was standing quietly, chewing hay, she slapped it on its flank and shouted, "Stand," in a rude, exasperated voice. "Why so? Because." Then, in a barely audible voice, she answered his question.

"Because, for instance, another overseer lives in this settlement—maybe you know him—Mikhail Nikolayevich, last name Raguzin. This Raguzin beats and disfigures his wife to the point where it's frightening just to hear—her screaming can be heard throughout the whole settlement. She is always covered with bruises; he beats her with whatever comes to hand. And the woman, you have to know this, the woman is very good—stately, even beautiful. Hardworking, too! She can't waste a moment without doing something. She dug her kitchen garden herself, she raised a pig by herself—the lard alone weighed over a hundred pounds—and they have a cow, as well."

Juravlev interrupted her. "She has no one to blame but herself. Why doesn't she apply to the court?"

"Our commander, too, says, 'Apply to the court. Get a medical certificate from a doctor and they'll give him five years.' They'll give him. Yes, they'll give him, but what next? He will be sent to a prison camp and she—she wil have to raise the children herself. She has three little ones. How do you think she'll be able to feed them? So she suffers."

She had finished milking before she finished her story about the sadistic overseer. Squeezing the pail between her legs and resting her arms on her knees, she remained seated. Then she stood up to her full height and the stall again seemed crowded. From the ceiling a white, rime-covered piece of straw, looking Christmas-like, floated slowly down. "So that's the history with the geography," she said, breaking the silence with difficulty. But, from her tone, he guessed that she was smiling. "Yes," was all he could answer.

5

The tension and constraint disappeared as soon as they got back to the house. It was pleasant to feel how the heat of the room enveloped them, gradually warming fingers, jaws, and cheekbones heavy with cold. Warmth penetrated inside them, too. Somehow, all the talk and all the standing in the crowded, frozen stall had brought them together. Together they burst into laughter when she said, "A nightingale can't be fed by telling fables—it's time for supper."

In the bottom of his small green trunk there was a small bag containing sugar and honey cakes. Juravlev took them out, but she protested so fiercely that the curls on her head began to jump. Smiling, he merely waved his hand and set them down on the bench. It was obvious that she liked to work around the house and that cooking gave her pleasure. Leaning a large square loaf of bread against her chest, she cut several thick slices. She put a wooden bowl of pickles and salt cabbage on the table. Then she opened the door of the stove. From its large black mouth a steamy fragrance of food forced itself into the room. Using two old rags, she removed the cast iron pot and set it on the table with a solid thump. It was *shchi,* Juravlev's favorite cabbage soup. Taking hand-painted spoons, already half-peeled off, Olga put two of them on the table. It was only then that Juravlev noticed the girl wasn't there.

"Where is your daughter?" he asked.

"Sleeping. Her place is above the stove."

Together, sitting side by side, they ate from the single pot. Everything seemed to amuse them—the way the brine spurted from the pickles in lively crooked bursts, the way their spoons pushed each other in the soup. In her sleep, Nadyusha stirred and muttered indistinctly. Stopping their spoons, they listened silently.

"You say *'kolkhoz,'*" he said in a quiet voice, as if continuing a previous conversation. "Without any notice, I land on the doorstep. Surprise, everybody, here I am! Oh, there is no doubt they will enroll me and take me in. But it's March already. When will I be able to get money out of my job? Maybe in September, God willing, if there's a harvest. And even that would be on account. How will I live for seven months without money?"

"But you said you had a family," she reminded him.

"Yes, my family," he answered, smiling grimly. He rested his spoon on the pot, bottom up. "How much can they have? Last year, *kolkhoz* members were given less than a pound of grain for each working day—and, since the girl is not considered a worker, she's not counted. So, here I come, with one bag of food—a bag you say will soon be empty. What next? They're not only struggling themselves; suddenly they've got a permanent guest—a husband and a father. You think they'll really say, 'Hooray, a breadwinner has fallen from heaven'? Or will they simply tell me to go to hell? And, if they do, what do I do next? You're an overseer. You know what it is to be a 58. How do you answer that?" Still smiling grimly, he looked at her and shook his head.

Handing him his spoon, she said, "Eat. Don't be upset."

He took a bit, then put the spoon back down. "How can I not be upset?"

Pushing the pot aside, she brought out a green bowl filled with milk and began to sip it from the spoon. "Eat," she reminded him.

"You see," he continued, as if he hadn't heard "I'm supposed to be free, but there's no place to go."

"True," she answered "In that case, you have only one choice."

"What?"

"The plant."

Juravlev scoffed openly. "People who went to my city wrote they were allowed only three days when they returned from prison camp. Then they were told to move on."

"Don't scoff. We have nothing in common with the city out here. Have you heard about the glass plant?"

"You mean the new one?"

"The new one," she repeated. "It is only four kilometers from here. They're desperate for workers. They'll take anyone! Many who live in this settlement walk there to work." Trembling with renewed expectation, Juravlev longed to believe her, then reality set in. Shaking his head he said, "They'll never take a 58."

"Never, never!" she mocked. "I give you a way out, and you say 'never.' If I didn't know, I wouldn't say. Tomorrow, get to the administrative region as fast as you can for your passport. The day after, go to the plant."

"I'd go there in a minute," Juravlev exclaimed, "if I thought it was true."

"If I tell you it's true, it's true. The locals who work there say there are a lot of 58s. They're rolling in 58s. True, they don't have a dormitory—most people rent part of a room. Others live in this settlement and go there every morning. If you ask, I will lease you space here." The offer was made before she realized she had made it. Then, self-consciously, she laughed.

Her last words didn't penetrate immediately, since Juravlev was so astounded at this sudden opportunity. He was thinking of what a miracle it would be—and that, if he set off at dawn, he could walk to the region with plenty of time to spare. If he were not detained with getting his passport and if, perhaps, a passing car would give him a ride, he might be back by tomorrow evening and could count on another night's lodging. Olga's words suddenly sank in. More than another night. He took her arm and held it for several moments in his hard fingers. "You will lease me part of this room?" he asked—looking at her flushed face, her large sparkling eyes, the rosy blouse and the full arm still resting in his hand. "And why not?" she answered, averting her gaze.

After supper, she removed and washed the dishes, then swept the floor. Juravlev strolled into the courtyard. The roosters were singing to one another and the settlement was already asleep. Because of that, the night seemed even darker. Invisible clouds swept the sky and the stars became scarce. Returning, he hung his coat over her sergeant's jacket. Olga was moving toward the bed, carrying a half-awake Nadyusha. Kissing her and whispering to her, still not looking at

Juravlev, she said, "Here is my man; we will sleep together. For you, I made a bed over the stove." Juravlev understood and respected her reserve.

"Keep my belongings until I return," he said. "If I'm lucky, I'll manage to get everything done and be back tomorrow night."

She tried to control her trembling voice.

"God protect you," she said.

The Letter

I HAVE JUST managed to drive him out—you know, of course, of whom I speak. On the floor there is an angry, crumpled piece of paper with two words on it, "Damn you!" With these words I had started my letter to you, to give vent to my rage. But immediately I thought—it is always possible—I thought you might only throw the letter away without finishing it, and I must, I have to talk to you before saying good-bye.

My thoughts are so confused, I'm not sure I can control them. I want you to know in detail, though, how I have banished him. I want you to know with what difficulty I discovered all I had to learn. All that I will come to later—but first I will begin at the very beginning. It is not important that you know the beginning as well as I do, I cannot do it any other way. Otherwise, I will become confused again and damn you again and the pain will win. Even now it is difficult for me to put my thoughts in order—but perhaps I've already said that.

Do you remember when our romance started? At the same time that I received your first letter, I got three more, also from strangers. A good dozen had come several days before. They were all loathsome; I barely skimmed them. Only afterwards did I realize that in our world—in a world of exiles—for many men the newspaper announcement of a divorce often served as a want-ad for a husband. They offered to meet me, they quickly tried to assess the size of my living space. Some were even more presumptuous. They began their letters with the personal "Hello, Klasha," as if they already knew me—or, even more intimately, "Dearest Klava, don't grieve."

But then your letter arrived. Should I even bother describing the impression it made on me, why I distinguished it from all the others? All that you already know from my response and everything that followed. Though the letter came from a prison camp, I was positive it was written by an innocent victim—by that time we already knew that even completely guiltless people could be trapped. Yet, if you had not written a second time, everything would have ended with only a casual hello between strangers, everything would have drifted away like smoke—like smoke from the cigarette I am smoking right now.

To flourish, feelings need both time and substance. Your further letters provided that. I could recite them, literally, because I read them over and over and learned them by heart. As you can see, I am not hiding my emotions. On what else can I now depend? What else would compel me to send this letter, to tell you truthfully and simply all that has happened—to talk to you as I would talk to myself?

In your first letter, there was nothing definite, no word about the future. But there was both wit and heart—and a melancholy that touched me deeply. Then, suddenly, in the eighth or ninth letter, one sentence leaped from the page:

"In three months, I will be free."

Can you imagine how those words excited me?

Three months, ninety days—how few, yet how infinite. Beside myself with joy, I paced about the room. I addressed you with tender words, persuaded you that three months, if you used your creativity, would not seem long at all.

Then, with difficulty, I forced myself to come to my senses, to approach the mirror. Mercilessly, I examined my face. I saw the wrinkles around my eyes and lips. Cruelly, with a heartlessness I could not understand, I deepened them and multiplied them.

Thirty-three years, and what years! I said to myself. You have grown ugly and faded and, as far as your soul and your feelings are concerned, who cares? Not even he cares.

It was then that the idea came to me to send you my picture. In my letter, I remember, I tried to treat it lightly. "Look what an old lady I am, I'm thirty-one years old." (I'm sorry. I subtracted two years. My hand grew stiff and could not draw two threes.) Then the days of waiting began—even now, recalling them, I shiver. I'm far from being ugly. Like most women, I know my value and voice it openly, without pretense. Still, I was nervous. Ah, how nervous I was. Suppose—tastes are capricious—that you didn't like me? And to such an extent that you no longer wished to write and would end our correspondence. At the same time, was it not strange that I never had doubts about you? As you can see, I never asked for your picture—your letters were your likeness.

I know how long you've been imprisoned, know how difficult it is for you now. And despite that, I dare ask you, do you know what it means to wait? I think the impatience I suffered you've never known. It is inherent only in women. In my mind, I went with my picture, went from the city in which I live and went to be with you. Along with my letter, I entered the camp. For me, a resident of Siberia, it was not so difficult to imagine the camp; I have seen many of them—true, only from the outside—God has spared me so far. Along with my letter, I walked through the desolation enclosed by fence and wire, walked past all the barracks until I entered yours. Then, in my mind, I walked further, walked out of the picture you took in your hand, looked at you and smiled.

Oh, after all that has happened, how hard it is to tell you these things!

You know the rest, I don't want to try your patience. Only a few days passed and your answer arrived. I confess without shame that my cheeks and ears were glowing, that my heart was pounding painfully. I felt, at the most, seventeen—and I was happy. You liked my picture, and you wrote more than a few flattering words. While reading them over and over, I suddenly realized it was now only two months until your release, and there was no end to my joy. Not quite two months until we would meet!

After that, the time passed differently. I don't want to say that it flew or rushed by, but this period began something new in my life. It strengthened my confidence and my feelings toward you—yes, my feelings.

It was at that time I took the next step. You thanked me and wrote how greatly it was appreciated but it was not really necessary. Even so, I meant to repeat it again and again. You must understand, I had to do something for you, even though it seemed insignificant. I refer to the parcel of food I sent. I savored finding the box, buying the food, and the way I brought it to the post office, and how it was tied, and the postal order I wrote and the wounds of sealing wax they poured in my presence. All that I savored, all that brought me nearer to you in a dear and different way.

In misfortune, as in good fortune, everyone behaves the same. In the end, everyone does the same thing. I drew a calendar and, every night before going to bed, I treated myself by crossing off another day. I believe that all who know how and are accustomed to waiting, do this, and I don't doubt it is something with which you are familiar. For me, crossing off the days had yet another effect; it made me younger and reminded me of my childhood—of one particular event I must tell you, so please hear me out to the end.

When I was nine years old, the Christmas tree—how can I put it right—was not yet "rehabilitated." My father decided to risk celebrating (only for his own children, of course) both the forbidden Christmas and the half-forbidden New Year. I learned that we would have a Christmas party a month before the event. "A full month!" I exclaimed with distress. I was young and naive. I had not yet learned the tormented sweetness of waiting. But the days began to fly from the months like leaves from a tree, the month was laid bare and, by squeezing shut my eyes, I could already see its end. Besides, we began to prepare for the event well in advance. We did everything ourselves. Christmas tree ornaments could not be bought, so we made them. Even the candles we made ourselves. My grandmother was still alive then. She went to a church and managed to collect some candle ends about the size of a child's little finger. All the long month we worked to prepare for the festival, and all the long month we were filled with festival joy.

Why do I remember this? Because the last two months have provided me with the same kind of joy, but it has been joy coupled with anxiety at the same time. I have learned it is necessary to know how to wait—yet still keep a sense of anticipation as the longed-for moment approaches. Oh, how slowly the months dragged on, but oh, how fast they flew by! Three days, two days, one day! And the fact that after all these days happiness would come I didn't doubt.

My God, even now I cannot accept the fact that all that went straight to hell! But surely you see that I am no longer a simple child, surely you see the situation was not simply my imagination. From your letters, I felt that you, too, were waiting, and that you were nervous as well. Only now do I recognize the reality—it was merely a diversion and you were carried away.

I have reached this point and, once again, anger sweeps over me. Once again I want to damn you, and I refrain with difficulty. Forgive my loss of self-control, but one thing I know with certainty—one should not do what you have done. There is a limit to every game and to go beyond it is mean and merciless.

What else can I say to you about these, my heartfelt hopes? I have said enough. But then the last day arrived and the last night. What can I say about those? I should probably stay silent. Suddenly, I fear you are reading my letter and laughing. Suddenly, I realize that I know nothing about you, nothing. My heart grows cold and I want to tear up these pages and finish our romance without another word. How could you? How did you dare?

No, I mustn't continue this way. I must finish this letter and send it to you. It may not be as important for you as for me, but for me it is absolutely necessary.

In your last letter you mentioned by which train you would arrive, when approximately you would ring the front doorbell. (I warned you, "Three rings. Don't forget, I live in a communal flat.") At the appointed hour, I sat in my room and it was not the alarm clock ticking off the seconds, it was my heart, each second very fast and hard. I sat. I listened. I waited. Then the rings! I counted them, I counted each of them. There were a full nine, each different—five short and one long, seven short, and on and on. Each ring shot through me. I sat rooted to the spot by the first three rings, rooted until an additional fourth or fifth ring resounded, and I knew it was not you. Finally your ring was heard. It could belong to no one else.

And you, Nikolay Semyonovich, had arrived.

We have a long, half-dark corridor cluttered with boxes, bicycles, folding beds, trunks, baskets, and suitcases—and with only one small twenty-five watt bulb to light it. (On a more powerful one, not all of our tenants could agree!) With numb feet I went to the outside door. I opened it, and you crossed the threshold. You pulled off your cloth cap. In the half-light I saw your shaved prisoner's head, the brightness of your dark eyes and the rucksack on your shoulders standing up like a hump. Awkwardly, you held out your hand, and I understood your awkwardness. I attributed it to natural trepidation and, in this case, to timidity as well.

I, too, was timid. "Come in, Nikolay Semyonovich." These words I pronounced barely audibly and led the way along the narrow, dimly lit tunnel. Walking behind me, you said, "Oho! She remembered!" The voice was hoarse, indistinct, cracked, even a little too familiar. But for your familiarity I instantly found explanation. Shyness is expressed in different ways, I explained to myself. And as far as your voice being hoarse and cracked: "The man's worked chopping down trees at thirty degrees below zero and colder, so what do you expect—that he should speak with the soft voice of a singer, crooning lullabies?"

How often we see and hear what we would like. To your appearance (which I have to say, and you would have to agree, is not so attractive, not so intellectual), I also reconciled myself completely. I just melded it with your thoughts and your letters and the image, however strange, proved to be part of the whole. You were clear to me and whatever failed to fit I simply ignored.

What, you would ask, did not fit? Oh, trifles—for which, I repeat, I found an immediate explanation. Entering the room, you threw your rucksack into the corner and asked me in slang, "So?

What's the story?" To be frank, I do not admire common phrases, and one might easily assume they do not exist in your vocabulary, either. But he is self-conscious, I said to myself, he is nervous. So, also from nervousness, I burst out laughing and answered in the same way. "As you can see, *we* are the story."

Continuing to justify your coarse words, I said to myself—You try to live in his condition for ten years and not only would you forget good manners, you would probably crawl on all fours. Then you, Nikolay Semyonovich, examined my room inquisitively—too inquisitively for the first time. Glancing at the mirrored closet, you reverted to slang again. "Very classy," you said. Noticing, I reproached myself for having noticed. "Dear and good one," I thought to myself, "you are self-conscious and embarrassed, but you are so clever. Try to calm yourself." It was necessary to stop my excessive scrutiny, so I began to get busy about the apartment, to prepare breakfast. I had wanted you to enjoy yourself and, to show off a little, I had managed to find a supply of foods which were not easy to buy. I set a little snack on the table with a bottle of Malaga. You said, "Oho!" and began to rub your hands in an anticipatory and unpleasant manner. All this time you eyed me openly and again I thought—"How would *you* behave after ten years of confinement?" Then you winked and brought out a quarter-liter bottle of vodka from inside your *moskvichka*. (Why is a prison-laborer jacket of that sort called a *moskvichka,* after the capital of our country? As a mockery, perhaps?) "Here it is," you said and, with excessive pride, slammed the bottle on the table.

Is it worth repeating all your words, is there any sense? I hurried to feed you, I kept waiting and wondering, "When will you finally become yourself and speak in the words that are so familiar to me?" I forgave you everything, without question. "What is that?" you asked, when I offered you coffee. "We never had that." Then, paying no attention to the glass near your place, you took the vodka, tilted up the bottom, and began to drink from the bottle. You drank about half, swallowed a bit more, screwed up your eyes to see that exactly half was left, and then handed the bottle to me. "Come on," you said, and I burst into laughter. Yes, I burst into laughter, took the bottle from your hand, poured a few drops into the glass, and drank. As you can see, I was ready to reconcile myself to every peculiarity.

Meanwhile, the vodka began to have an effect on you. I suggested we switch to Malaga. With one hand you took the bottle I offered, with the other you stroked my arm, which was bare to the elbow. Your hand was rough, clammy, unpleasant—and your nails were dirty. Instinctively, I pulled back and, for the first time, looked at you with reproach. "Well, well," you said and snickered. I was suddenly uncomfortable. It was not the manner your letters had led me to expect.

I am telling you too many details, excessive details. You are aware of how gradually an impression builds and, by accumulation, suddenly becomes clear. Somehow, of course you can guess why, I got the desire to look at your internal passport. It was a vague but insistent urge, so I turned our conversation in another direction. I began to speak of certificates and identity cards. Then I showed you my own papers and passport. I had totally forgotten that I had removed two years from my age and now it would be revealed. You read the passport attentively, turning every page. That gave me the right to ask for your passport in turn. It had been granted to you only the previous day since, like all prisoners, for the past ten years you had no identity at all.

My request excited no suspicion. The vodka and wine were working together well. There was no suspicion, none—quite the opposite. You even decided to boast about your valuable new book. You took the small, dark green document from the pocket of your cotton-lined prison pants. To do so, you had to unbutton them, which you did with no particular modesty—without even turning away. By this time, I wasn't surprised, you had already been too familiar. "Look! Read it!" you insisted.

Obviously, studying your passport revealed nothing. It was certainly in your name, Nikolay Semyonovich Avdeev; there was no deception there. But with each moment my suspicion increased. Carefully, I studied your every movement, weighed your every word. The contradiction between my former correspondent and my current guest kept growing and growing. I began to use deception. I wanted to learn the truth, every bit. I should have acted more quickly because by this time you were drunk and losing control of yourself—as if you ever had any.

I listened and responded—frankly, not always to the point. Finally, I said, "We need more snack food. Here is money, and here is a piece of paper. Write down what I tell you to get, and then you can go and buy it." You agreed instantly. You liked my generosity, and it would have been surprising if you had not.

Casually, I removed a hundred-ruble bill from my purse. Then I handed you a note pad, gave you a pen, and asked you to write. I chose difficult words deliberately, but for what? The very first letters you wrote, even the way in which you held the pen, confirmed what I already knew. No, it was not you, Nikolay Semyonovich, who wrote me those letters.

My first instinct was to show you the door, to drive you away without any excuse. Our apartment, like most communal ones, is overcrowded and—had you resisted or started a fight—there would have been enough people to throw you out. Something restrained me, and now I am content I managed to keep control.

With difficulty, you scrawled the list and, having finished, staggered off to fulfill the order. On leaving, you tried to embrace me. It wasn't so easy to restrain you.

And so our feast continued. I behaved cautiously. Stealthily, I approached the question by degrees. I burned to know who had actually written Avdeev's letters and just how the insane plan had started.

Nikolay Semyonovich continued to insist, inept liar that he is, "Why, I wrote them myself, me," then added, "and indeed, well done, weren't they? The expert, he's a real pro." A primitive man, Avdeev didn't forget to boast of his own merits in that business. "Don't think it was him who tracked you down in the newspaper. It was me. Him, the expert, I only asked to scribble the letters. He was the scholar among us; he wrote the complaints for our guys. He even wrote to Kalinin, wrote to Shvernik! To tell the truth, it's pointless, that kind of complaining, but look at one letter and your heart breaks. He's a real pro. Imagine! For a long time he insisted he didn't want money from me to write these letters. I give him five rubles, and he doesn't take them. What do you do with him? Finally, he gave in. He said okay, but even then he never took any money. What a nut case!"

In that way, my queries continued. Step by step, imperceptibly, I wormed everything out of him: your first name, patronymic and last name, your age; that you are single and that your term will be over in just one year. Only then—as if rewarding myself for my disappointment, vexation and pain—only then did I express my true feelings.

To get rid of him, a thief to whom prison is like his own home, was not easy. He resisted. He was actually offended! "Why?" he complained. "You wrote—wrote, sent me your picture. You send me your picture and then, for no reason, it's good-bye? Is that how you honest people behave?" Yes, he blamed it all on me. He said all the intelligentsia were like that—if you were not in prison for political reasons, they didn't give a damn about you. Then he turned on me, accused me, and said maybe I sympathized with the counterrevolutionaries myself. Finally, he began to swear at me. For you, who are familiar with camp vocabulary, it is not hard to hear how he cursed.

It lasted a long time. It was difficult for him to get used to the idea that some simple female, whom he himself had found in the paper, some simple female wanted to make a fool of him! He raged and grumbled. He talked nonstop. You got your share as well—according to him, the letters should never have been written the way they were. Finally, I threatened him, and only after I threatened did he leave, cursing everything and everyone in the world—but, after ten years in prison, he was not eager to meet the militia.

It is late now. I have covered many sheets of paper with writing. My hand aches, my heart aches. Just now I have picked up and put on the table the crumpled piece of paper. In the light from the table lamp, it looks like a many-sided Chinese lantern, as if it were shining from within. On it I make out the words, "Damn you!" With those words I began my letter, and with those I was going to end it. But even as I did before, I reject them now as well. Your letters have almost become a part of me, even though you signed them with another person's name. I needed them, they were necessary to me. Were? I know that I need them now as well, and I will need them in the future—that, without them, life will be lonely and difficult for me.

It will be impossible. You acted badly, I think you will agree. But you did it without bad intentions—at least that is what I hope.

No, I cannot damn you. My hand and my pen refuse to write those cold, thorny words. I've become so used to your letters, I cannot even imagine how I will break myself of the habit of receiving them, how I will live without waiting patiently for them. The pain of meeting Avdeev, the pain of that disgusting charade will fade, and then what will be left? No. I cannot accept that.

Please don't think I force myself on you, no. I don't want to guess about the future, to build plans, to feed hopes. How often these plans and hopes collapse, how often they are unfulfilled. I ask you for little. I leave the future to the future, to its own capricious, twisted ways. You too, I believe, know how willful destiny can be, how inconsistent. I repeat, I ask for little. I just ask that we continue our correspondence. I hope the letters will be the same, and I will find in them the same ideas and insights. But now those letters will not be signed with that unfortunate alias, but with your own name. You will sign them yourself, as I myself sign my letters and will sign them in the future—if, of course, you agree to answer me, to write me again . . .

The Neighbor

1

YAKOV IVANOVICH, THE Moscow floor polisher, was sentenced by the *troika* to ten years, on a completely trumped-up charge. The principal witness against him was a pensioner in his communal flat—Marya Gavrilovna Potapova—called by her middle name, Gavrilovna, for short.

In interrogation and transfer prisons, as well as in camp, Yakov Ivanovich heard many stories about malicious informers. There were cases where father informed against son and son against father, or brother informed against brother and wife against husband. One person, for instance, was in prison because he was betrayed by his fiancée who, he swore, was insane about him. But, as the saying goes, one does not suffer from somebody else's misfortune, so all these stories flew past Yakov and failed to touch him. Only his own misfortune preoccupied him, gave him pause, and made him grieve.

Once—it was perhaps the fourth or fifth year of his term— Yakov Ivanovich, among other convicts, was unloading a barge filled with bricks. It was a night in late autumn and the sharp wind slashed like a knife, shards of ice cut at them and the Yenisey River—difficult even when normal—had now gone berserk. The barge rocked violently from side to side, often almost overturning, and the water was like a giant wall that pushed through your legs and pulled you with it. Wet and cold and hungry, bending under an unbearable burden and unable even to find a foothold, Yakov was struck with a sudden burning.

"I want to look Gavrilovna in the eye, to say nothing, not a word. I just want to look her in the eye."

Yakov was a person with a well-developed conscience, and it seemed inconceivable to him that Gavrilovna would be able to withstand such a gaze. For what reason? What had he done to her? She knew very well that her whole testimony was false. How could she have done it? Yes. He would say nothing. He would simply look her silently in the eye.

The vision began to recur frequently and, in recurring, gave him comfort. Whenever the work got too hard, or grief overwhelmed him, or his clothes were so worn they were no longer warm, or his cough was so severe it seemed he would die in that cursed land and rot there forever, Yakov Ivanovich would picture Gavrilovna and the way he would look her in the eye and the way she would squirm, not knowing which way to turn from the pain and shame. And he would ask her only one question. "Why? What harm did I ever do to you in my whole life?"

He felt her disquiet, and he himself was disturbed, but he couldn't do it any other way, however difficult it was. A person must be made to understand what he has done so he won't do it again—so he will tell his children and his grandchildren. But, since Gavrilovna had no relatives at all, he would usually end the imagined meeting with his betrayer by declaring firmly, "It is unforgivable, for no reason—for nothing at all—to destroy people."

2

To live in captivity without something to console you is difficult, especially if you feel you have been accused unjustly and are serving your time for no reason. Many convicts take comfort in contemplating revenge. Perhaps that is why so many find solace in the popular story of the prisoner who, after finishing his term, set out to find his betrayer. Roaming from city to city, from village to village, sifting every clue like sand through a sieve, he finally finds the culprit. And, after unleashing all the pent-up rage in his soul, he destroys him.

That the gentle Yakov Ivanovich could never permit himself such revenge, even in his thoughts, goes without saying. But his longing to confront Gavrilovna and to look her in the eye grew stronger and stronger, returning constantly to his mind, enveloping him more and more.

So in this way time passed, and finally the last year began, then the last month, and then it was the last week.

From time immemorial, when Kalininskaya oblast' still carried the pre-Revolutionary name of Tver'skaya guberniya—and even now in our own time—the village of Verbinino has supplied Moscow with its floor polishers. Yakov Ivanovich was from that village, that was where his family lived. At the end of his term, he was not permitted to return to Moscow, but only to the place where he'd been born.

At his release, Yakov Ivanovich was fifty-five. Much had happened during the past decade. His daughter had married, his son had served in the army. And who knew how his wife had managed to work their small piece of land and still to contribute to the *kolkhoz?* There was much to think about. But sitting in the train, throughout the whole journey, for seven long days, he thought of nothing but his meeting with Gavrilovna. He would follow the dark, curved corridor to her door and she would open it. After that, everything would happen as he had seen it, every detail would be as he had imagined. Acutely, he felt her consternation and concern.

"After all," he continued, justifying himself as if he were arguing with a stranger, "she deserves it. Ten years. Ten years! Only think how much has happened."

But he couldn't think—not yet—neither about the past nor the future waiting for him in the freedom. His stay would be brief in Moscow—only time enough to transfer from one train to the next. But there would be time enough to see Gavrilovna. Besides, whose fault was it that he would never have time in Moscow again? Gavrilovna's! She was the culprit!

3

Having checked his things, Yakov hurried to the tram, catching the same number he always took to his flat on Bezbozhny Street.

To prevent dirtying passengers with his floor polishing equipment, he used to stand outside on the rear platform. He had been standing a good half of the way before he realized he was no longer carrying a bucket and brushes, so he entered the tram and took an available seat. There was nothing else to do, so once again he began to mull over the preposterous case they had brought against him. From what had they fabricated it? As if the director of the firm for which Yakov polished floors would ever have given him those—what had they called them—Trotsky leaflets, and as if he would ever have concealed them under his jacket, against his body. As if he would ever have given them to the director of another company, who would have then distributed them to his clients. Of course, it was useless to explain that in his whole life he had never seen such leaflets! Had never even heard of them! And Yakov, though he was summoned in the day and summoned in the night, and threatened over and over, had maintained this position, had maintained it throughout: "I know nothing; I saw nothing."

It was at that time that Gavrilovna's testimony appeared. And, while they read it to him, he could only shrug his shoulders in utter disbelief. My God, what wasn't in that testimony! Concealing leaflets in his shirt was only the beginning. It charged that Yakov concealed leaflets everywhere and constantly spread harmful propaganda. To Gavrilovna herself he kept saying, "You wait. You'll see what we will make happen." And, cursing everything and everyone in the system, he gave her leaflets to read and started swearing.

That would have been the proper time to demand a confrontation—but Yakov Ivanovich didn't yet know about confrontations and the possibility of demanding them. The only thing he could think of, while her testimony was being read, was to ask to see her signature. Frequently, on the day when her pension was delivered, Gavrilovna was out and left him her book, so he knew her signature well. Alas! Gavrilovna's testimony was signed by her own hand, there was no doubt. And here Yakov Ivanovich was so aghast he could only shake his head and hold out his hands in shock, and the investigator said, "There. You see? So why do you deny it?" Yes, that's exactly how it was. He realized he had said these words aloud and looked around, but the conductor called out the stop. Yakov Ivanovich hurried to stand up. Here it was! Bezbozhny!

4

From now on neither the sidestreets nor the houses nor anything else in Moscow could have meaning for him—Yakov Ivanovich knew that and had already accepted his exile, yet he lamented and tried to remember those scenes there was no sense in remembering. The first step of the staircase in his building was still broken and, nostalgically, he nudged the broken part with his toe. Was it surprising that the list of tenants on the door to his old apartment was new? Some people had moved, some had passed away, and he, Yakov Ivanovich, had been arrested—so his room had been given to someone else. Nervously, he took out his glasses in order to scrutinize the list. He read the name of the new inhabitant listed under his former number. He read it several times—Bryukhanov, A. E.

Suddenly, a knife of ice pierced him and he broke into a cold sweat. He helped his eyes by running a trembling finger along the list. His heart sank. Why had it never occurred to him once during those ten years that Gavrilovna—who had been old even before his arrest—that Gavrilovna could die? How old would she be now, if she were alive? He closed his eyes in panic. There had been war, there had been want, what little food could be found had been rationed, there had been misfortune and, finally, there had been death. The thought of her dying immobilized him. Unable anymore to look at the list, he groped for the bell and rang two times. Usually, from curiosity or perhaps from idleness, Gavrilovna would open the door for every ring. Straining to hear, he was elated—yet still tense—when the sound of familiar footsteps echoed in the hall. He had time only to notice that one heavy burden had fallen from his shoulders when the original took its place.

Meanwhile, the footsteps behind the door stopped. As was her habit, Gavrilovna switched on the hall light to see where she was going, then turned it off to save electricity. As was also her habit, she rattled the keys. Then the top lock turned, the bottom lock turned, and the door swung open.

What happened next was exactly as he had pictured it all those long years.

"Who do you want?" she asked, and let him in before he answered—another familiar habit. She didn't look too much older, but she had gained weight and to her two chins had added a third. Moving a bit, she looked at him attentively without recognizing him. Was it possible he had changed that much? Or, perhaps, her eyes had weakened. Unwillingly, he pulled off his prison cap.

"Hello, Gavrilovna."

Immediately, her demeanor changed. Her eyes became joyful; her face suffused with happiness; and, in ecstatic exuberance, she began hopping from one foot to the other.

"Yakov Ivanovich!" she exclaimed breathlessly. "Our dear, our darling! We have waited for you and now you are here!" And she began to sob, pressing her sleeve against her face. "Thank God I have been able to see you alive!" Again, she shifted from one foot to the other. "What am I doing? I've completely lost my mind! Let's go, let's go, my dear one. I will heat the kettle, and we will do as we used to, we will have tea together. I know how worn out you must be. What a hard time you've had!" Unable to continue, she covered her flushed face and gasped with emotion. "Let's go, let's go," she repeated, sobbing and stumbling as she moved along the curved corridor.

Dazed, with drooping head, Yakov followed her. "Careful," she warned him, "Folomin puts his trunk right outside here. What can one do with him?" And Yakov automatically sucked in his breath and squeezed by. Somewhere in the apartment, just as it had long ago, a door squeaked—announcing it had to be mended.

"See? Here is the small hook for your jacket," she reminded him. Those words, and the fact she expected him to have tea with her, stopped him. He entered the room without removing his jacket.

She was already bustling about the table, taking the napkin off the bread plate and removing the lid from the butter dish. Then she took the kettle to heat on the communal stove down the hall.

"Marya Gavrilovna," he said, forcing out the words and unable to look at her, "how could you have testified as you did?" His throat closed so tightly that his voice could scarcely push through. "You knew it wasn't true. How could you have possibly done it?"

"What? What are you talking about?" she asked. Then, guessing, remembering, she slapped her hands against herself. "But I did nothing," she assured him and, grasping a chair, sat down. "They called me to this large office—they sent me a notice so, of course, I went. They said, 'Tell us everything just as it was.' So I told them the truth—how we live in the same apartment, right next door to each other, and how we take turns paying the rent—one month I go to the bank, the next month you go; and how we pay our share for the gas and electricity and never argue about it—whatever is asked, we pay. And this man in charge—what do you call him?—he's listening and writing, listening and writing. Oh my God, what an intelligent man, my dear, how fast he wrote—I'm talking, and he's going like a typewriter. Then he gives it to me to read, as it should be. Thank God I took my glasses. And though I'm not very good at reading handwriting, still I notice that it seems different, it's not what I told him. And he sees that I'm going to question it and says, 'Now don't you worry, Gavrilovna, just sign.' Then he explains, 'It's all the same. You'll never see Yakov Ivanovich anymore. He won't live in Moscow again, and it won't do him any harm,' and he pats me on the shoulder. So what can I do? Here is an important man, an educated person. In his position, who am I to tell him what should be done?" And she continued to describe how learned the investigator was, using words of respect and admiration—the kind she usually reserved for really educated people like accountants, cashiers, or receptionists in the doctor's office. "But let's talk about something important, my dear. Finally, you're here, after all these years! Now sit and wait. I will get hot water and we will have tea together."

The Semyonovs

1

THE NIGHT BEFORE, his left palm itched—it meant success and good luck. True, it had itched before. A year ago and two years before that as well. But at that time Sergey Mikhailovich Semyonov didn't attach any importance to it. What success can there be in camp? What good luck? This time, however, he scratched his palm with pleasure, luxuriating in it, and even—as is the custom—spitting a few times. Then, the next day, when he was called to the office, he thought about his itching palm of the previous day and looked at it as if it were a companion. He looked at it again on his return, limping and panting with excitement. His palm hadn't let him down. Was it really possible that everything was going to change now and go well? After all, he needed so little. He hadn't come from Moscow or any other large city, so was it surprising that after ten years of confinement they would allow him to return to the little town where he once lived?

It was in this calm, understated way that he planned to break the news of his good fortune to the barrack. But his self-control lasted for only two syllables. No sooner had he uttered them than his emotions whirled him up like a tornado, and he rained down every detail, especially that had he not been permitted to return home, exile would have been tantamount to his death.

"Because, judge for yourself," he said, turning his head from side to side, seeking their assent. "Judge for yourself. What would I do in exile? How would I live? For a mere corner of a room—not even a full one—you have to pay, for heating you have to pay, for food you have to pay—and with what? What could I do? Let's say I'm a night security guard in a small village store—even without me there are crowds of people out there looking for work like that. Besides, truthfully, how good a security guard would I be? They'd come, tie me up, hit me on the head, and I'd be finished. No, exile is not for me—it means certain death. I was ready to say it, even to the commander. 'Do whatever you want, but into exile I will not go!'" He finished in such a defiant, though completely improbable, way that his voice broke. "And I wouldn't have gone, ever! I would have just thrown myself in front of the gate and hung onto it, crying 'I won't go!'"

He didn't need to belabor the point. After serving their terms, more than half the convicts there would be sent into exile. And besides, it was obvious that any "I won't go!" was mere bluster. But his listeners were silent. No one had the heart to disillusion him.

He was nearly seventy and prison had taken its toll. He was faded and wrinkled, as small as if he'd been shrunk, and stooped over; his scalp was covered only with wisps of down, and his mouth was so toothless that even when his lips were closed it looked as if he were grinning at himself. The main point, of course, was that the old man was delirious, drunk with happiness, and at such a time one could be forgiven for saying whatever nonsense comes to mind. An Estonian pastor, a huge man with a beard like Moses', even delivered a parting benediction. On behalf of everyone there, he blessed the guest—for by now he was a guest—and beseeched God to grant him a good trip and a better future. The very next day, Sergey Mikhailovich Semyonov began to prepare for his departure.

Oh, these departures! Before his final release there were still five full days—to pack his poor possessions would take only a few minutes. In order to pass the time, Semyonov packed and unpacked, moved his things from place to place and moved them again, aired out his small trunk and, knocking on it, tested it constantly to make sure it was still strong—all the while recounting the story of his life. He was even provided with a listener—Shikhanevich, a hatter from Lvov, who occupied the space opposite him. And Semyonov, sitting on his upper berth, shuttling his worthless belongings about, grinned his toothless grin and recalled the past—embroidering his importance just a bit. By some stroke of luck, he'd managed to save the jacket from his old uniform. Only the buttons were missing. They had been metal and so were removed by a strict overseer during a search. Inspecting the jacket hanging over his spread fingers and shaking out the folds, Semyonov told how he had been head of the regional postal service, and how many post offices had been under his command— some even with a telegraph. His office had been right in the center of the region, a separate hut with felt padding on the walls to keep out the noise and even a telephone. Ensconced in this hut, he'd be able to communicate not only with places throughout the region but even with Moscow—with any city in the entire Soviet Union! Suddenly, as he heard his own words, it seemed almost miraculous—even to him—that all this had been real. At that time his wife had still been living. At that time his son had been working in the headquarters of the local agricultural department and wasn't just some nobody; he'd graduated from the famous Timiryazev Agricultural Academy in Moscow. At that time his daughter had been in her fourth year of middle school.

"When they came to take me," he confided to the hatter, "my old woman was the only one who guessed the reason, and she fainted dead away. There she was, stretched out on the floor with her eyes rolled up in their sockets. And suddenly I realize that I cannot go to her anymore—it's as if I am not her husband, not the host in my own home anymore, that I am already a prisoner. Thank God, my son kept his head and helped her."

His toothless mouth half-open, he fell silent and sank into thought.

"You have good children," Shikhanevich said, "they don't forget you."

Regarding Semyonov's children, Shikhanevich could judge only by the parcels they sent, parcels which arrived infrequently. But he was a kind person and wanted to say something pleasant to the departing one.

Semyonov reacted brightly. "Oh yes, oh yes, I have wonderful children." And he began to tell the little he knew from their letters—the son had gotten married, the daughter had graduated from school and was now working—but listening to himself, the words sounded somehow dull and distant—as if he were repeating someone else's story, and it was not very interesting. He was the first to notice this, and fell silent. What was he like, this son who was now thirty-five? What was his daughter-in-law like? Or his daughter? He couldn't even imagine. And suddenly he remembered a story about his son—when he was a small, mischievous six-year-old who had swallowed five fifteen-kopeck coins.

"He is unable to cry, he can only mumble 'm-m-m-m' and wave his hands, and he's red and gasping for breath and his eyes are popping out," he said, and his own eyes began to pop in the same way his son's had all those years ago. "Can you believe it? My wife and I are so stricken with fear, we are not only unable to help, we are even too terrified to get close enough to try. Thank God, our neighbor ran for the doctor, Dr. Melamed. What a man he was! He flew to us immediately. My Misha was already turning blue. So what does Yosif Isaakovich do? He squeezes Misha between his knees to prevent him from shaking and pokes a finger deep into his mouth. I could only shut my eyes, I'm so sure this is the end. Then I hear the doctor say, 'I'll take one of these in remembrance,' and he explains that all these coins were stuck in Misha's throat and could easily have strangled the boy."

"Oh my God," exclaimed the soft-hearted Shikhanevich, "of course, they could have strangled him." He wanted to continue, but Semyonov interrupted him. His story wasn't finished yet.

"And Misha?" he chuckled, then seemed as if he would burst with laughter. "Misha grabbed the money. 'You can't have them. I've eaten them! They're mine!'"

"Mine," repeated the hatter, who was so touched he could hardly continue. "So, Semyonov, you have managed to survive all this." And a bit later he said, "My people have a prayer—'Thank you, God, for letting me live to this very moment.' It applies directly to you. May you live now, at home among your family, until you see your grandchildren born." Suddenly, his face changed, and he pretended to be strict and solemn. Lifting his forefinger, he said, "I have only one request, Sergey Mikhailovich. Make sure your grandchildren don't swallow what they are not supposed to."

And Semyonov responded in the same solemnly joyous way. With his straight face and faded eyes, he looked at the hatter and nodded. "Yes, yes. I promise, comrade Shikhanevich."

2

As with all prisoners who have just been released, Sergey Mikhailovich was longing to talk, to tell of his experiences. He was dressed in his prisoner's pea coat and grubby boots, his shabby convict cap with the wild flaps, and his cotton pants tied at the ankle with the white string that immediately conveyed to any passenger that he'd just been released from camp. It would have been nice, during train stops, to walk along the platform, to get a breath of fresh air, to visit the food stand and buy a small white roll or a sandwich with smoked sausage—the kind Semyonov saw other passengers bring back to the railway car. But in his pocket he had no passport. Instead, there was a certificate he could exchange for legitimate documents only at home. So he sat silently at the window and pined. And, because he had nothing else to do, he looked more often than necessary into the bag where he'd stored his provisions—his day's ration of bread and herring and a paper cone packed with sugar. To the bag he had tied a large iron drinking cup, but for boiled water he asked only one peasant woman who carried a copper pot with her—and her he asked infrequently, with a timidity and servility uncharacteristic of his past.

Somehow passengers kept appearing and disappearing, one replacing the other, and it took him a while to realize that not everyone was traveling to the end of the line. The woman with the water disappeared, too, but he didn't noticed it until his throat became parched. Her place remained unoccupied for a long time, but then a large woman appeared who had worked herself into a sweat carrying two huge bags. While the train was standing, she was continually handed smaller bags from the outside—which she dragged on board and stowed above and below the benches and in every place she could find. As long as the train stood still this procedure continued, while she continued to search for every available spot to put them. Removing a headkerchief as thick and beautiful as a tapestry, she straightened her hair with a curved tortoiseshell comb. Then she sat near Semyonov, all the while panting heavily and casting suspicious sidelong glances at him. It made him very uncomfortable, especially when their eyes met, so he pressed his face close to the window. Beyond, it was beginning to turn blue. Soon, he could not tell one thing from another, everything blurred and became black. The fifth night was coming—the next to the last of his trip.

Tomorrow I'll be home . . . A bit later he repeated the words, moving his lips, and then waited—but the thought never flowered. It was compressed into those five words. He recalled how a bright powerful stream of memories had poured over him when, seven or eight years ago in his sleepless hours, he had begun to think about being free. It was not true that convicts never dreamed of the future. Even when he had been severely ill, even in the hospital, Semyonov used to imagine how he would leave through the gates of the camp, how he would catch the train, and how he would talk to his neighbors on the trip and they would rejoice with him and wish him luck. And not only the train! Several times he was somehow returning home along the Siberian post road in a sleigh drawn by horses and, though he understood it was just a dream, with ice-cutting clarity he kept seeing the same bearded coachman with his pockmarked face and the horses—one big and dappled—traveling swiftly on horseshoes that sparkled. And everything around was sparkling—the snow like diamonds on giant pine trees against a blue sky. Now he felt that something must be wrong with him because his thought "Tomorrow I'll be home" didn't go anywhere.

"It must be my old age," he decided. "Now I will rest and maybe, as used to happen in camp, my thoughts will leap forward." He stretched out on his back, but still nothing happened. So he tried to imagine tomorrow, the next day. "Here I am, entering the house," he prodded his hopes, but still they went nowhere. "No. One cannot force things. It must be a matter of age. Is that surprising? I'm nearly seventy. That's a big figure."

Somehow, he was able to relax and, in relaxing, was able to reconcile himself to his age. Every age had its shortcomings. But no matter, as Shikhanevich reminded him, he had survived until this long-awaited moment and the train was flying toward it. Tomorrow he would be home. Putting his hands under his unshaven cheek, he wished himself goodnight and fell asleep.

He was awakened by a terrible racket and didn't know right away what had happened. Then he could see that, inside the car, his female seat partner was scurrying about, making loud noises. He could hear her swearing, "The bloody thieves!" followed by a stream of profanity. In the dim light of the bulb one could see her skirt flying as she checked above and below, bending and lifting, looking for her belongings. Once her head appeared near his—he was sleeping on an upper berth—and he was stunned by the hatred on her face as she glared at him and his clothing. Raising himself with trembling hands, he reached for his small trunk and the bag of food on which his head was resting. His neighbor, lying opposite him, lifted himself as quickly as Semyonov. Below, two people were deciding how best to deal with the thieves—to kill them on the spot or deliver them to the militia. One of them began to boast about how they had once lynched a young gypsy—not much more than a boy. The small thief was finally cut down and, as he lay there, crumpled and coughing, he died with blood-tinged foam bubbling on his lips. Semyonov's neighbor in the berth across from him was also listening. A hairy man with penetrating eyes, he heard the end of the story and turned toward Semyonov, inspecting his prison apparel with a look Sergey Mikhailovich feared was suspicious. Unable to restrain himself, Sergey Mikhailovich smiled unnecessarily and said, "We politicals also suffered from the thieves." He paused for breath and finished, "For us, too, they made life impossible."

3

Looking around, with his small trunk and small bag in hand, Semyonov walked along the streets of his home town. The light frost forming on his face was already a lenient sign of spring. "It's just the same here as it was in our place," he thought, meaning the camp in Siberia. It was dusk. He recognized every house. For reasons he couldn't identify, he dallied, looking at all the lighted windows. "This is the Babichevs. They're having tea," he said to himself. "And there is Timofey Ivanovich." In spite of himself, he slowed his steps, stopping more and more often. "Hi there! Hello!" he practiced aloud and then grinned self-consciously. He realized that the words coming to him were empty, and he felt their unimportance. "It's good the children haven't been evicted," he thought. Who had written him about that, his daughter? His daughter-in-law? Who and when? What difference did it make, the letters were all mixed up in his mind, and he hadn't been able to distinguish their handwriting. "Hi there! Hello!" What else was there to say? He couldn't think of anything, and maybe it wasn't important he did.

When he came to the house where he had lived, he waited outside so long that he felt uncomfortable. But even here his thoughts were scattered and incomplete. Again he remembered that the family hadn't been evicted, hadn't been touched, and that was good. The moon hovered just above the building, just above the fence. The shutters were closed but through the thin slats there radiated a bright honey light. "The electricity works well, much better than in our place," Semyonov thought as before, meaning Siberia and the light in the barracks. Woodenly, he walked up the steps of the porch, put down his trunk, and placed the small bag on top. Only then did he find strength enough to knock on the door.

Very soft steps echoed in the corridor, and a melodious voice asked, "Is that you, Mikhailik?" Semyonov had no time to answer. The door flew open and in a bright lighted square, as if in a frame, a young woman stood. At once he noticed her beauty, her happy blue eyes, and full smiling lips between which wet and very white teeth sparkled. Robed in a light housecoat, her arms bare, her whole figure—from the short blond hair to the arm resting against the door—radiated peace and some special contentment. A light, delicate scent seemed to surround her.

It lasted no more than a second. Sudden fear distorted her face, her eyes became sharp, and her lips trembled. "Oh!" she gasped and began to slam the door shut but, changing her mind, put it on the chain. Only afterward did she ask, "What do you want?" There was no doubt that she was Liza, his daughter-in-law, but somehow he asked for Mikhail. Now she asked, "What for?" No sooner had she asked the question than she gasped again, but this time it was in a different way. She was joyful and excited and began to sparkle as before.

"You! You're Sergey Mikhailovich! Yes?" Now she opened the door wide and stared at him. And the more she stared, the more she smiled.

"Yes! Yes! I recognized you from the old pictures!" With surprising strength, Liza lifted the bags and, letting him pass, followed after. Excited, she asked questions and then immediately answered them herself. Why didn't he telegraph them about his arrival? Oh, of course, who knows when the telegram would have arrived? She crossed the dining room, passed in front of her father-in-law, and entered the bedroom. Sergey Mikhailovich followed her slowly. Here, under the blue silk lamp shade, there was a soft light—bluish as well—and the same delicate scent he had detected in the corridor seemed even stronger here.

"Look," she said with loving pride and, as if apologizing for her rapture, smiled. "Look. Here is your grandson. He is almost six months old." Then, unable to restrain herself any longer, she began to babble to the baby the way all young mothers do. "Here is your grandfather, your grandfather Sergey Mikhailovich has arrived and Vasilyochek doesn't even know—he's sleeping, my dear silly little son, sleeping and sleeping and sleeping."

Moving aside a bit, she invited his grandfather to come closer and looked at Sergey Mikhailovich with joy, asking, "Isn't he wonderful?" The child stirred slightly. Regretfully, Liza tiptoed into the dining room. There with warmth and excitement, she was eager both to ask for information and to give it.

"So how did you guess that first time that there was a letter for you in the box of sugar cubes?"

It had been her idea, she professed proudly, to put a brief note between the layers of cubes in the small box of sugar. Who would untie and examine a box of sugar cubes? Another time, shen she left for the city, Mikhailik had given her a hundred-ruble bill and asked that she send a money order to his father. Again, she had opened the box of sugar and cleverly placed the bill between the layer. Then she had closed it again, tying it with a thin yellow string. Sergey Mikhailovich had, of course, received it? He nodded and she clapped her hands just like a child.

"How did you figure out who the parcels were from?"

Yes, when the censor had asked him about that—it was 1949, and both during and shortly after the war almost no one in camp had received parcels—Semyonov had been unable to give a clear answer. Naturally, he named his son, but the censor shook his head. He also made a mess of the question, "Where are you expecting to receive a parcel from?" The censor had sneered, "Are you trying to tell me you don't know from whom or where you might get a parcel?" Finally the censor himself said, "It's from someone named Rudneva, from the city."

"So I remembered," grinned Sergey Mikhailovich, "and the next time I answered in the proper way."

Listening to the story, her face changed frequently. It became sad and a bit alarmed when her father-in-law could name neither the family nor the city from which the parcel had been sent. But at the happy ending, she began to sparkle again.

"That was my maiden name, Rudneva," she smiled. "I drove to the city, bought some food, and sent it to you. Last time, two months after the baby was born, I asked a friend of mine to sit with Vasilyok." She blushed with sudden embarrassment. "I pumped milk so she could feed him three times from the bottle. And if you only knew," she continued excitedly, standing and taking several steps, "If you only knew how happy Mikhailik was when I showed him the receipt for the parcel. 'Now I can eat peacefully,' he said."

Basking in her warmth, Semyonov suddenly realized he had never once asked about his son or daughter. But what was there to ask? Now he asked, as if he did so every day, "Are Mikhail and Nina still at work?"

"Mikhailik?" she repeated and pursed her lips. "Oh, he's always busy. Always busy! You know that he is now a chief? And it upsets me. Not a night passes but there's a meeting, or he has to travel out of town for a few days. He is always gone." It seemed to her that her father-in-law was perturbed at this news, and she added, "No. Don't worry. He didn't go anywhere today. He will be here soon." Then her conversation took a new direction. "Oh, I'm talking and talking, and you've just finished a long journey and want to eat and drink." She stood up and went immediately to the kitchen. Standing near the door, remembering that she hadn't answered his question, she added, "Nina couldn't find a job here, so she is in the Oreshkino area, working there. At the New Year she was here to see Vasilyok and wrote you a letter. And I put a letter into the box of sugar you received."

4

The hot tea tired him, and everything seemed to be happening in a warm haze. The samovar sung cozily. It began on a very high note and then, lullingly, soporifically, switched to a purr and a hum. It was obvious that Liza was so talkative because she was so often alone. "Life has no mercy on anyone . . . " Had his daughter-in-law uttered the phrase? Or perhaps, while listening to her, he had that thought himself? In '43 there was a moment in the city of Kharkov when the Germans had been beaten back by the Russians. And though Liza was then just twelve years old, she and her mother were able to fight their way east. But even behind the battlefront, with a sick mother, it was difficult and they were hungry all the time. She pressed her palms to her cheeks and looked sadly at Sergey Mikhailovich. Recalling adversity disturbed her, and she fell silent. "No," she shook her head as if trying to shake off the past, then looked at her father-in-law again and smiled shyly. "It is better if I tell you how we met, Mikhailik and I, and how at once we both . . . " she choked and tears sparkled in her eyes, " . . . and how at once I liked him."

But even there she interrupted herself.

"Oh, I keep talking and talking," she said. "I talk, and you—tired after your journey—do not take anything. Please. Eat. I made the cake myself. Mikhailik would be very upset if he knew that you ate so little. And look how late it is, and he's still not here! It's the sowing campaign. Do you have any idea how many problems they have?"

Now, after she mentioned Kharkov, he recognized her Ukrainian accent, especially when she used certain words. Silent, she stood, then sat again. Her idle hands bothered her, and she began to move everything on the table toward Sergey Mikhailovich—the pie, the bread, the butter, and the cheese. So as not to distress her, Semyonov began to eat, even though he was no longer hungry. Looking at him, she nodded her head approvingly, and he was reminded how she had looked at Vasilyok when she bent over the cradle.

Suddenly, Liza lifted her head and came to life. It seemed that she must have exceptional hearing; she appeared to be listening to silence. "He's coming! Mikhailik is coming!"

But Sergey Mikhailovich didn't hear anything for a long time. Hurrying, she rushed into the corridor and opened the outside door, letting the cold air pour in.

"Come and guess who's here," he heard her voice calling. "I will not tell you! I will not tell you, you must guess!"

Mikhail couldn't guess, so she wouldn't let him pass. Their playful bantering could be heard throughout the corridor. Finally, teetering on her toes as she teased him, she led him toward the dining room.

"But how can I be expected to know?" he asked, with the indulgence of an older person speaking to a child.

"Even now you don't know?"

He moved Liza aside slightly, passed around her, and only after that exclaimed "Father!" and rushed to Sergey Mikhailovich, who rose in confusion—with the saucer from which he had been sipping tea still in his hand.

Like his wife, Mikhail began to ask questions. How had his trip been? What day had he been released? Had he had enough money for the journey? He looked at the table and, with reproach in his voice, said to his wife, "You could at least have offered him a cutlet or some fried eggs!"

She gasped guiltily. "But I didn't know what Sergey Mikhailovich could eat. I'll bring something right away!"

Sergey Mikhailovich stopped her. He was full, he said. They were silent for several long seconds.

"Why am I sitting here?" Liza said, coming to her senses. "You haven't had your dinner, Mikhailik!"

"No, stay, stay," said Mikhail and, like his father a moment ago, stopped her.

He wanted to sit silently near his guest, gazing into his face. With grief and a heavy heart, he saw more and more how much his father had aged—how his hands trembled and his head nodded involuntarily. He was almost decrepit. Mikhail glanced at his wife. He wondered what they had been talking about before he arrived. Of course, Liza must have told him how she had been in labor with Vasilyok for three days and three nights, and what a good baby he was, and how he already understood everything. Or maybe they, as he did now, had also been sitting in silence.

But Liza was unable to be silent for very long. Smiling, she looked first at her husband and then at her father-in-law. She was thinking how hard it was to believe—that Sergey Mikhailovich hadn't seen her Mikhail for ten years. And she had not had time enough to tell him anything.

Proudly she announced, "Since last year Mikhailik has been a member of the Regional Party Committee." Then, recalling Mikhailik's own words, she began to recount in detail how he had been chosen as a candidate, and how he had been overwhelmingly elected.

She chattered for a long time. Only at the very end did she begin to feel self-conscious and to pronounce each new word with difficulty.

She was intuitive and, as always, sensed her husband's mood. What had happened? She hadn't boasted, and she hadn't said anything wrong.

But Mikhailik had grown increasingly gloomy. Nervously twitching his shoulders, now the right and now the left—oh, how she knew his habits!—he began to pace back and forth across the dining room floor. His eyes were unseeing—that she also knew very well—so hard was he concentrating on something. On what? Abruptly he asked, "Did my father come in through the front door?" "Yes," she answered, perplexed. She then decided the more she told him in detail about Sergey's arrival, the sooner his mood might revert to normal. It must be his father's miserable appearance and the way his head shook that upset him so much. "Oh Mikhailik, Mikhailik," she thought and, with pity for both of them, again began to tell the story of how Sergey Mikhailovich knocked, how without asking she had opened the door. "And immediately, something flashed in my mind and I stared, and I knew. Here's Sergey Mikhailovich!"

Was Mikhailik listening to her? He continued to pace from corner to corner, as before lifting now one shoulder and now the other. Then he stopped in front of his father.

"On the way from the train station did you meet anyone you know?" Instinctively, Sergey Mikhailovich felt compelled to answer in detail. "No one living saw me. What happened, I thought? Has everyone already gone to sleep? Only the Babichevs were up, having tea. I saw them through the window."

Without waiting for the end of the rambling answer, Mikhail again began to pace. The expression on his face was that of a man suffering deeply. He knew that his father and wife were watching him and waiting with growing concern. He also knew that whatever words he was about to say, no matter how carefully chosen, would be loathsome and abominable. But it was impossible to be silent any longer. "In '40, when you were taken," he said, appealing to them both and avoiding their gaze, "In '40, when you were first taken, I immediately proclaimed that I disowned you—and last year, when they elected me to the bureau, Kozyrev asked me twice whether the situation had changed. Both times I said no. I knew, of course, that they couldn't prove anything—the parcels had always been sent from another town and under another name."

"Yes, yes," Liza interrupted happily. "You remember, I even told everyone I had a brother in Kharkov and that I was going to the region to get food and to send him a package." She smiled at Sergey Mikhailovich, as if reminding him of their earlier conversation.

Mikhail listened impatiently. "Of what importance is that now?" he asked as soon as she was silent. "None! Now my father is here!"

Tortured and distressed, he looked at her. She smiled at him uncomprehendingly. Three years of marriage had convinced her that men didn't understand even the simplest things and got upset over nothing.

"But my God, Mikhailik," she assured him, "you can explain! After ten years your old father has come to his son. What can be more natural? And of course they will understand—even your Kozyrev."

Until Liza spoke, Mikhail had been standing at the window. When she said they would understand, even Kozyrev, he turned toward her and curled his lip sarcastically. Several times he stared at his watch and gradually his stricken face became cold and decisive. He narrowed his eyes. "It is impossible for my father to stay here," he said to his wife. Appealing to Sergey Mikhailovich, he said, "You yourself must understand that." With unsteady fingers, he looked at his watch again. "In forty-five minutes, a train will leave for Oreshkino. You must go to Nina. Here is money. I will send more every month."

And Sergey Mikhailovich understood, and knew that he had always understood. Gently, he nodded agreement. Then, seeing five hundred rubles in his son's hand, he said, "Oh, no. I don't need that much." But Mikhail didn't listen. Firmly and awkwardly, he forced the money into his father's pocket. Only Liza, with wide-open eyes, looked at her husband. "But Mikhailik," she reminded him, "you know very well that Nina . . . "

"I know! I know everything!" he interrupted and glared at her so sternly that she stopped in mid-sentence. "You must take my father to the train and you must hurry. You will be late."

5

Only returning from the station did Liza give way to her tears. She walked quickly, almost running, sobbing like a child. She had to see Mikhailik as soon as possible.

About twenty steps away from their house, her husband called to her. He was in his fur coat, hat, and boots. "The train has already left," she said. "I'm not going to the station," he replied. She was so concentrated on her thoughts that she forgot to ask why he was in the street and how he could possibly have left Vasilyok alone. The words tumbled out.

"You know, Mikhail, you know very well that Sergey Mikhailovich can not live with Nina. It was because of him she couldn't find a job here."

"I was at the telephone center. I just spoke to Nina. She will take father to Bebutovo. We have an aunt there."

Liza was still crying and trembling. He took her into his arms.

"Liza, he will be all right. I told Nina not to begrudge him any money and to find him a room with heat. And you will be able to visit him once a month. The city is a small one, quiet and far away. No one knows us there."

And because she continued to tremble, he continued to plead, continued to justify himself. "What could I do? What could I do? There is no other way."

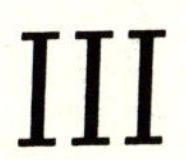

Seven Slashes

"Seven Slashes" was the first story Stonov smuggled from Siberia. It details mercilessly his seven days in the cabinet, while he was held in Lubyanka for interrogation, and should perhaps have been Part One of this edition. But, separated into several envelopes and posted by several people, it is the only story of which a large segment was lost.

The Stonovs surmise that one of Dmitry's allies may have looked inside the letter. Frightened by its theme, he destroyed the contents. It is also possible that whomever opened the envelope saw only the cigarette papers and cared little about what was written on them. In Russia, at the time, good quality cigarette paper had greater value on the black market than powerful literature. Much of this extraordinary account may well have been wrapped around cheap tobacco, only to vanish in smoke.

Psychologically, despite the many times he tried, Stonov could never bring himself to reconstruct the missing portions—only "Day One" and a fragment of "Day Seven" survive. This collection would not be complete without them.

1

OF COURSE IT was a hoax—a cruel, inhuman hoax. But Mironov had already been in interrogation prison for five months, and he knew to what length the investigators would go.

Coming back to the cell, he inhaled his cigarette deeply with the profound pleasure of the deprived. During interrogation, smoking is forbidden.

"What happened?" his cell mates asked eagerly.

Mironov said, "I thought, my friends, that I would never see you more—not today, tomorrow, or the day after. My major was angry and more anxious than ever to find fault. He shouted, stamped his feet, pounded his fist on the table, and even raised his baton as if to beat me. Over and over he would thunder, 'Confess, shithead prostitute! Confess, shithead prostitute!' you know the way they do. Once, sneaking up behind me, he whispered in the voice of death, 'I will put you under the press.' Then he called in another investigator to help—Gavrilyuk. Together they shouted in two voices, beat on the table with two fists.

"Finally Gavrilyuk said, 'We've bothered with him enough. My advice? Just lock him in the cabinet and next time he'll be on his knees, begging to confess. Write the order. I will bring it to the commander for his signature.'

"My major spat upon his hands, as is his habit. Then he reached for a sheet of paper, tore it into four pieces, and took one part. Bending his head to one side, he wrote several sentences in a labored hand. Gavrilyuk grabbed the sheet and left the room. Returning, he tossed it on the table and said, 'It's done. Now I'll call to see if a cabinet is free.' He dialed the prison, listened, then threw down the receiver. 'Busy!' He called again and again and again, no fewer than five times. With each call, he flung down the receiver and said, 'Busy! Busy! Busy!'"

His cell mates considered each other calculatingly. "No fewer than five times?" they asked. "Maybe even more," Mironov responded. "Finally, sick and tired of the telephone, he slammed it down and told me to get the hell back to my cell—they'd make the arrangements later."

"So now," Mironov said wryly, "here I am, back home with you."

Again, his cell mates looked at each other, then they smiled. "Your major was bluffing. They wanted to terrify you, to put a gun to your head." Quickly, Mironov agreed. "Of course they did! I myself guessed that at once."

Yes, Mironov had guessed it himself—though not at once, as he tried to assure his friends. The first time was when Gavrilyuk returned and placed the paper on the table. Mironov was farsighted. Though the distance was great, he had managed to see the commander's signature. It was short and consisted solely of initials. "Gavrilyuk signed that paper himself" flashed through his mind. The thought returned repeatedly: the short calls, the casual manner in which he dialed, and the dramatic way he slammed down the receiver. It was as if they were playing parts in a play. "Oh yes," he repeated, "I guessed it immediately. It was clear they were bluffing."

And yet, on that very evening and on that very night, waking suddenly, Mironov found himself shivering with cold. What if it hadn't been a threat? What if the commander had really agreed to the cabinet? But the evening passed, and the night passed, and the following day and several more, and Mironov still had not been taken.

In the cell, where boredom is the rule and nothing ever happens, the investigator's threats were soon forgotten. When, after five days, Mironov was called, he didn't doubt it was just the usual interrogation. He didn't doubt it as they led him down the long corridor, walking on rubber runners that muted the sound of footsteps. At the end was a counter. He didn't doubt that the overseer would search him and then hand him to the duty guard, who would take him to the major.

But when Mironov came to the counter and looked at it casually, his heart enlarged with sudden pain. On the counter was the quarter piece of paper, signed by the commander.

2

Every convict is assaulted with the same cold panic whenever he's taken from his cell. Mironov was in this panic as well. But now, added to the panic was anger at his fellow prisoners. He had believed them when they said he shouldn't worry. "I told you," he accused them, "I knew. I knew." The duty guard led him into the wire cage. He was alone only for a moment. A young stoop-shouldered lieutenant entered. He was carrying the same piece of paper and was followed by two guards.

The charges on the paper were brief. The stoop-shouldered lieutenant read them perfunctorily: "For provocative behavior during investigation, seven days in the cabinet."

"What behavior? What provocation?" asked Mironov desperately.

"You know better than I do," answered the officer and hurried out. The guards hurried as well. Lifting Mironov by both elbows, they swept him down the steps, down and down past several floors and then, on the last—the lowest—they stopped. The corridor was half-dark. At the end, under a dim bulb, they searched Mironov and told him to take off his clothes. Bewildered, Mironov took off his jacket. "Faster," ordered the guards, "take off everything." His fingers wouldn't obey and opened the buttons awkwardly. "Everything, everything," they hurried him, "leave only your socks and your underwear."

They pushed Mironov thus clad into the cabinet, and then they locked the door.

Mironov took a shuddering breath. "So . . ." he whispered thoughtfully. Looking around, he saw that the box was a rectangle—very high, without windows, and just three feet in every direction. On the ceiling, caught in a metal net, blazed a bright bulb. Into the wall opposite the door a bench had been built.

Perspiring, yet chilled to the bone, Mironov sat. He sensed he was doing something he had never done before; his hands were tucked beneath his buttocks and he was sitting on them for warmth.

Under the stark light he scrutinized himself with a level of attention he could not explain—seeming to see for the first time the fleshy, aging body on which there hung a blue knit shirt and shabby longjohns held together with a single broken button.

Without willing it, he heard the singsong words of a childhood story beating on his brain. "Once upon a time, there was in the world a small boy named Lyovushka. Blue-eyed, with freckles on his nose, he was his parents' only child, looked up to by his comrades, prized by all his acquaintances and prized equally, perhaps, by all the world. There was not a person who met him who did not exclaim, 'Look! Here is Lyovushka!' Everyone was pleased to see him, everyone loved and spoiled him. As a youth, when he became 'Lyova,' everyone still loved and spoiled him. And, almost without a ripple, when he got older and became 'Lev,' he still remained the most capable, the most witty and resourceful, the most admired and unique. Whenever his mother would proudly display his drawings, he'd duck his head and smile diffidently, embarrassed by the lavish praise. But no one doubted for a moment that one day he would become a very important artist and his work would be seen by millions."

Mironov listened to the steady stream of words tattooing in his head. Underneath them he sensed a layer of poison, but still he was touched to tears. Breathing heavily, he stood. Since it was impossible to walk in any direction, he shifted from one foot to the other. Another click sounded in the eye of the door. Mironov sat, and again, though he blocked his ears and shook his head, the words continued to resound.

"Lev Vasilyevich Mironov didn't become an artist. He became an architect, greatly respected and admired. In the whole city there might be only a few who failed to know it was he who had designed and built the theater, the post office, and the magnificent railway depot. Then swiftly and suddenly, in one dark disastrous moment, all that melted away forever. Forever! Vile people roared at him in vile, repellent voices. Who was this miserable puffy man in his blue underwear and striped socks? Lev Vasilyevich Mironov? Nonsense. Nonsense. Lev Vasilyevich Mironov had vanished from the face of the earth forever. In his place, with his hands beneath his buttocks, sat a good-for-nothing convict—no longer called person but prostitute.

Agonized, Mironov cried out, "Stop! No more, no more!" The peeping eye opened sharply. The guard shouted in a loud voice that flattened against the wall, "It is forbidden to speak!" The words with which he answered would be the last Mironov would utter while he was in the cage. Like a little boy caught in mischief, Mironov flushed and said, "I didn't know." Hearing himself, he wondered from where this weak, whining sound of a supplicant had suddenly come—the voice of a slave. Maybe Lev Vasilyevich had not just vanished a moment ago. Maybe he had been lost for a long time. "I won't do it again," he whispered and wanted to weep.

3

Dark green and white paint divided the cabinet into two parts—dark green on the bottom, white on top. Obviously, the cabinet had been neglected for a long time, and the paint was cracked and peeling. It created peculiar silhouettes—a fat man with a cigar in his mouth, a camel with two humps, the thin branch of a leafless birch tree.

With a start, Mironov began to notice scribbles on the wall. Because they were not immediately apparent, it was necessary to search for them—which is probably why they had escaped attention. He could not believe it; they were everywhere—near the bench, around the door, smothering the side walls—brief messages containing only two or three letters followed by a few numbers. What had impelled those who had sat here before to scratch their initials and the dates of their entombment? Mironov remembered the mountains. In the Crimean and Caucasian mountains, there were thousands of triumphant messages left as talismans by travelers who had come from all over—visitors from Moscow and from Leningrad, from Kaluga and Mtsensk, from Kiev and remotest Vladivostok. A man with either paint or knife climbs a mountain merely to carve his name. Why? Is it recklessness, excess energy, or the urge to make himself immortal?

But here it's not the same, not the same at all, Mironov continued to think. A man cannot remain unrecognized for long, even when he's buried in a box. He needs to feel the touch of a friend, to have a comrade or even an acquaintance acknowledge him. "I am here," says the brief message, "I am buried, but I hear and see, I feel and think, so I am alive." Then other voices respond, a whole league of people from whom freedom has been stolen. "We are here, we are with you, you are heard!" Who were these predecessors? His eyes ached from the unrelenting light, the dead silence roared in his ears—or maybe it was merely the sound of blood beating its way to his heart. Mironov realized that his brain demanded exercise, or he would go mad. Looking at the words on the wall, he tried to recreate his companions, those miserable men who had suffered in this box before him.

His eyes were held by one message in particular. The letters were small and spidery, "V. C.," obviously drawn by aged and trembling hands. The old man had forgotten, or merely been too feeble, to draw the date—he had barely scratched in the year. Mironov could picture him. He was a man who had been frightened the whole of his life, with big suffering eyes, a beak nose, and a beard touched with gray. Without realizing it, he had for most of his days been locked in the cell of his own fears. Every night, before closing his eyes, he would cross himself under his greasy blanket and say, "Thank God, another day is done." It would almost seem that arrest had released him from this torture and that now he could devote himself to survival. But no. He begged, scrambled, and crawled before his captors. In the cabinet, silently crying, with a sick heart that suffocated him, still he would plead, "I'm alive. I beg you, please, let me return to my previous fears and exist in my previous pen." And why, permit me to ask you citizen V. C., why?

It was not V. C. who answered. It was the fat man who had been staring at Mironov for a long time from his place on the wall. "And why, permit me to ask you in turn, why from the vast array of all these available signs did you pick the most pitiful and the most insignificant? What drew you to this miserable "V. C."? Does it occur to you that this man, to whom fear is a constant companion, is a man who somehow mirrors you? Is related to your own secret insecurities?" Mironov cut him off sharply. "Let's stop finding fault with each other. We have to spend seven days and nights together. Seven days and nights—that's 168 hours, 10,080 minutes, over 600,000—more than a half million seconds!"

The thought of time amplified to six digits overwhelmed him. In this glaring, airless silence, even the seconds seemed different. Stammering, Mironov began to count, got to ten, and then gave up. The sterile silence assaulted his ears, the walls began to press in on him, and he found himself gasping for breath. He must not go mad! It was essential that he think about something else, anything but time. Yet, despite his efforts, thoughts about time went round and round, like a noose encircling his neck. "I am done," he conceded in defeat and again set his mind to counting seconds. Silently, the signatures on the wall began to flicker before his eyes. He begged them, "Help me. Tell me how one even begins to live through this."

4

There was no *parasha* in the cabinet. Mironov asked to be taken to the toilet. Stepping out in the corridor, he felt unfettered, and it was much easier for him to breathe. But how good it was in the foul-smelling toilet! To him the air seemed full and clean. The sun was rising beyond the open window. Behind the bars there was a lilac sky. And the sounds!—what a symphony of wonderful sounds! Purposefully and melodically, the water splashed into the urinal. How manly it sounded as it traveled through the thick black pipes. Outside in the square, life was asserting itself. Each car spoke in its own way—he could distinguish the sound of tires as they braked and slowed, then slid across the asphalt. In spite of the early hour, the square seemed to explode with activity. The trams, endlessly warning passersby, sounded insistent bells. Even the wind, the autumn wind of early morning, whispered a radiant noise. Standing at the urinal, Mironov could see a sink reflected on a wall around the corner. Realizing it was not visible from the peeping eye, Mironov moved to it quickly and quietly. Sensually, he splashed his face and chest and, still careful to check that he couldn't be seen, cupped water into his hands and hurriedly swallowed it. God! He didn't want to leave! Again, he returned to the toilet and sat. Inhaling deeply until his chest was full, he savored the air. Even more, he reveled in the sounds. It had to be about six in the morning, no less. "After all," he thought, "after all, twelve hours have passed. How many more remain? When I go to the cabinet, I can count there."

But when he returned, the small space gripped him like a vise. Deafened by the silence, his mouth open and gasping for stale air, he stood in the middle of his tomb. Stretching his arms, he tried to extend them to their fullest. It was not possible; the distance was too small. Rage enveloped him and he wanted to stamp his feet against the floor. "No! It's not to be borne. What monster devised this obscenity?" He thought of all the ordinary people who happily made their homes adjacent to this seemingly innocuous place of horror. "All of you decent citizens, raising your children and prattling about truth and justice. How do you dare live without guilt, right next door to this building?" Rage had exhausted him and, still sweating, he lowered himself onto the bench. Rocking from side to side—because sitting had already become awkward—he realized that, until quite recently, he himself had belonged to those good people babbling about honesty and respect for humankind. Huge monoliths like this in the middle of the city had never deterred him from living quietly and immersing himself in his work. Then he meditated on his colleague—the architect who had built or remodeled this building—who didn't rely on guesswork but had used the most up-to-date equipment to estimate the exact cubic feet of air needed for survival. An expert, he came to the conclusion that breathing would be difficult and felt it his duty to inform the authorities of this dangerous condition. "What? Difficult to breathe?" asked his superior. "Perfect! That's exactly what we need! Exactly what is necessary!" The architect simply shrugged his shoulders. He could do no more. He shrugged his shoulders and turned to the next task.

But what about the jail physicians? The whole staff of doctors, nurses, and aides? Mironov turned his thoughts toward them. For two months, an epileptic student had been sitting in the cell. With every day his health deteriorated. His seizures came more often, his falls to the floor bruised his whole body, for long hours he lay in a coma. How many times did the convicts beg that the student be taken to the infirmary? But the doctor, that gray old man, had never considered it necessary even to answer them. And the student had not been alone. There had been the artist who was consumptive. After every interrogation, blood would rush from his throat. The doctor would check his temperature then casually move away. At night, this same clean, perfumed doctor would sit in the circle of his family, and his three-year-old grandson would come to him, babbling words that touched his heart. Filled with love, the old doctor would toss him up in the air and, in tossing, skillfully notice that the boy's legs were a bit bowed. Alarmed, he would say to his daughter, "You know, dear, you should remember to give him the cod-liver oil I gave you so he won't get rickets."

And what could be said about the rest of them—the vast staff of investigators, detectives, secret agents, stenographers, typists, rude and ignorant guards?

Strange, the larger the callous circle of indifferent people grew, the less agitated Mironov became. Of his recent anger no trace now remained. Now, over and over, he turned his attention to the past twelve hours and subtracted them from the frightening figure 168. But now that figure no longer existed. "156 is less!" he consoled himself, "and even that number keeps changing. It diminishes every moment."

So, he went on, what was I thinking about? Ah, yes. People. I won't include Tolstoy, who wouldn't be silent when accused people were hanged even hundreds of kilometers from his home in Yasnaya Polyana. I'm talking about ordinary, so-called decent people—a common country doctor, for instance, who would consider it a duty to raise his voice in the presence of his peers to prevent a violent and unjustified killing. Where are they? Has mankind really degenerated so completely? No. Nothing is that simple. It's more fundamental—and the main point is not to judge. Everyone is guilty. All of humanity—and I among them. But, despite everything, I still believe in God. "Oh, God," he whispered, "we are so intimate, tied together in this place, in these circumstances, I must tell the truth. I must say what I think and feel. I have never believed in a hereafter glittering with gold and diamonds. But I do believe in decency and I believe that evil must disappear." "And love will return to the earth," snickered his memory. "It will," he insisted, "and love will return." They were the banal words of the poet Nadson but somehow, here, stripped of pretense, they spoke to his soul.

And the time passes. And the time passes. This idea kept returning to him and soothed him. At least two more hours had passed. Morning must have come. There were no windows, but he could see the golden fall sun and feel the crisp air that is so easy and joyful to breathe. Why not ask to go to the toilet again? I can sit, rest, and breathe to my heart's content.

He knocked. The eye slid open immediately, as if the guard had been standing there all the time. "Permit me to go to the toilet," Mironov requested. "It is not necessary to take you to the toilet every minute," said the guard. Mironov began to explain, "But you are mistaken . . . " when the eye was slammed shut, and he had no time to finish. "This fortunate man has his own way of counting time. For him, every two hours is just a minute," thought Mironov. "We'll wait. We'll wait."

5

Mironov sat patiently, as if he were a supplicant in a reception room with his hands held submissively in his lap. He sat this way for one hour, perhaps two—even three. It was probably close to dinner time. Surely by now he could visit the toilet. But he continued to postpone the request, as if testing the limits of his own tolerance. It was painful to sit any longer, so he stood and began shifting from one foot to the other. Then he sat again. Then he thought, Now I can ask to be taken to the toilet.

At this point, the peeping eye opened without his asking. In the half-dark slit, the bright eye and mustache of the guard appeared. He was a new one; the previous man had been clean-shaven. The words Mironov heard him say were absolutely insane, considering the time of day. He heard him say, "Lights out." Lights out. "Go to sleep?" He didn't understand. The bright eye of the guard looked pleased, even his splendid mustache seemed to smile.

Mironov decided the mustached one was joking and responded in the same lighthearted way. "Maybe it's not time for lights out, but it's certainly time to go to the toilet."

Even in the lavatory, understanding came slowly. When he finally understood what had happened, he was horrified. He was shocked. He was ready to weep with despair. Behind the bars of the window sat not the morning sky but the evening sky and the city, with the same noises as before. Cars honked. Trams rang, sounding their bells. People murmured in the crowded streets.

Idiot! Ass! He had confused everything, mixed everything up! He had only been sitting a few hours, a few paltry hours—and he had been ready to swear he had been there most of the day and part of the night. Fool! How difficult was it to figure out that he would not have been kept that long without at least a bit of bread or a sip of water. He had understood nothing. Nothing! He was trapped inside an animal's den, where every second was equal to an hour; where all day and all night the eternal bulb would burn with unnatural brilliance—itself trapped in a wire cage. No. He was doomed never to leave this coffin; the stuffiness would suffocate him and, dying, he would still be blinded by the deadly, dazzling light. "Lost!" he moaned. Now he heard, "Lights out." Locking the door of the box, the guard said, "Lights out." Mironov didn't answer. Perspiring profusely, he shifted aimlessly from one foot to the other, repeating the same refrain in his head, "Lost. Forever lost. Forever lost."

Mironov brought himself up sharply. It was crucial that he take control of himself. And at that, some demon lurking inside mocked him, scoffed and ridiculed his stupidity. Lost, forever lost—but he could control himself, couldn't he? The demon shrieked with laughter, doubling over with glee. "Look at him, a fat man in blue underwear with blue longjohns barely covering his bow legs, bathed under the brilliance of an eternal light. Look at him—and what does he want? To take himself in hand!" Mironov steeled his resolve. "I will. I will. I will do it," he swore.

Curling his body with difficulty almost in a fetal position, Mironov lay on the narrow bench and wished himself good night. "Good night, Lyovushka," he said, in an inaudible voice. After saying those words, a man is supposed to turn on his side and feel the lips of a beloved brush the top of his head. The fleeting memory barely touched his consciousness. He ached to sink into oblivion and actually did.

When he awakened, he remembered neither where he was nor what had happened. Standing a hand's length from his face was a pair of boots. Raising his eyes, he saw a stern chin and a splendid mustache lit by the rosy light of the corridor. "It is forbidden to sleep on the floor," said the guard. Still half-asleep, Mironov mumbled "Yes." "You may sleep only on the bench," said the guard. Mironov mumbled "Yes." "If you want, you can put your feet up against the small wall opposite; many people sleep like that." "Yes, yes," said Mironov, struggling to rise.

What he really wanted was to lie with his face turned to the wall, but his bent knees prevented him from assuming that position. Curling up as before, he closed his eyes. Vaguely, he felt there was something unpleasant happening and it was necessary to sleep, to sleep, to sleep as long as possible.

6

The wake-up call brought with it a measure of relief, but the relief was not immediate.

As usual, when one is awakened by command, the desire is always to sleep at least a half hour more. Mironov's body ached. The light was especially bright on his waking eyes, stinging them with pain. Mironov realized he must limber up each morning or his condition would worsen. As he had done the previous night, he began to shift from one foot to the other. It was necessary, too, to check his feet and see if they were swollen—he had heard that happened frequently to convicts in the cabinet—but somehow he was too lazy to bend. Then, remembering how some of his cell mates sometimes exercised in the morning, Mironov forced himself to squat. No, his feet were in order.

And now what? He could count seconds. He could hold up each hand, spread the fingers wide and, as he bent each one over, count the seconds. The thought repulsed him. No, by no means would he ever count again. Once and for all he must force himself to understand that here, under the everlasting electric light, time was distorted. It didn't allow itself to be counted. It was endless.

So, what now? Answering himself, he said, "Really, Lev Vasilyevich, what a nuisance you are to me!" At that moment, the eye slid open and the guard pushed through half the usual ration of bread and one cup of boiled water.

Mironov wasn't hungry that day, nor would he be on those that followed; still—without knowing why—he was overjoyed by the sight of the bread. For several long seconds he lifted it in the palm of one hand, then shifted it to the other. Now he had to divide it into three parts—breakfast, dinner, and supper. Taking his time, he scored it evenly then tore it into three equal pieces. Unwillingly, he forced himself to let them go, placing each on the bench with an equal distance between them.

What had happened? Absolutely nothing. He, Mironov, had been given his earned ration of bread, that was all. So why was he so excited, so overjoyed?

Suddenly, it swept over him. He was sentenced to the box for seven days and nights. During these seven days and nights, he would receive seven daily rations. Bread. The bread could be the measure of his time! One portion had already been received—therefore one day no longer existed. Now it was truly possible to subtract it from the total number—and now he had a new number—not seven but six.

Mironov looked quickly at the eye. It was closed. Decisively, with a burst of speed that was no longer characteristic of him, he rushed to the wall near the bench. There, with his thumbnail, he scratched a line no longer than a match—one slash. "Done!" he exclaimed with exuberance. Incredibly, he was happy. The slash was visible from three feet away. He sat on the bench. By turning his head, he could even see the slash while he was seated. Upon awakening, he would be able to see it instantly. . . .

9

. . . chilled . . . his skin streaked with perspiration.

It was an inexplicable and unfounded premonition of disaster. The disaster was such that it was impossible to think about it without deadly horror sweeping through him in a matter of seconds. He turned abruptly toward the slashes. Shimmering, they shook before his eyes and, in order to calm them, he had to touch each one with his finger. Somehow, he began counting from left to right. Here is today, the last day. Here is yesterday and the day before yesterday. Each slash he counted he covered with his trembling hand, so as not to count it twice. In such a way he came to the seventh—and froze in sudden fear. He tried, but could not say the number. His tongue could only hiss.

He refused to believe it. He refused to believe either his premonition or his eyes. The catastrophe had exploded in just this instant and, only by steeling himself, could he block it from consciousness for one brief moment. Squeezing his eyes shut, he shrank as if he were going to jump. Then, shivering with cold, he peered again at the first slash.

It was not like the rest, it was shorter. It was shorter and slanted. Together with the crack in the wall, the slash made an angle. Did it have any connection with the six others—the ones Mironov had drawn himself? He could find neither words nor thoughts. He could only whisper over and over, "It's too much. It cannot be. It cannot be."

He distinctly remembered that this morning there had been seven slashes. Yesterday there had been six! All this time, every time, he had included the first slash in his count. From where, then, did this doubt suddenly come?

He thought, "First of all, I have to calm down and figure it out," although he knew perfectly well that even to think about being rational was impossible and that both his ability and his will to reason were destroyed. Struggling, he went on, "I remember, I remember. I drew the first slash while I was standing and, I remember, I was in a hurry and very excited." It was as if he were trying to justify himself but knew, at the same time, that he could prove nothing. "Yes, I was in a hurry, I was excited," he continued to repeat, "do you understand? If a man is excited and writes something even while turning around to see if he is being watched, then in such a case . . ." He stopped.

His arguments were unconvincing, even to him. Yes, he had been excited, in a hurry—but what did that have to do with the slash? Something else now cried for attention—had this decapitated slash been drawn by him, Mironov? "Yes or no? Yes or no?" he demanded of himself. Then, with a cold cruelty and a desperation he had never expected, the answer tore from him in agony, *No!*

He knew then with certainty—he could not spend one more day in the cabinet, it was totally impossible; his death was inevitable. He knew then with certainty, I am done. I am doomed.

For the first time Mironov understood that the vortex would suck him up into death with the same energy it had thrown him into life. Irrationally, he rushed toward the slashes, driven to scratch several of them—even a dozen—to mix up the count more completely. Swiftly, he aimed his fingernail at them. Only blind instinct forced him to stop his hand, to tear it away from the wall and to fight for his life.

He pounded on the door. According to his calculation, the mustached guard should now be on duty. "He is responsive, a simple but kind soul," Mironov tried to convince himself. "When he noticed that I had fallen off the bench and was sleeping on the floor, he came into the cell and woke me politely. He suggested I lay on the bench and even remembered to remind me that I could brace my feet against the wall. Despite the fact that he works in an interrogation prison, he is still a responsive and good person. He . . . The door was opened by a young guard Mironov knew from before, when he had been in the prison cell. In order to give more severity to his already stern face, he always frowned, spoke abruptly, and barked orders.

"To toilet," Mironov said loudly, the first words that came to his mind. Before answering, the guard adjusted his tunic, knit his brows, and demanded, "Polite treatment, please." Again, he tugged at his tunic and, still not looking at Mironov said, "You don't know prison rules?"

"It is necessary for me to go to the toilet," repeated Mironov, desperately muffling his voice.

The sunlight crossed the toilet like a slanted column. It was long past noon. Mironov stood at the urinal for a while. What could be expected from this severe youth? Despairing, Mironov returned to the cabinet and tried yet again.

"For the last time I have visited your toilet. Today my term is over."

"No small talk," barked the guard.

No. Nothing could be expected from this one. "No small talk," the guard repeated, rubbing the fold at the bridge of his nose. In truth, with the same severity, he might have said, "Yes. For the last time. Very soon you will be thrown out of the cabinet." Or he might simply have nodded in agreement. But he did nothing; he only shouted and forbade Mironov to speak. Maybe he thought that the convict wanted to confuse the count, to cheat him out of twenty-four hours. He knew perfectly well who should sit in the box, and for how long, though he cut off the conversation. So what was there left to do? Nothing! Nothing!

Mironov removed his undershirt. But he could not bear to look at his body—at the dark nipples, at the ribs beginning to arc from their cage—so he pulled it back on again. Then, stealthily, he crept to the door and put his ear to the cold metal. He had never done that before and he didn't know why he was doing it now. In such a way, leaning against the door, he stood for a long time. His swollen feet grew numb, and he lifted first one then the other. His heart pumped, and it seemed to him that his head knocked against the door with the same rhythm. Finally, he heard footsteps. They were the steps of the mustached overseer. He had miscalculated only slightly. "He will certainly speak to me openly, he will sympathize with me—but I won't ask him directly, I will be devious and he will reveal what I want to know without realizing it."

It was necessary that he knock immediately. He moved from where he was and sat down. Only then, coughing loudly, did he lean over and rap on the door. The mustached man appeared.

"Be kind, citizen overseer," Mironov said, "put me on the list with the investigator for tomorrow."

He pronounced "for tomorrow" clearly and distinctly, so there could be no mistake. What guard would put a convict on the list "for tomorrow" if, in an hour or even less, he were to be released? The mustache blinked understandingly, then took out the folded copy of his daily log from the top of his boot, licked the tip of his pencil, and requested officially: "Last name, first name, patronymic."

Overcome with despair, Mironov was unable to answer. "I have perished," he moaned and slipped into the abyss.

10

Indifference engulfed him. If he could have analyzed that indifference, it would have terrified him much more than his previous fear and the catastrophe which followed.

He sat with his head drooping down, practically between his spread legs. His arms hung lifelessly at his side. On the wall, toward his left, were the seven slashes. It was possible to make them out again, to try to check them again, but he sat as if paralyzed, without moving or even turning his head. The slashes no longer interested him. How could anything possibly interest him now? In his youth he had never been able to face the fact of his death; it had maddened him. Never, even in the years that followed, could he think quietly about his end. But in prison, among strange people on strange beds with straw-filled pillows, the thought of death was never far away. The postmortem, the protocol, the legal papers and finally— in the late night—the body with the nameplate on the ankle rolling inexorably toward the crematorium. While the surrounding city slept, a truck with a crate was rushing down the road. Inside the crate—growing cold, growing stiff—would be his body. The flame, the all-consuming flame, then the ashes—cast into some unknown pit or just tossed into the wind. With great difficulty, struggling against an immobilizing lassitude, he lifted his shirt and looked at his chest.

It was about to become a handful of ashes.

He listened to his thought but was completely unmoved by it. It melted as quickly as it materialized. There was a family he loved, who lived less than a kilometer away from where he was entombed. It was an unattainable place, and he would never see them again. Never. But even that failed to arouse any emotion. Even that failed to terrify him. He wanted only to sit motionless and never move again.

The guards appeared in the cabinet. In the glaring light he saw their polished boots, inhaled the scent of their shoe polish. They could shoot him or hang him; it was all the same. They had brought his clothing. Dimly, he wondered why. They ordered him to put it on. The harsh voices hurt his ears. How difficult it was to dress, to force himself to act. How exhausting to pull on the prison pants, to pull the boots over his bloated legs.

11

Looking as if he had aged twenty years, hardly shifting his swollen feet, he shuffled over the threshold of his cell.

Even his fellow convicts—who had experienced everything—looked at him with fear and grief. But not a single one of them had the courage to approach the bed on which he lay.

Afterword

Based on Conversations with Anna Stonov

ONE SUNNY AFTERNOON, vacationing by the Black Sea, Anna Idlin climbed a mountain and found Dmitry Stonov waiting for her on top of it. Six years older than she, he was a dashing correspondent and a sophisticated Muscovite. At the age of twenty-four, she was in her last year at the University of Kharkov where she had worked her way through college by teaching literacy at night in the railroad school. Though the pay was minimal, working for the railroad provided one advantage—a railroad pass. It is the same pass to which Juravlev refers so wistfully in "In the Freedom"—two trips a year, go wherever you want. Underpaid and often undernourished, Anna had decided to use the pass and give herself one last luxury before graduation—a week by the Black Sea.

It took Dmitry one year to convince her to marry him but, from the moment she did, she became his best friend, confidant, and an unfailing source of strength. A biologist, she taught fourteen hours a day at three different schools, helping to support the family all the while Stonov wrote and all the time he was in prison.

Their son Leonid was born in 1931. Ten years later, Anna's sister Bella, who had remained in Kharkov when Anna had married Dmitry, was shot by the Germans because she was Jewish. She had married a gentile, however, who was lost in the war. Their orphaned baby had been taken in by her paternal grandparents, but they were in constant fear not only for the child's life but also for their own—should someone report them for harboring a Jew. The Germans retreated in 1943 (the retreat to which Liza refers in "The Semyonovs"). In 1944 Anna heard that one of her friends—a talented pianist named Elizabeth Loyter—had been booked to play a concert in Kharkov. Anna asked her to try to find Yelena, which she did. A tiny, frightened four-year-old, she was dressed in rags and covered with lice. Elizabeth took her back to the hotel, fumigated her thoroughly, found her clothing, and carried her back to Moscow where the Stonovs adopted her.

Yelena was not the only person to benefit from the open arms of the Stonovs. It was said that Anna singlehandedly nourished most of modern Russian literature—since the Stonov apartment was always open to writer friends whom she felt a compulsion to feed. She was even teased by her family because once, after the family applied for emigration, the apartment was guarded by two members of the militia who stood outside their door for most of the day. Anna finally invited them in for supper because she felt sorry for them. It should be recorded that they refused her invitation.

It was to this apartment that Yanis came—the woodworker-farmer in "After the Death." He did not die in camp; rather he was released two months before Stalin's death and visited the family on his way back to Riga. It was Yanis who described to Dmitry the horrors of the Soviet invasion and the deportation of people there. Stonov likened the ravages against the weak on the train to the ravages perpetrated in prison against the dead. Yanis was able, incidentally, to report that Anna's novel method of smuggling money to Dmitry had been successful. Although it was possible to send funds through the post office to prisoners in Siberia, there was no guarantee they would ever be delivered. As Stonov has Liza describe in "The Semyonovs," Anna would send Dmitry small boxes of sugar cubes—concealing a slim bill or letter under one or two layers. Yanis was not the man, however, who said the Soviets had lengthened his life by giving him twenty-five years, when he was sixty-five. That man, whom Dmitry met at the Kacha labor camp described in "Single Combat," was named Fishman.

During the twenties and thirties—after Lenin's death in 1924 but before Stalin became supreme dictator—several hundred thousand Russian emigrés returned to the Soviet Union filled with idealism and lured by the promise of real socialism. Dmitry met those who joined the Union of Writers. With few exceptions, they would all later be arrested and accused of espionage. Stalin feared that they, having been raised in a democracy, had no compunctions about openly criticizing what was obviously a failing system, and he wanted no reports sent to the West. In truth, it was the foreigners who were the first to recognize that Stalin represented the death of the dream, and they were a threat to him—as were those returning soldiers who innocently praised German cows or Dutch tiles or American planes. They, too, found themselves imprisoned, as are several of the convicts in "The Correct Man." Dmitry met many of these former idealists in camp—such as the doctor in "The Jewish Melody" and Voronov in "In the Late Hour"—and their plight haunted him. It was during this same period (1937-38) that Stalin also arrested and killed most of the top-level officers in the Red Army for fear they would unite against him. One of them—an intellectual and a violinist named Marshal Mikhail Tukhachevsky—was a rabid Communist and very capable. Hitler managed to neutralize him by duping Beneš, the president of Czechoslovakia. He had information leaked to Beneš that Tukhachevsky was a German informant. Beneš, a friend of Stalin, notified him, and Tukhachevsky was shot. The charge, of course, was false. Stalin's frenzied purge soon left the country without military leaders but, one month after war against Germany was declared in July 1941, some who were still alive were released and sent to the front to run the campaign.

There was a real Chinese man in Dmitry's interrogation prison. Rather than supply a translator, the investigators subjected him to sleeplessness. Sleep-deprivation was one of the most effective tools of the KGB because, within ten to fourteen days, the victim would go mad. The KGB also utilized psychological warfare. Although they knew perfectly well who they were coming for in the middle of the night, the guards would wake everyone and subject them to terror, as they did before taking Sooee away for further questioning. Stonov describes this in excruciating detail in "How We Return Home." Dmitry was not only touched by Sooee's tragic plight but also saw something larger in him. He saw him as a symbol of the Russian people themselves—a whole nation of victims who were unable to understand their condition and who were inarticulate in the face of oppression.

Until the day she left for America at the age of eighty-six, Anna Stonov served as chairwoman of the Board of Wives of the Union of Writers—five hundred women for whom she was counselor and advisor. It was a job she held for fifty years. One of the women who became a good friend was an artist, Eva Pavlovna Rosengolts. It was against Eva's brother—Arkady Rosengolts, the people's commissar of foreign trade—that a famous case had been brought in 1937. Although careful examination of security provisions proved that no such activity could possibly have taken place, he was accused of having put glass in the flour produced by a particular mill. Rosengolts was sentenced to a long term in prison that was the equivalent of death. Stonov heard more about Rosengolts in camp, from convicts who had been there a long time, and knew he had been shot and executed. The bizarre aspect of the whole affair intrigued the writer who visited a flour mill and did research there before finishing "The Flour and the Glass." Rosengolts was survived by two daughters. One of them married the son of Enver Hoxha, the Communist leader of Albania, and moved to that country, where she gave birth to her children—and still lives.

Prior to the Revolution, the Tsar and the Russian Othodox Church had been one. Immediately after the Tsar's overthrow, the Communists moved to suppress religious influence. Priests were arrested, and most churches were either turned into storage places or leveled. Although the concept of religion as "the opiate of the masses" became a basic tenet of communism, many kept their faith, even if they could not acknowledge it openly. It was only in 1941 that the church was granted a brief respite. Stalin, who had fears about winning the war against Germany, felt he needed the church in order to flame a feeling of patriotism that would inspire and motivate men in uniform to fight against the Nazis. In return for this concession, the church agreed to turn over to the state most of the money collected at services. This agreement was also the background against which many imprisoned in Siberia for religious reasons were allowed to live, even though they had been sentenced to hard labor. It was, ostensibly, the reason that a fanatic like Kropnik in "Single Combat" was not killed by camp command.

The ruthless shrewdness that typified every moment of Stalin's reign was never more poignantly depicted than in the character of Igor Shevelev in "Vasily Vasilyevich." Whenever Stalin arrested and executed a man who had children, the names of his offspring were kept on file. Certain that they would be in sympathy with the dead parent and thus someday be an enemy of Stalin, most were arrested on reaching majority and sent to Siberia. One of these was an eighteen-year-old college student with whom Dmitry shared a cell, Vladimir Magaziner. Dmitry took him under his wing and tried to care for him. After Stalin's death, when both had been released, Vladimir not only visited the Stonovs frequently but also met his first wife through them. Magaziner became a noted engineer and now lives in Israel.

Anna remembers vividly how their lives changed after Dmitry's arrest. Whereas before their door was always open and the house was always full, they suddenly became pariahs. One day she ran into an old friend in the street—Natasha Bianky, the wife of the novelist Aleksandr Pis'menny. Natasha said, "Don't be insulted, Anna, if we don't come to see you. We can't. The KGB has already called and asked about our relationship with you." Although "The Correct Man" is a sardonic depiction of a society gone mad, it was stimulated by one of Anna's cousins, a colonel in the army. Anna recalls, "Just prior to Dmitry's arrest, he had visited us, as he used to do quite often, and accidentally left his military cap. After Dmitry was taken away, he had to retrieve it. He had his wife call and request that we bring the cap out to them on the street because they felt it was dangerous to step into the apartment."

Mysticism, along with religion, was forbidden by the government since it contradicted Soviet ideology. Like all intellectuals of his generation, Dmitry despised the very thought of "fortune-telling." Prison opened Stonov's mind to a wide variety of things he had never before considered. Anna suspects it is not unlikely that the character of the acerbic Aleksey Vasilyevich in "The Prophet" was really based on Dmitry himself.

After the war, the divorce rate rose so alarmingly that Stalin was disturbed. He felt it reflected badly on the image he wanted to create of the perfect life under the Revolution. To make a divorce more difficult to obtain, it became mandatory to place a prominent divorce notice in the newspaper. Gradually, these notices began to serve another purpose. They served as introduction to someone who might provide a better place to live. Nor was it unusual for well-educated people like Klava in "The Letter" to correspond with a prisoner. As she writes in the story, "By that time we already knew that even completely innocent people could be trapped."

During the three hundred years of their rule, the Romanovs executed two hundred and fifty men for political reasons. Since only the nobility were allowed to govern and their defection was rare, that small number of executions is understandable. But in less than seventy years, from the Revolution to Perestroika, nearly seventy million people were executed or died in labor camps under Communist rule. The tragedy was that only a few of the so-called political prisoners were there for actual dissent. The vast majority had been imprisoned by virtue of secret and usually false testimony. An occupant in a communal apartment who simply wanted more space could accuse his neighbor anonymously to the KGB. Anna notes, "It was recognized that Russia's lack of leadership in the scientific field was partly due to juniors who insinuated charges against respected and responsible seniors, leaving a vacuum of knowledge and experience that lasted for decades." But it was not only in regard to apartments and leadership positions where envy and greed could lead to disaster. Although a theory that explains Raoul Wallenberg's disappearance was accepted in Russia as perfectly reasonable, it seemed so bizarre to the West that it was immediately discounted. It is now gaining some credibility. Certainly as late as 1989, when the Stonovs spoke to Wallenberg's brother in Moscow, the matter was being taken seriously. It is said thatWallenberg was kidnapped in 1944 and kept hidden in Siberia simply because Brezhnev—who was then the political commissar in Hungary—had wanted his car.

Brezhnev, at that time forty-years old and stationed in Budapest, had a passion for automobiles. Wallenberg's mission of rescuing Jews from the Holocaust was no secret, and few Russians cared. Certainly, his activities were easily traced, since he was always driven around Budapest in his private car—a large, white, very expensive European model. Brezhnev is said to have wanted the car desperately and to have made Wallenberg several offers. When, one day, Brezhnev seriously tried to convince Wallenberg to trade his car for Brezhnev's fancy jeep, Wallenberg laughed at him. Shortly afterwards, he disappeared. But Wallenberg did not disappear alone. Not only did his driver vanish with him but his car disappeared as well. Witnesses, who swore initially that they saw the car in Brezhnev's garage, later refused to come forward. Brezhnev's rapid rise in the Politburo, plus his exceptionally close ties to the KGB, would certainly explain why—despite the fact that Wallenberg's detainment in Russia has been widely documented—no record of him exists anywhere.

Stalin's death in March 1953 energized Stonov. Like the narrator of "The Murderers," he began to write an unending series of appeals for reconsideration of his case. Fearful that his efforts alone would not be significant, Anna and Leonid were among the first to organize their own campaign. They started by recruiting a committee of prominent writers to work for his release. Only four of eleven people asked had the courage to agree. In the meantime, they wrote dozens of letters every week to every member of the Politburo—including Molotov, Malenkov, Khrushchev, and Kaganovich. It was their great good fortune that Molotov happened to read one of their letters when it became politic to demonstrate new liberalism to the West. Molotov sent the letter to Roman Rudenko, the Soviet equivalent of attorney general. Rudenko waited three months, but finally forwarded a request to the Supreme Soviet asking that the sentence be revoked. It was not until the end of 1953 that the Supreme Soviet reconsidered Dmitry's sentence, but that did not result in his release. It meant only that his case would be sent back to the KGB for reinvestigation. The KGB immediately asked that Anna come back before them. Knowing they would again try to convince her that the sentence had been justified and that she should still renounce her husband, she was loathe to return. Despite all the pressure exerted on her to divorce Dmitry when he was arrested and taken to Lubyanka—scores of wives in her position did so—she never deserted him. Later Dmitry told her of the many prisoners whose wives had done that and of their despair in camp and the loss of their will to live. It is Juravlev's unspoken fear in "In the Freedom."

When Dmitry was brought back to Lubyanka in 1954 for reinvestigation of his case, he shared a cell with a famous economist named

Moissey Markovich Gindin. Gindin had been imprisoned for seventeen years. His wife Sofia was fifteen years younger than he and about forty years old at the time. Anna used to see her in Lubyanka when she brought food for Dmitry. (Contrary to the policy in 1949, the jail administration now permitted relatives to bring in food.) Although each of them made a practice of speaking to no one in the prison's reception area, Sofia was so beautiful and seemed so intelligent that Anna once decided to wait for her outside the building and find out who she was. Her story was a sad one. Gindin had been arrested when she was twenty-three and their daughter was only one. After ten hard years as a single woman and mother, she decided to remarry—convinced that her former husband would never return. And even if he had survived until his release, he would be exiled from Moscow forever, and she knew she would not want to live elsewhere. It is important to understand that life in Moscow was infinitely superior to that in small provincial cities, let alone in remote villages.

When Stalin died and Gindin was returned to Lubyanka for reconsideration of his case, Sofia immediately asked her second husband to leave. They never saw each other after that. In the meantime, she was distraught. She was afraid that Gindin would learn about what she referred to as "her betrayal" and be unable to forgive her. The economist, of course, had heard about her remarriage but never reproached her. "In a way," Anna observes, "it was a happy story because many of the wives turned away from their imprisoned husbands forever. Later, if the husbands survived, they led a miserable life. They were worn out, sick, and exhausted—with no place to live, no place to work, with no civil rights, and no legal protection."

Returned to Moscow via transfer prisons, Dmitry Stonov was locked up in Lubyanka from 4 July to 20 August 1954, while all previous witnesses against him were called back to retestify. All but one recanted their previous testimony and said they had been forced to perjure themselves out of fear. Only one refused to recant and that was Antonina Shapovalova, clearly the Tonya of "How We Return Home."

Dmitry Stonov was finally released on 20 August—seventeen months after the campaign for his freedom began. Because the Stonovs were among the first few aggressively to pursue release, it was almost two years sooner than other prisoners whose families had not taken early action. Eventually, the tide became so overwhelming that prisoners were no longer brought to Moscow for retrial. Instead, special commissions were formed and sent throughout the country, and cases were heard in camp. Only at the end of 1955 and the beginning of 1956 did most political prisoners begin to return home.

When Dmitry rejoined his family, he returned to the same luxurious three-room apartment he had left in 1949. Other prisoners were not so lucky. In "The Semyonovs" Sergey Mikhailovich cannot believe the family's good fortune in having been able to keep their house until he learns that his son has renounced him. It was a common practice. Hundreds of ads were seen in the newspapers and heard over the radio every day, affirming such repudiations. But Anna had always resisted pressure to divorce Dmitry and no one in the family ever considered turning against him. How, then, had they managed to save their choice apartment in the House of Writers—an apartment that even included a phone? Once again, the Stonovs found themselves engaged in a landmark effort.

It was the practice of the KGB to seal off any space vacated by a convicted person and, usually, to reward one of their spies with it. "Dmitry was arrested at 1:00 A.M. The KGB searched our apartment until the following noon. They made a long inventory of his belongings, which we still have. Then they wanted to lock and seal two of the three rooms, leaving only one for the three of us. I began to beg them not to seal the children's room. Leonid was eighteen at that time, practically an adult, and Yelena was nine. It was not good for them to share sleeping space. The officer screamed at me, 'I'll lock it out of spite!' I stopped asking and said, 'Do what you want.' I don't know what influenced him but he locked only Dmitry's study." It was at this time that an old acquaintance—a lawyer named Semyon Zaslavsky—came to their aid.

Before the Revolution, Zaslavsky had owned his own lavish eight-room apartment. Afterwards, the apartment was expropriated, and he was allowed to keep only two rooms. All the others were assigned to different people, one of whom was Dmitry Stonov. Stonov was an intellectual, and thus acceptable to Zaslavsky. In addition, on two occasions Stonov had helped his friend hide valuables from the authorities. Now Zaslavsky advised the Stonovs to fight the KGB. The mere thought was terrifying, but the old lawyer kept up the pressure.

What the KGB was doing, he told them, was illegal, and they would never show up in court to defend it. "If you go to court," he advised, "you'll win." The Stonovs decided to proceed—primarily because Anna insisted that Dmitry would someday return and not be able to write were his study taken over. Theirs was the first case of its kind ever brought, and they won it. As the canny pre-Revolutionary lawyer had predicted, the KGB never appeared. When word of their victory got out, so many people brought suits that, within two years, the law was changed—making the KGB, the Defense, the Interior, and the Foreign Affairs Ministries exempt.

"Seven Slashes," of course, is autobiographical and totally authentic. When Dmitry returned from the labor camps, he told his family in detail about Lubyanka and the tortures and humiliations endured there—about the brutal investigators who wrung out "avowals of guilt" by different and very effective tortures that only few people could endure.

The cabinet had been one of them. It was a tall box, no more than three feet square, and so precluded the occupant from ever stretching out. The cabinet reserved for Dmitry was not in Lubyanka, however, but in the Sukhanovka Prison—a terrible special-punishment jail near Moscow. Dmitry could never bring himself to reconstruct those parts of "Seven Slashes" that were lost in the mail. Anna herself so empathized with his pain that, to this day, she refuses to read the story.

Kathryn Darrell
Chicago, Illinois
Summer 1995

Dmitry Stonov, 1917, year of the Bolshevik Revolution.

Dmitry Stonov, WWII, 1943, photographed on the Soviet/German front.

House of Writers, 17 Lavrushinsky Street, Moscow, where Dmitry lived with his family from 1937 until his death in 1962—excluding two years on the front and five and one-half years in prison.

СОЮЗ
СОВЕТСКИХ
ПИСАТЕЛЕЙ
СССР

Фотографическая карточка и личная подпись члена ССП СССР.

т. Стонова

СОЮЗ СОВЕТСКИХ ПИСАТЕЛЕЙ СССР

ЧЛЕНСКИЙ БИЛЕТ № 662

Тов. Стонов Д. М.
состоит членом союза советских писателей Московской организации.
Время вступл. в ССП 1/VI 193 г.
Председатель правления ССП СССР
Секретарь правления

Certificate, Union of Soviet Writers: co-signed by its Chairman, Russian writer Maxim Gorky and its Secretary, Stalin's emissary, Alexander Scherbakov, 1934.

Dmitry Stonov, and his wife Anna, at home in his study, March 1949, one week before his arrest.

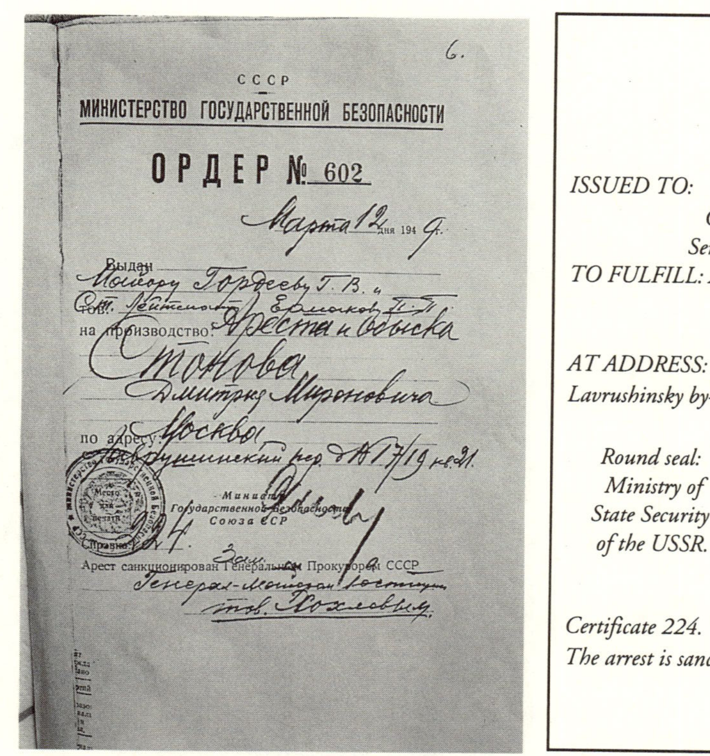
СССР

МИНИСТЕРСТВО ГОСУДАРСТВЕННОЙ БЕЗОПАСНОСТИ

ОРДЕР № 602

Марта 12 дня 1949 г.

Выдан Майору Гордееву Г.В. и
тов. Ст. Лейтенанту Ермакову П.П.
на производство Ареста и обыска
Стонова
Дмитрия Мироновича
по адресу: Москва
Лаврушинский пер. д. № 17/19 кв. 21

Справка:

Арест санкционирован Генеральным Прокурором СССР

USSR.
Ministry of State Security.
WRIT no. 602.
March 12 day, 1949 yr.

ISSUED TO:
Comrade Major Gordeev, G.B.
Senior Lieutenant Yermakov, P.P.

TO FULFILL: Arrest and Search
STONOV
Dmitry Mironovich

AT ADDRESS: Moscow,
Lavrushinsky by-street, House Number 17/19, Apt 21

Round seal:
Ministry of
State Security
of the USSR.

Minister
State Security
USSR
V. Abbakumov (signature)

Certificate 224.
The arrest is sanctioned by Vice-General procurator of USSR
General Major of Justice
Comrade Khoklov.

Writ for arrest, 1949, and English translation.

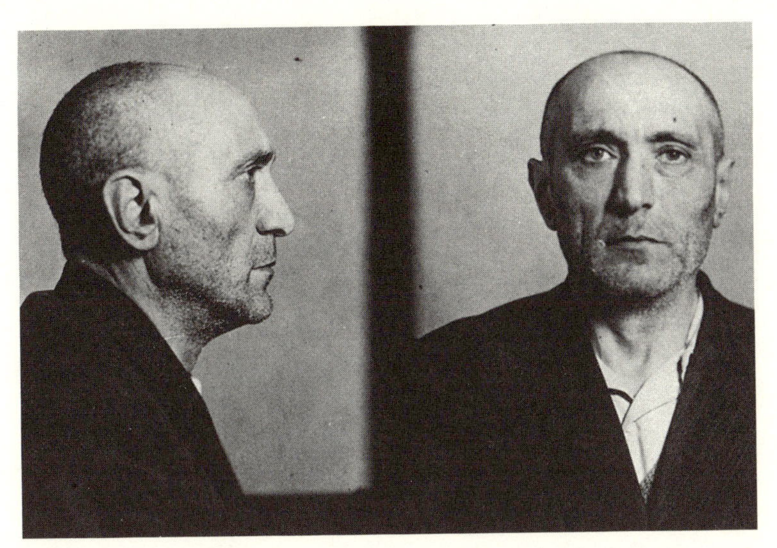

Dmitry Stonov in the Ministry of State Security jail, on Lubyanka Square in downtown Moscow, March 1949, days after his arrest.

The building on Lubyanka Square was ostensibly only the headquarters for the Ministry of State Security. But inside, there was an enormous interrogation jail, the setting for "Seven Slashes." A high wall on the roof concealed prisoners who, when permitted, could take one twenty-minute walk per day.

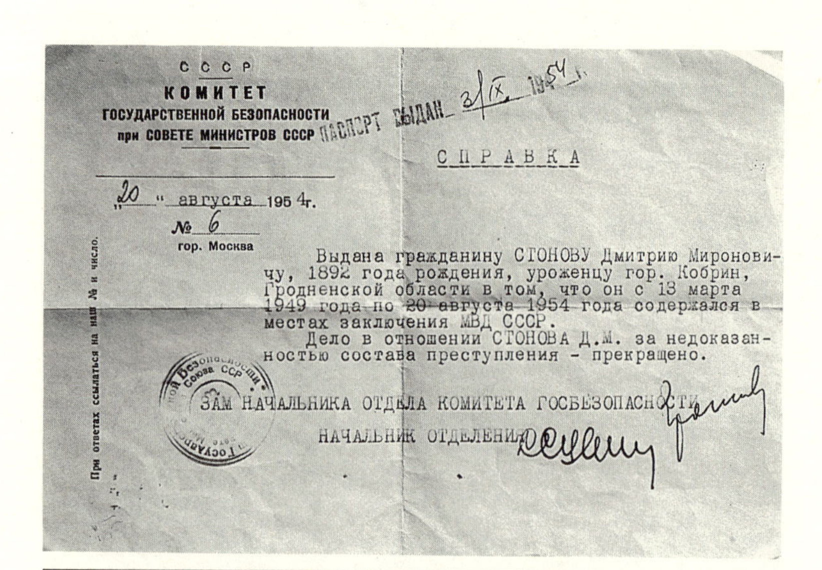

СССР
КОМИТЕТ
ГОСУДАРСТВЕННОЙ БЕЗОПАСНОСТИ
при СОВЕТЕ МИНИСТРОВ СССР

ПАСПОРТ ВЫДАН 3/IX. 1954 г.

„20" августа 1954г.
№ 6
гор. Москва

СПРАВКА

Выдана гражданину СТОНОВУ Дмитрию Мироновичу, 1892 года рождения, уроженцу гор. Кобрин, Гродненской области в том, что он с 13 марта 1949 года по 20 августа 1954 года содержался в местах заключения МВД СССР.

Дело в отношении СТОНОВА Д.М. за недоказанностью состава преступления - прекращено.

ЗАМ НАЧАЛЬНИКА ОТДЕЛА КОМИТЕТА ГОСБЕЗОПАСНОСТИ

НАЧАЛЬНИК ОТДЕЛЕНИЯ

При ответах ссылаться на наш № и число.

USSR
COMMITTEE
STATE SECURITY under COUNCIL OF MINISTERS USSR,

20 August, 1954 yr.
No. 6
City Moscow.

Issued to citizen STONOV Dmitry Mironovich, 1892 year of birth, born in the city of Kobrin of Grodno Region, that he as of 12 March 1949 year to 20 August 1954 year was kept in places of detention of Ministry of Internal Affairs USSR.

The case in reference to Stonov D.M. for absence of any proof of the commission of a crime—is discontinued.

Round Seal: Committee of State Security and Council of Ministers of USSR

VICE COMMANDER OF THE DEPARTMENT OF THE COMMITTEE OF STATE SECURITY
COMMANDER OF THE UNIT (Signatures)

Cerificate of release and English translation: Stonov's date of birth was actually 1898; his parents had falsified it as 1892, so he could escape serving in the Tsar's army.

Dmitry and Anna Stonov with their son Leonid in Moscow, August 1954, one week after Dmitry's release.

Yelena Stonov Krichevsky, 1970. Born 1940. Adopted 1944 by the Stonovs. Her mother, Anna's sister, was shot by Germans in Kharkov because she was Jewish, and her gentile father perished in a Nazi prison camp. Yelena died in Israel on May 3, 1995.

Dmitry Stonov's grave in Moscow's Vvendensky cemetery. The stone, designed by the now famous sculptor Yuriy Chernov, features a bas-relief of Dmitry's profile with the author's distinctive signature beneath.

Stonov Chronology

1898	Born 8 January in Bezdezh, Byelorussia
1905	Witnesses arrests of *muzhiks* by Tsarist regime
1908-1912	Attends commercial college in Brest Litovsk
1912-13	Moves to Lodz; works in weaving factory
1914	Spends the year wandering
1917	Becomes a Bolshevik
1918-20	Fights in the Red Army in the Civil War
1920	After war, moves to Poltava; becomes a newspaper correspondent; founds magazine *Raduga*
1921	Quits Communist party; leaves Poltava for Moscow; works as correspondent for several newspapers, including *Izvestia*
1925	Publishes first book, a collection of short stories—*The Fever; By His Own Hand* quickly follows
1927-38	Publishes *Hundreds of Thousands* (1927), *People and Things* (1928), *The Raskin Family* (1929), *Stories about Altay* (1930), *The Blue Bone* (1932), *Out of the Circle* 1936), and *Esterka* (1938); contributes regularly to Maxim Gorky's magazine *Nashi Dostizhenia*
1942-44	Drafted into army; fights on the Soviet/German front
1944	Demobilized because of injury; in Moscow, works at Informburo, Radio Committee, and Literature Institute
1947	Publishes *Early Morning*
1949	On 13 March arrested and imprisoned for several months in Lubyanka; spends seven days in "the cabinet"; in September, tried in absentia and sentenced to ten years in a Siberian prison camp
1949-50	Sent to prison camp for scientists and engineers in Krasnoyarsky; begins to write "In the Past Night" on cigarette papers
1950	transferred to labor camp near the city of Krasnoyarsk in Krasnoyarsky Kray; meets Victor Kagan and develops life-long friendship
1953-54	In March 1953 Stonov family tries to get his case reconsidered; on 20 August 1954 Stonov is released
1955	Begins travels to Byelorussia, Lithuania, and the western Ukraine
1959	Publishes *Teklya and Her Friends;* writes *City of Our Fathers* and *Stories* (published posthumously)
1962	On 29 December dies of heart attack

Notes

Foreword

p. vi: **KGB:** the Soviet secret police, established in 1917 originally as the Cheka; in 1922 it was renamed the OGPU or the GPU (united department of political police); the GPU was abolished in 1934 and absorbed by the People's Commissariat (later Ministry) of Internal Affairs, or the NKVD (later the MVD); The MVD was responsible for the detection of subversive elements, supervision of prison and labor camps, and "reeducation" of political offenders; more recently, it has been called the MGB and finally the KGB, the Committee for State Security.

Muzhiks: Russian for peasants; *kulaks* were prosperous or even wealthy peasant farmers, who sometimes used the labor of the poor peasants. It was against the *kulaks,* who strongly opposed the collectivization of agriculture, that the communists directed their venom.

p. vii: **"The year 1905 was one that flashed by . . .":** refers to the December 1905 Revolution, a series of mutinies and strikes brought about largely because of the losses Russia was incurring the Russo-Japanese War, and resulting in short-lived winning of some civil rights and the establishment of the Duma, or Parliament.

Civil War (1918-20) broke out in Russia after the Bolshevik Revolution in October 1917, which overthrew the Provisional government of Aleksandr Kerensky. Two main factions were involved: the Communist Red Army and the opposition White Army or White Guards. By 1920 the Communists defeated the Whites and consolidated power.

Tolstoy, Lev Nikolayevich, (1828-1910) is one of the greatest Russian novelists, philosophers, and mystics famous for such works as *Anna Karenina, War and Peace,* among many others.

p. viii: **"In 1921, he . . . changed his name":** It was fashionable at that time for writers to take pseudonyms reflecting their sympathy and concern for the poor Russian people. Most pseudonyms had sad connotations; e.g., Gorky, bitter; Bedny, poor; Golodny, hunger; etc. The name Stonov adopted is taken from the Russian word *ston,* or moan.

Maxim Gorky (pseudonym of Aleksey Maximovich Pyeshkov, 1868-1936) was a prominent Russian writer of short stories, novels, and plays. His writings reflects his Marxist devotion to social realist style and subject matter—society's outcasts. Probably best known in this country for his play *The Lower Depths*.

Union of Writers: founded in 1934 under the direct auspices of the Communist party. Members had to accept and promise to promote communism. Stalin frequently used writers to help in education and propaganda.

Bulgakov, Mikhail Afanasyevich, (1891-1940): a Soviet writer born in Kiev. He wrote several plays, novels and short stories, including *The Master and Margarita* (1938). When Soviet officials determined that a number of his works were too outspoken, they withdrew them and did not lift the ban until the sixties.

p. ix: **Informburo** was the information agency of the Soviet Union.

massive arrests: Members of the Jewish Socialist Bund and Zionists were targeted early by Bolsheviks. Under Stalin, quotas were set for Jewish admissions into universities and the workplace; members of the Jewish Antifascist Committee, who had distributed anti-Fascist propaganda during WWII, were arrested in 1948-49; and in 1953, a "doctor's plot" was supposedly uncovered and Jewish doctors were charged with conspiring to kill army, party, and government leaders by using incorrect medical procedures—which led to the widespread dismissal of Jewish doctors.

Abakumov, Victor S., formerly the Minister for State Security under Stalin, was executed in 1954.

p. x: **Siberian prison camp:** Under Stalin, the major NKVD camps were in the northern European part of Russia (Arkhangelsk, Vorkuta, Komi); the Ural; Siberia (especially Krasoyarsky Kray); Russian Far East (Yakutia, Kolyma); and Kazakhstan (Karaganda, Akmolinsk). Sixty or seventy million perished in Stalin's camps.

Krasnoyarsky Kray is located in the Central Siberian plateau, extending across the Siberian steppe, forest, and tundra to the Arctic Ocean—directly east of the Yenisey River, stretching from the Taymyr Peninsula south to the Tuva Republic. Krasnoyarsk is the capital of Krasnoyarsky Kray.

p. xi: **When completed, the manuscript:** Throughout his life, Stonov struggled with the order of the stories in "In the Past Night," arranging them and rearranging them over and over. Until the day he died, he was never satisfied with it. The translators, too, worked on the sequence constantly. It is their fervent hope that, in the light of history—having divided the stories into those of detainment and those of supposed freedom—they have now achieved something close to what Stonov sought.

p. xii: **Zoshchenko,** Mikhail (1895-1958): a leading prose satirist during the twenties and thirties. Anna **Akhmatova** (1889-1966) was one of the outstanding Russian poets of the twentieth-century. In 1946, the two were attacked and their work was banned by special edict of the Central Committee of the Communist party—the ban was in effect many years after Stalin's death.

p. xiii: **Howard Fast** (1914-): the two books to which Stonov is referring are *The Passion of Sacco and Vanzetti: A New England Legend* (1953), and *The Naked God: The Writer and the Communist Party* (1957).

p. xiv: **Chekhov,** Anton Pavlovich (1860-1904): considered one of the most prominent Russian playwrights and short story writers; known for his psychological insight into character and his subtlety of style.

Bunin, Ivan Alekseyevich (1870-1953): an important Russian poet and novelist who was noted mainly for his prose writings; he was the first Russian to win the Nobel Prize in Literature (1933).

Nagibin, Yury Markovich (1920-94): a prolific short story writer born in Moscow. Besides his patriotic war stories, Nagibin authored a number of works in the more personal Chekhovian tradition, focusing on the subtleties of human interaction rather than action or plot.

"After the Death"

p. 3: ***Kolkhoz:*** Stalin's collectivization efforts called for converting all independently owned farmland either into collective farms *(kolkhoz)* or state-owned farms *(sovkhoz).*

p. 4: **"That was not how it was in '44":** The Soviet Union annexed Estonia, Latvia, and Lithuania in 1940 under the agreement with Hitler. In June 1941, a week before the beginning of Soviet-German War, the Soviets had forcibly deported thousands of the Baltic people to Siberia. Later, in June 1941, German troops occupied the Baltic states. In 1944, the Soviets were able to oust the Nazis, occupying the Baltic states themselves and soon initiating the second massive deportation of the native population to prison camps.

p. 8: **October Revolution** refers to the Bolshevik Revolution of October 1917, not the earlier democratic revolution of February of that same year.

May Day was established in 1889 by the Second Socialist International as a holiday for radical labor; under the Bolsheviks, it became a very important day in the Soviet Union.

p. 9: **capo Kazashvili:** After the Bolshevik Revolution in October 1917, titles of persons were no longer capitalized in an attempt to abolish ranks—hence, capo Kazashvili.

counterrevolutionaries indicates, in this story, persons dedicated to overthrowing the Bolsheviks.

"The Jewish Melody"

p. 17: **Pogroms** were organized massacres of Jews in Russia. They were carried out under both the Tsars and Communists during the Civil War.

p. 18: **the first Five-Year Plan** was Stalin's plan for industrialization and collectivization adopted in 1928, with the main objective of industrialization the USSR. Subsequent Five-Year plans became a regular feature of Soviet economic planning.

"The Flour and the Glass"

p. 40: **Yezhov,** Nikolay I. (1895-1939): the infamous head of the NKVD (Ministry of Internal Affairs) from 1936 to 1938 who devised particularly sadistic methods in order to further Stalin's program of "The Great Terror." In 1939 he himself was shot in the basement of Lubyanka. In December 1938 he was replaced by Beria as People's Commissar for Internal Affairs and the following April he was arrested. His followers in the NKVD had mostly been purged by the end of 1938. Of course, the new people's commissar that replaced him was Lavrenty Beria, as bad as Yezhov.

p. 41: ***Obkom*** refers to the regional committees of the Communist party. **patronymic** is a name derived from the first name of one's father, part of the usual Russian system of address.

"How We Return Home"

p. 53: **"Listen to him. It sounds as though he's trying to sell everyone on going to prison":** The image of the camps conveyed by the narrator in this passage is identical to the image the Soviets successfully conveyed to the West during the thirties and forties. Anna Louise Strong, lauded in the thirties for her books and insight into the Bolshevik world, observed that "The labor camps have won a high reputation throughout the Soviet Union as places where tens of thousands of men have been reclaimed. So well-known and effective is the Soviet method of remaking human beings that criminals occasionally apply to be admitted." ("Witness to Revolution: The Story of Anna Louise Strong," aired by PBS on 10 January 1986).

"Single Combat"

p. 61: **Article 58**, points 10 and 11, from the Russian criminal code, made it a crime to disseminate anti-Soviet propaganda or to agitate against the Soviet system in any way. The people arrested under this law are known as "political 58s" or "politicals." Those sentenced under those points of the

Article were sent to distant labor camps for class-dangerous elements requiring a more severe regime.

p. 62: **Shushkina** is the feminine form of the surname Shushkin.

"Vasily Vasilyevich"

p. 69: **interrogation prison**: an important aspect of the interrogation process, aimed at breaking down prisoner resistance to confession. The average prisoner was held in such prisons from a few months to years. Methods used to obtain confessions in these prisons included subjecting the victims to inadequate sleep ("sleeplessness") and food and temperatures just a few degrees above freezing. Customarily, interrogations took place at night; a prisoner who had just fallen asleep would be awakened and taken to a room where a very bright light was focused on him. Interrogators would ask the same series of questions designed to exhaust and confuse the victim; ordinarily, such interrogations were repeated ten to twenty consecutive nights. Many prisoners would be physically tortured as well.

p. 70: **kolkhozniks** refers to those who live on a *kolkhoz,* or collective farm.

p. 72: **". . . I was not taken for political reasons"**: political prisoners, those arrested under Article 58, were considered much more dangerous to state security than common criminals, and were separated from prisoners serving time for various nonpolitical crimes.

p. 77: **MVD,** the Ministry of Internal Affairs. See note to page vi, on KGB.

p. 79: **the Supreme Soviet**: organized in 1936; formally the highest organ of state power and the only legislative body in the USSR, it was in fact absolutely powerless and completely controlled by Stalin and his successors.

"The Correct Man"

p. 80: **transfer prisons:** those prisons in which people already sentenced were held while awaiting transfer to the camps. Physical conditions tended to be worse in transfer prisons, but rules were less strictly enforced.

"Then, finally, . . . you're exiled to a remote region": those who served time in prison camps were often sent into internal exile afterward.

p. 83: **Denikin,** Anton (1872-1947): member of the Tsar's Army and well-known Russian general. In 1918, after the Revolution, he organized a resistance group, the "Russian Voluntary Army." It was comprised of ex-Tsarists and White Russians who struggled against the Bolsheviks. Defeated in 1920, Denikin escaped to the West and later died in England.

Wrangel, Pyotr (in Russian, Vrangel; 1878-1928): a well-known career general under the Tsar, he later commanded the Russian White Army during the Civil War (1918-20) and raised an army of his own in an attempt to defeat the Bolsheviks from the Ukraine to the Black Sea. Unsuccessful, he escaped to the West in 1920, where he founded the anti-Stalin "Russian Political Union," dedicated to liberating Russia from the Soviets.

p. 87: **Nekrasov,** Nikolay (1821-77): noted Russian poet of the second half of the nineteenth century. Some of his best work effectively describes the degradation of the peasantry.

"The Prophet"

p. 91: **Kol'tsov,** Aleksey Vasilyevich (1809-42): famous Russian poet who imitated folk songs and whose work has been compared with Robert Burns's.

Vlasov, Andrey (1901-46): Soviet general famed for his bravery and strategic brilliance in the beginning years of World War II. In 1942, after Vlasov's army had been completely surrounded by the Germans, he and what remained of his men were taken to Germany as prisoners of war. In Germany, aware that Stalin would never forgive him for being captured and still resentful over the fate of his parents, Vlasov organized the Russian Liberation Army with the goal of freeing Russia from Stalin. Vlasov was caught by the Red Army in 1945, in Czechoslovakia. He was sentenced to death and shot in 1946. From then on, many Russian soldiers who had been German POWs were stigmatized with the name *Vlasovtsi* (Vlasovites). On their return home, many thousand of them were shot by Stalin, and hundreds of thousands were put into labor camps and forgotten.

Bandera, Stepan (1908-59): leader of the West Ukrainian Nationalist movement. From 1943-47 he fought first against the Germans and then against the Soviet occupation forces to create and maintain an independent Ukraine. After the Germans were defeated by the Russians, Soviet divisions were deployed against Bandera. Those soldiers not killed by the Soviets were captured and sentenced to labor camps.

cossacks from the Don, . . . the Kuban: fought with the White Army against the Bolsheviks in the Civil War of 1918-20 and so became enemies of the communists.

Stalin, Josef Vissarionovich (real name Dzhugashvili; 1879-1953): born in Gori, Georgian SSR. After Lenin died in 1924, Stalin won the power struggle with his rivals and established by 1927 an absolute dictatorship by "purging" other Bolshevik leaders. Stalin was head of the Politburo of the Communist party. He was known for his implementation of the first Five-Year Plan in 1928, the exile of Trotsky (1929), his horrible brutality in the purges of the Communist party (1936-38) and the Army (1937-38), and his collectivization efforts called for the "liquidation" of kulaks (independent farmers) who resisted his efforts to make all farmland into collective farms *(kolkhoz)* or state-owned farms *(sovkhoz)*. Industrialization and collectivization won at a tremendous cost in human life and liberty. He was the principal organizer of the Great Terror and the Friendship Treaty with

Hitler in 1939, which changed the history of the world. In 1941, he took over the premiership from Molotov. He in turn was succeeded as premier by Malenkov upon his death on 5 March 1953.

p. 92: **Beria,** Lavrenty Pavlovich (1899-1953): the dreaded Soviet Secret Police chief who replaced Nikolay Yezhov notorious head of the NKVD (the Russian secret police) from 1938-49. Later, he served as deputy premier in charge of the Ministries of State Control and Interior (MVD), in charge of terror. Arrested in July 1953, he was later executed.

"In the Late Hour"

p. 96: **White Guard . . . Red Army:** During the Russian Civil War (1918-20) the Red Army of the Communist regime was opposed by the Whites, a diverse group.

p. 98: **soviet council,** or *soviet:* Officially, at that time, the soviets and the Communist party, were separate and distinct. "Soviets" were central and local legislative and executive authorities. It was the intention of the Revolution that these groups would govern Russia, giving a voice to even the smallest communities, but all the time, the soviets were completely under the Communist party control.

Anna Karenina . . . Onegin . . . Bazarov: all famous fictional characters from nineteenth-century Russian literature. Anna Karenina, of course, is the eponymous heroine of Lev Tolstoy's novel (1875-77). Onegin is the hero in the famous epic poem, *Yevgeny Onegin* (1823), by perhaps the greatest of all Russian writers, Alexander Pushkin (1799-1837). And Bazarov is the hero of the novel *Fathers and Sons* by Ivan Turgenev (1818-83).

Lomonosov, Mikhail (1711-65): considered the Russian Leonardo DaVinci. A renowned scientist, artist, poet, writer, and historian, he was recognized throughout the world. Lomonosov founded the Russian Academy of Science as well as Moscow University, which now includes his name in its title.

p. 99: **Komsomol,** or the Young Communist League, was established in 1918 and comprised young people between the ages of fourteen to twenty-six. It conducted activities under the leadership of the Communist party, which it assisted in propagating policies among Soviet youth. Komsomol members were enlisted to help not only in various national causes such as industrialization, collectivization, and eradication of illiteracy but also in the defense against the Nazis in WWII.

p. 100: **GPU.** See note to page vi, on the KGB.

"In June of '53"

p. 106: **Amnesty** was proclaimed to commemorate Stalin's death in 1953—but it extended only to criminals, not to those imprisoned for political reasons. This release of millions of felons resulted in a crime wave of unheralded proportions.

"The Murderers"

p. 110: **Stolypin trucks,** named for Russian prime Minister Pyotr Stolypin (1862-1911), were a common method of transporting prisoners after they had been sentenced. Prisoners were crammed into railway cars—usually cattle cars—or "Stolypin trucks," which were narrow penal wagons holding from twenty to thirty people in a six-man compartment. Often the trip took months.

"The Letter"

p. 137: **Klasha . . . Klava:** diminutives of Klavdiya (Claudia). In Russian custom, it is considered too familiar and a breach of etiquette for strangers to addresss one by one's nickname unless they are asked to do so.

p. 139: **"rehabilitated":** a wry reference comparing the fate of Christmas trees (as well as Christmas and other religious holidays) under the communists to that of prisoners. Refers to the process by which prisoners can get their cases reheard; if they are found innocent they are released and considered "rehabilitated," and they are restored to good repute.

p. 144: **Kalinin,** Mikhail Ivanovich (1875-1946): Russian communist leader and revolutionist, was the first president of the USSR from 1919-46 (officially, the chairman of first the ZIK—the central executive committee that preceded the Supreme Soviet—and then the Presidium of the Supreme Soviet of the USSR).

Shvernik, Nikolay Mikhailovich (1888-1970): Soviet political leader. Under Stalin, he served as head of Soviet trade unions from1930 until his appointment in 1946 as chairman of the Presidium of the Supreme Soviet. After Stalin's death, he was again put in charge of trade unions.

"The Neighbor"

p. 147: ***Troika:*** Established originally in the 1920s, *troikas* were broadly invoked on Stalin's orders in 1934 and had the power to impose any sentence, including the death penalty, in all provinces and their republics. They consisted of the NKVD chief as its chair, the provincial or republican party first secretary, and the chairman of the local executive committee (or a representative from the prosecutor's office). Generally, the NKVD chief authorized the sentence; the others added their initials only as a formality after the fact. The defendant was not present at the proceedings and there was no pretense at a trial. Most political prisoners were sentenced by *troikas.*

p. 150: **Trotsky,** Leon (real name Bronstein; 1879-1940): Russian revolutionary leader and statesman under Lenin. Under Lenin, he served as the commissar for foreign affairs and then commissar of defense. He organized the Red Army in the Civil War. He headed the Leftist opposition to Stalin after Lenin's death, but when Stalin gained power, he was expelled from the party in 1927, exiled to Alma-Ata in 1928, and ordered to leave the USSR in 1929. He lived in many places before settling near Mexico City in 1937, where he was assassinated on Stalin's orders.

"The Semyonovs"

p. 161: **Mikhailik:** a diminutive of Mikhail.

p. 162: **Vasilyochek:** like Vasilyok, a diminutive of Vasily.

"Seven Slashes"

p. 176: **Lyovushka . . . Lyova:** diminutives of Lev. Of the two, Lyovushka is the more endearing and therefore appropriate for children.

p. 181: **Yasnaya Polyana:** the estate of the prominent writer Lev Tolstoy (see note to page vii).

p. 182: **Nadson,** Semyon Iakovlevich (1862-87): a well-known Russian poet.

Afterword

p. 193: **Tukhachevsky,** Mikhail N., Marshal (1893-1937): Russian Civil War hero. In June 1937, he and other army commanders were arrested, tried, and executed on manufactured charges. Accused of espionage in behalf of Germany and Japan, anti-party conspiracy, cooperation with Trotsky, and so on. He and many of his co-defendants were later "rehabilitated" by Khrushchev between 1955-58. More than 35,000 officers, about half the officer corps, were killed in Stalin's purge of the army officer corps.

Beneš, Edvard (1884-1948): the right-hand man to Masaryk, was foreign minister (1918-35); premier (1921-22); President of the Czechoslovakian Republic (1935-38 and 1945-48). He went into exile after the Munich Pact and headed the Czech provisional government in London during the Second World War. After the War, he was reelected president of the liberated Czechoslovakia and resigned after the communist coup d'état in 1948.

p. 195: **Pis'menny,** Aleksandr Grigoryevich (1909-71): twentieth-century Russian writer of novels, short stories, and novellas.

p. 196: **Raoul Wallenberg** (1912-47?): Swedish businessman and diplomat, best known for his heroic efforts during WWII. In his capacity as the first secretary of the Swedish legation in Hungary, he organized the rescue of approximately 100,000 Hungarian Jews slated for deportation to Nazi death camps. Taken after Soviet troops entered Budapest on 17 January 1945, he was sent to a Soviet prison camp on manufactured charges of espionage, and then disappeared. Soviets later admitted his innocence, but claimed he died of a heart attack in 1947; however, some reports over the years have indicated he is alive.

Brezhnev, Leonid Ilyich (1906-82): Soviet statesman who succeeded Khrushchev as first secretary of the Communist party while Aleksey Kosygin was premier; he became president of the USSR in June 1977.

p. 197: **Politburo:** main political and executive committee of a Communist party.

Molotov, Vyacheslav Mikhailovich, (real name Skriabin; 1890-1986): politburo member (1921-30); secretary of the CPSU Central Committee (1930-41). He was prime minister from 1930 to 1941, until Stalin officially took over the premiership from him. From 1939 to 1949 (Molotov together with Ribbentrop signed the Soviet-German Pact in 1939) and again from 1953 to 1956 he served as foreign minister. One of the principals of the Great Terror, he was Stalin's chief adviser at the Teheran, Yalta, and Potsdam conferences. Molotov was appointed, together with Beria, Bulganin, and Kaganovich, to the post of First Deputy Prime-Minister in March 1953.

Malenkov, Georgy Maximilianovich (1902-88): a particular favorite of Stalin and one of the orchestrators of the Great Terror, Malenkov was involved with the purges in the thirties and forties and Stalin's collectivization efforts. A member of the Politburo and deputy prime minister from 1946 to 1953, he succeeded Stalin as prime minister (1953-55). When Malenkov resigned his posts in 1955, he was appointed deputy premier and served until 1957.

Khrushchev, Nikita Sergeyevich (1894-1971): After serving as first secretary of the central committee of the Communist party from March 1953, he became premier from 1958 to 1964. His denunciation of Stalin in 1956 led to the de-Stalinization of the USSR and the rehabilitation of many prisoners. In October 1964, he was replaced by Brezhnev as first secretary and Aleksey Kosygin as premier.

Kaganovich, Lazar M. (1893-1992): principal figure in the Great Terror, member of the Politburo, and intimate of Stalin. Served serveral times as the peoples commissar of transportation during the thirties and forties.

p. 198: **And even if he survived until his release:** Under the "Minus 100" law, political prisoners freed without forgiveness or rehabilitation (for example, those who were released for physical incapacitation after serving their terms) were prohibited from ever living in the one hundred largest cities in Russia. Of course, that especially included Moscow.

p. 199: **that even included a phone:** In 1937, when Stalin built special living quarters for people in the arts, those in the House of Writers were especially desirable. Not only were the apartments spacious, in terms of what was then available in the country, but each unit had its own phone. Later, those phones proved to be a mixed blessing. It was true they allowed the writers ease of communication, but they also allowed the KGB to keep track of their activities.

p. 202: **Sukhanovka Prison:** about twenty miles outside Moscow, it was called "the dacha" by prisoners who regarded it as one of the worst. Consisting entirely of isolation cells, its regime was especially strict.

***

The preceding notes are based upon personal interviews with Anna, Leonid, and Natasha Stonov, as well as the following scholarly texts: Conquest, Robert. *The Great Terror: A Reassessment.* Revised edition of the 1970 edition. New York: Oxford University Press, 1991. Dmytryshyn, Basil. *U.S.S.R.: A Concise History.* Fourth Edition. New York: Scribner's, 1984. Geller, Mikhail and Alecksandr Nekrich. *Utopia in Power: The History of the Soviet Union from 1917 to the Present.* New York: Simon and Schuster, 1992. Pipes, Richard. *The Russian Revolution.* New York: Vintage Books, 1991.